CELEBRATING EDMONTON'S
QUEER HISTORY

Cruising
the
Downtown

Edited by Kristopher Wells and the
Edmonton Queer History Project Team

With a foreword by
Elizabeth Massiah and Michael Phair

NeWest
PRESS

Contents

We begin this book and our exploration of Edmonton's queer history by honouring the way Indigenous Peoples of Turtle Island have traditionally acknowledged the land at the start of gatherings, ceremonies, and events since time immemorial. We offer our own land acknowledgement as an opportunity for shared reflection about space and place, decolonizing historical assumptions, and engaging in shared learning; and in recognition of Indigenous lands, treaties, and peoples that comprise amiskwacîy-wâskahikan.

We respectfully acknowledge that much of Edmonton's queer history has occurred on Indigenous land within Treaty 6 Territory, which has been the traditional gathering place for Nêhiyawak (Cree), Anishinaabe (Saulteaux), Niitsitapi (Blackfoot), Métis, Dene, Inuit, and Nakota Sioux.

We thank our community Knowledge Keepers, Elders, and Two Spirit peoples for the teachings and gift of being able to share these stories with you.

FOREWORD

Joining with hundreds of others from across the province and country, we came to Edmonton as a lesbian woman and a gay man and very quickly became actively involved in the city's emerging queer community in the 1980s and 1990s. We found our way into the "gay" establishments of the time—GATE, Womonspace, Common Woman Books, Flashback, the Roost, Boots 'N Saddle—and when we could find them, we quickly joined many "gay" organizations focussed on sports, religion, advocacy, women, and drag, most of which are referenced in this book.

These years were also a time filled with challenges, which included Conservative governments led by Peter Lougheed and Ralph Klein; the Individual's Rights Protection Act (IRPA), which actively excluded protections against discrimination for gays and lesbians; and a city council and police service that were either unaware of or hostile to people like us. Both of us were out of the closet and well aware that we could be fired from our jobs, refused housing, and subject to harassment from the police like many other members of our community. Most of the six hundred thousand Edmontonians at that time, including the media, likely thought there were no so-called perverts in Edmonton or were hostile when they encountered us.

Under the Alberta Human Rights Commission's banner Alberta for All we gathered and organized with others in our community to advocate for human rights protection and to remove the sense that we were second-class citizens. In support of these efforts, we helped to create the Gay and Lesbian Awareness (GALA) society with the mission to end discrimination, raise visibility, and celebrate our lives and communities. Delwin Vriend was a GALA member when he was fired from the King's College (now the King's University) for being gay. Delwin's case was a galvanizing force that led us to organize, advocate, and agitate all the way to the Supreme Court of Canada.

On July 1, 1984, the first publicly known Edmontonian with AIDS, Ross Armstrong, was diagnosed and hospitalized. Two days later, the two of us and four others met and formed the AIDS Network of Edmonton (now HIV Edmonton). We took on the tasks of organizing support for people infected with AIDS, educating the public about the virus, and advocating for equal rights to protect all of us, particularly people with AIDS. The community's response to AIDS was pivotal for us and for Edmonton. Our small group grew to include hundreds of volunteers in the fight to end AIDS and secure appropriate healthcare services, community supports, funding, and fundamental human rights. Throughout the 1980s and into the 1990s, virtually every gay and lesbian organization, bar, and business contributed to ending AIDS and achieving critical human rights victories. We also remember a time when a member of the Alberta Legislature put forward a motion to put people with AIDS in prison camps. For everyone in our community, it was a terrifying and emotionally draining period of our lives—a time of illness, dying, and death of friends that brought out every ounce of strength, courage, and resilience we could muster.

We also remember the community's incredible energy, including challenges, successes, disappointments—and, of course, all the fun we had over those years. We even enjoyed the activism we did, the meetings with politicians and media, the countless letters we sent, and the petitions that collected hundreds of signatures. Those moments were all worth it when they led to victories like the establishment of the Gay and Lesbian Police Liaison Committee to improve community relations, and when Delwin won his landmark case before the Supreme Court of Canada, which extended human rights protections for all of us based on sexual orientation.

This commemorative book celebrates what was accomplished in Edmonton by so many within the queer community. We know that much more needs to be done, and although victories can be reversed, we are guided by the renowned lesbian author Jane Rule, who famously stated, "Politics is like housework, just when you think it is done, it needs doing again!" We are watching and standing ready, armed with the lessons of the past, to help protect and build our community's future.

Liz Massiah and Michael Phair

PREFACE

We recognize the word *queer* is a powerful term that is still offensive to some and that has been reclaimed by others. We use *queer* as an all-encompassing descriptor for a wide variety of sexual and gender identities, expressions, desires, and same-sex attractions in both the past and present. We also use queer as an intersectional way to examine issues of power, privilege, and identity and as an insurgency to resist the power and oppression of hetero- and cisnormativity, which have often attempted to erase and silence our lives and existence.

Cruising the Downtown explores Edmonton's queer history in the context of downtown Edmonton. We've divided the book into six sections, which explore aspects of 2SLGBTQ+ history and queer life in the heart of the city. You can read the book in the presented order or skip to the sections and entries that grab your attention. You can also use the book to supplement the Edmonton Queer History Project's downtown map and create your own personalized walking tour.*

As a way to help this history come alive, many sections of the book include personal reflections. Some reflections are written by the history makers themselves and offer unique perspectives on our city and community.

However you use or read the book, we hope you'll find a story that resonates and be inspired to share it with a friend. Enjoy cruising through Edmonton's queer history!

* See https://www.edmontonqueerhistoryproject.ca/the-map

ACKNOWLEDGEMENTS

The sections and chapters in this book are all part of a collective effort researched and written by the Edmonton Queer History Project team with support from the Canada Research Chairs program and MacEwan University. In particular we would like to acknowledge and thank Darrin Hagen, Dr. Michelle Lavoie, Rob Browatzke, Remi Baker, Morgan Evans, Michael Phair, Kyler Chittick, and Japakaran Saroya for the writing, research, and passion that went into developing these stories. Some individuals took the lead on writing drafts of particular chapters, while others worked on research, editing, and fact checking. This book is truly the product of a great team and community effort!

We are also grateful for the recognition the Edmonton Queer History Project has received from the City of Edmonton. We are also honoured to have been recognized as a finalist for the Governor General's Award for Excellence in Community Programming and to have received a National Trust for Canada Governors' Award in recognition of outstanding contributions to community, identity, and sense of place.

There is so much more history yet to be written and shared. We consider this book to be a modest beginning in an unfolding story about our resilient, diverse, and incredible 2SLGBTQ+ communities.

INTRODUCTION

Queer history is everywhere. You just need to know where to look to find it. When we reflect on Edmonton's queer history, it becomes evident that our community has needed to be both courageous and resilient to find a space and a place in our city. Our rich and storied past demonstrates that we've always been an essential part of Edmonton's social fabric, even when it wasn't safe for us to be visible, much less vocal.

Some of us came to Edmonton from small towns and First Nations reserves or were cast out of our own families. We came to the city to find others like ourselves. We hungered and searched for community, ultimately hoping to find love, laughter, and a sense of belonging. The closet was (and still is) a powerful force in many of our lives. Having to pass, hide, or deny who we are takes a toll on each of us in different ways. Some of us could never hide in the first place. Others had no choice but to fight back. Some of us didn't survive. All of us, in some way, have paid the price of homo/bi/transphobia. Over time and generations, we came together to build the community that we not only wanted but needed. We came because we believed our lives mattered. We made Edmonton our home.

Cruising the Downtown: Celebrating Edmonton's Queer History tells a story not only about the past but also about the present and how we might learn lessons from history that can help move our community forward in precarious times. It is a story not only of remembrance but also of hope—hope for change that is possible when a community comes together, supports one another, and takes collective action to build a more just and inclusive world.

In 1981, when the Edmonton Police Service raided the Pisces Health Spa and arrested fifty-six men, the spa managers, and the owner, the community came together, organized, and fought back. For some, this was Edmonton's Stonewall moment, when the community finally stood up to police harassment and oppression. Community meetings and fundraisers were held in places like the Roost (see page 238) and Flashback (see page 226). The bars, after all, were our sanctuaries and safe spaces.

The Imperial Sovereign Court of the Wild Rose (see page 46) held drag shows to help raise funds to support the "found-ins" and their ongoing legal cases. Gay Alliance Toward Equality (GATE, see page 18), the de facto gay and lesbian community centre, helped to organize lawyers and established the Privacy Defence Committee to bring forward a united public voice. Unexpectedly, the police raid also propelled Michael Phair into the public spotlight as an unlikely activist. Michael became an important and prominent community leader who would go on to become the first openly gay politician elected in Alberta's history and, in doing so, paved the way for countless others to follow in his footsteps.

Shortly after the Pisces raid, another monumental battle forever changed our community. On July 1, 1984, Ross Armstrong became the first Edmontonian publicly identified with AIDS. A former competitive swimmer, Ross was heavily involved with the Roughnecks, Edmonton's gay and lesbian sports and recreation group. Ever the leader, Ross became the public face of AIDS in Edmonton.

The community rallied around him. Several days later, a handful of folks gathered at Michael Phair's kitchen table and the AIDS Network of Edmonton was born (see page 34). Sadly, Ross passed away on July 1, 1986, two years to the day of his public disclosure. That was the reality then. There was no surviving AIDS. There was only death.

The HIV/AIDS pandemic took away a generation of our community builders, artists, friends, and lovers. However, as a result of this period of incredible grief and trauma, we also organized and built new communities of care and activism. We remained resilient and emerged even more committed to being visible and vocal. We were attempting not just to survive but to thrive. We fought not only for our survival but also for our dignity and respect.

For decades, groups like GATE, the AIDS Network of Edmonton, Metropolitan Community Church and Dignity Edmonton Dignité (see page 68), Womonspace (see page 178), and the Imperial Sovereign Court of the Wild Rose have been organizing and advocating for basic human rights protections for our community. They wrote countless letters to government officials, travelled to conferences and hearings, published newsletters and reports, and brought a very visible presence to the 2SLGBTQ+ community in Edmonton through the local media.

When Delwin Vriend was fired from his job as a lab instructor at the King's College for being gay, the community was ready to mobilize. They held media conferences, organized fundraisers, hired lawyers, and, most importantly, connected with allies who realized this wasn't just a fight for the gay and lesbian community but a fight for the fundamental human rights and dignity of all Albertans. Delwin's case would wind its way through both the court of law and the court of public opinion for seven long years before the Supreme Court of Canada ruled that sexual orientation must be read into Alberta's human rights legislation as a protected ground against discrimination. This landmark decision reverberated far beyond Alberta and eventually helped to pave the way for the legalization of same-sex marriage in Canada, leading to important legal changes around the world.

Everywhere you look around Edmonton, you can find remnants of queer history. This history can be found among our Indigenous and Two Spirit communities, who were here long before settlers arrived. Queer histories can also be traced back to our pioneers, trailblazers, and outlaws who sought to chart a new course by "going North." At its heart, Edmonton was a frontier town where a person could start life anew filled with endless possibility, adventure, and freedom.

We hope this book will provide a glimpse into our past and some of the people, places, and moments that have contributed to building not only the 2SLGBTQ+ community but our city. We've chosen to focus on the downtown core as this is where queer communities have traditionally been most concentrated and visible. In the late 1970s and 1980s, Edmonton even had the beginnings of its own "gaybour-hood" clustered around 104 Street, where the Roost, Flash-back, Boots 'N Saddle, GATE, and other businesses brought visibility, vibrancy, and a growing sense of community.

Our book is designed to remember and honour not only those who have made history but also younger generations of queer and trans people. Our community's history and our elders, activists, and leaders demonstrate that we can survive and grow older. Not only do we have a past; we have a rich and vibrant future. This future is possible only because of the people who have come before us and fought for the rights and privileges we enjoy today. We hope this book will encourage readers to traverse across generations with the understanding that history not only is found in the past but is critical to building a more just and inclusive future.

Thus, *Cruising the Downtown: Celebrating Edmonton's Queer History* is not an ending, but just the beginning. We know there are many more stories waiting to be discovered and told. We hope you will share yours.

PART 1

Building a Queer Community

Michael Phair Park

10124 104 STREET

In 2016, a pocket park in downtown Edmonton with grassy area, seating, and colourful artwork[1] was named after former city councillor Michael Phair. Mayor Don Iveson and Councillor Scott McKeen were present at the park's opening to unveil its new name. The dedication of this city park acknowledged Michael's long and distinguished career as a politician and community advocate and his many contributions to the city of Edmonton, especially in support of the 2SLGBTQ+ community.

Born in Wisconsin, Michael moved to Edmonton in 1980 to pursue a job opportunity in early childhood education. Previously, he had taught at Mount Royal College in Calgary, as well as internationally, training teachers in Nigeria and Ghana. At the time, he had expected to stay in Edmonton for only a few years, but he soon found himself at home. Michael hadn't been a resident long before he was arrested as a "found-in" at the Pisces Health Spa during the infamous 1981 police raid (see page 84). This late-night raid was not only a surprise but a terrifying shock, leaving the local gay and lesbian community feeling under attack. There had been similar police bathhouse raids in Ottawa, Montreal, and Toronto, but no one expected one to happen in Edmonton.

The Pisces raid led Gay Alliance Toward Equality (GATE) to organize a community meeting the next day at the Roost (see page 238). Michael was approached about speaking to the media, and after some indecision, he agreed to speak out, but only anonymously. He was working with young children, and being associated with this raid, or even being publicly identified as a gay man in 1981, could have ended his career.

The anonymity didn't work; people were able to identify Michael when the segment appeared on the local news. As a result, he decided that any future dealings with the media,

▲ Corny and Michael at Michael's famous community Christmas party
▼ Michael in the Pride Parade

about the Pisces raid or anything else, wouldn't be anonymous: he would stand visibly, vocally, and proudly as himself, no matter the cost.

As community outrage continued to build over the police's actions, Michael, along with Bill Cousintine, George Davison, and Andy Hopkins, created the Privacy Defence Committee, which sought to raise funds to defend those arrested in the Pisces raid. The community was now motivated and mobilized. Michael also helped to establish the Gay and Lesbian Awareness Society (GALA), which was the community advocacy group responsible for organizing and hosting Edmonton's Pride events, starting in 1984; prior to that, Pride events had been organized by gay community groups and bars. Michael knew that visibility and education needed to be key components to promote social change as the community organized to protect and defend itself.

In 1983, Michael landed in San Francisco for a year of postgraduate studies. Almost immediately, he attended his first AIDS-related funeral. The enormity of AIDS in San Francisco was surreal and devastating. When Michael returned to Edmonton, he hosted a social with some of his friends and gay and lesbian community organizers and leaders. The conversation quickly turned to the eventuality of AIDS arriving in Edmonton. When Edmonton's first case was identified in July 1984, GATE suggested the media contact Michael for a response. This action led to the formation of the AIDS Network of Edmonton (see page 34) around Michael's kitchen table.[2] Michael's home served as the organization's first headquarters until proper office space could be found.

Michael, along with Ross Armstrong and others, represented the AIDS Network of Edmonton in a meeting in Montreal in 1984, where discussion focussed on setting up a national strategy to fight the virus. This meeting led to the formation of the Canadian AIDS Society, with Michael serving as the first national chair. There was no money for this work, so the society operated out of the AIDS Network of Edmonton's office for its first year. Working closely with an ally in Ottawa, Michael organized the first national conference on HIV/AIDS in 1985. Serving as the chair for the Canadian AIDS Society, particularly in its early years, helped Michael understand the impact of AIDS on the gay and lesbian community and other vulnerable people across the country. That impact became especially evident at the second national conference held in Toronto in 1986.[3]

This early work was exhausting. Volunteers such as Michael were not only advocating politically but were directly engaged on the ground in supporting people living with AIDS, support that included everything from buying groceries to planning funerals. A huge number of volunteers contributed to this effort, including many gay men, lesbians, and heterosexual allies.

Michael's pioneering work with the AIDS Network of Edmonton was recognized with the 1984 John DeSmit Citizen of the Year Award from the Imperial Sovereign Court of the Wild Rose and the 1986 Citizen of the Year Award from the *Edmonton Journal*.

The fight against AIDS underscored the need to protect the human rights of all people. In Edmonton, this work was championed by GALA. GALA continually battled the provincial government to ensure 2SLGBTQ+ people received equal respect and protection under the province's laws and legislation. Groups of GALA volunteers would go to local bars with petitions and letters for the community to sign and forward to government ministers and legislators. Michael recalls an early meeting with the Alberta Human Rights Commission, where the delegates made sure they were well dressed and presented a professional front; Michael played a trick on his friend and colleague Maureen Irwin by showing up with a gold lamé purse and shoes—which he hid during the meeting, of course.

While some members of the commission were sympathetic, not all supported sexual orientation being added to the

Individual's Rights Protection Act, and without consensus the discussion never advanced past the minister of labour, as it was the minister's role to bring proposed human rights changes to the Alberta Legislature. Despite multiple meetings with two different ministers—first Les Young and later Elaine McCoy—GALA's petitions and letters to add sexual orientation as a protected right made no progress. In fact, quite the opposite occurred: the government issued a ministerial order explicitly banning the Human Rights Commission from accepting complaints from homosexuals.[4]

Michael's work with the AIDS Network of Edmonton, the Canadian AIDS Society, and GALA taught him about the importance of having a strong relationship with the media, something that he and others were able to use frequently to their advantage. This relationship enabled them to put human stories in front of the public, changing the narrative of AIDS from statistics to real people with faces, hopes, and dreams. Humanizing 2SLGBTQ+ people was a critical step in the long and ongoing struggle for human rights, especially in Conservative Alberta.

And it wasn't only the governments that needed to be fought. In 1989, when a downtown gay bar closed and reopened as a straight bar, the owners made it clear that gay people were not welcome in the new business. Immediately, Michael and others showed up to protest, their media allies in tow. The fact that a business owner could so flagrantly deny entrance to gay people stood as further proof that changes were needed to Alberta's Individual's Rights Protection Act.[5]

In the 1986 provincial election, NDP candidate William Roberts approached Michael to find out what Edmonton's 2SLGBTQ+ community needed from a government representative. It was the first time a politician actively courted the community and it proved to be successful. Roberts defeated the incumbent Conservative candidate and served as Edmonton-Centre's representative for the next two terms.

Recognizing Michael's skill with community organizing, MLA Roberts suggested Michael help Jan Reimer in her new mayoral campaign. After Jan was successfully elected as Edmonton's first female mayor in 1989, Michael worked closely with her and the city council as president of the Edmonton Social Planning Council. This experience, coupled with encouragement from Alderman Brian Mason, gave Michael the support necessary to try a run for a seat on city council. In early 1992, Michael once again convened a close group of friends and community leaders and asked for their opinions about running for city council. In general, their reactions were supportive and positive, but there was noted concern about whether an openly gay person could be elected in Alberta. No out 2SLGBTQ+ person had ever been elected to political office in the history of Alberta and only a few 2SLGBTQ+ politicians in Canada were out and visible at the time. On St. Patrick's Day, Michael decided to throw his hat into the race and announced his intention to run.

Being a gay candidate certainly earned Michael's campaign an extra degree of media attention. From the start of his campaign, Michael's priority was to run a good and fair campaign, win or lose, but as election day drew closer, he wanted to win! Community safety was a priority for the campaign, including issues ranging from community policing to lighting, signage, and traffic controls; another platform issue was open and accountable government. Michael's campaign met very little overt homophobia in the run up to the election, and when the final votes were counted, he made history by winning a tightly contested race.

During his five terms on city council (1992–2007), Michael achieved many great things, including the creation of the Edmonton Arts Council (EAC). The Arts Council took over the direct governance of city funding for arts and various festivals. A lengthy council debate almost saw the creation of the EAC rejected, but quick thinking on the part of Councillor

JASON SYVIXAY
Urban planner and 2SLGBTQ+ community member

How do we make queer history and celebration a permanent fixture of our city's fabric? How can queer identity and experience be meaningfully represented? As author Aaron Betsky notes, queer space is "not built, only implied, and usually invisible." Queer experiences are too often closeted and found in the shadows—away from public view.

As an urban planner, I often question to whom urban space belongs. Urban spaces are layered with important social meanings. They tell us about a city's values and provide a sense of who belongs—and who does not.

Michael Phair and his lifelong pursuit for the full liberation of 2SLGBTQ+ people in Edmonton has profoundly impacted how I view personal contributions to cities and communities. Every gesture, whether big or small, can help to challenge the legacy of oppression that members of 2SLGBTQ+ communities have been subjected to. And also how collective action premised on notions of equity and inclusion can create a sense of safety and belonging in our communities.

Michael Phair Park, named in recognition of Michael's many significant community contributions, recently received a visual uplift in the form of colourful confetti. This mural serves as a form of both resistance and community commentary—that Edmonton is a city that celebrates diversity in all its forms, centres queer expression and joy, and advocates for the full and equitable participation of everyone.

Like a burst of glittered confetti, I am hopeful that the legacy of Michael Phair, and so many other incredible community leaders, continues to spill out onto other Edmonton spaces—creating more opportunities for safe, queer expression and nurturing a sense of pride in place.

Sheila McKay led to a trial period for the new initiative. Its success was so overwhelming that it became a permanent organization, forever changing the landscape of Edmonton's arts community.

Michael's other significant accomplishments included being a champion for the environment and urban renewal, especially the revitalization of downtown and 104 Street. At the time, 104 Street was mostly undeveloped, with many less-than-desirable businesses. Incentives for developers helped bring new housing developments to the downtown core, and the grassroots work of community organizations ensured new developments respected the desired aesthetic and needs of the local community. Success meant navigating complicated relationships between developers, city administration, local businesses, and the people who lived in the neighbourhood. Michael became a skilled and seasoned mediator who wasn't afraid to put the needs of the community first.

One of the darkest periods of Michael's tenure as a city councillor came in the aftermath of the Delwin Vriend decision. Michael knew Delwin well, having worked together at GALA over the years. (It was at GALA's 1991 Flaunting It conference that Delwin's parents spoke publicly, for the first time, about having a gay son.[6]) Throughout the 1990s, Delwin's court case and ensuing legal appeals dominated Alberta's political landscape, community activism, and organizing (see page 105). This wasn't just a battle for Delwin, but for the human rights of the entire 2SLGBTQ+ community in Edmonton, Alberta, and across Canada.[7] When the final judgement was handed down from the Supreme Court of Canada on April 2, 1998, the victory for Delwin and the 2SLGBTQ+ community was cause for celebration. But what followed was a week of fear and anxiety for the community across Alberta as Premier Ralph Klein openly discussed the possibility of using the Charter's notwithstanding clause to exempt Alberta from the Supreme Court's ruling. Klein's comments gave tacit permission to the

BUILDING A QUEER COMMUNITY

political far right to spew the vilest of homophobia. It was open season on the 2SLGBTQ+ community.

As an out gay politician, Michael was on the receiving end of some of the worst of this abuse.[8] His office was bombarded with anti-gay phone calls and letters, many of which included death threats. Things got so serious that the Edmonton Police Service advised Michael to take different routes to and from work as well as having plainclothes officers stationed outside his home. A press conference the week after the Supreme Court's landmark decision gave Michael the opportunity to tell the world about the kind of hate he was receiving, making clear it was the Klein government, and particularly Stockwell Day, that had created the environment for such hatred to flourish.

Klein's decision that week not to use the notwithstanding clause brought this deluge of homophobia to an end, but the pain it caused Michael and others lingers even to this day. While sexual orientation officially became a protected ground against discrimination in Alberta, the real work of educating and changing people's hearts and minds was only just beginning.[9]

Despite public encouragement to run for mayor in 2004, Michael declined, and then in 2007 he announced he would not run for city council again. Although his long and storied chapter in politics was now over, it would not be the end of Michael's advocacy work. Michael quickly joined the boards of NeWest Press and the Pro Coro Music Society, as well as a group called Alley of Light, which had as its mission to rejuvenate the alley between 103 Street and 105 Street just north of Jasper Avenue. This group's efforts led to the creation of the city park that now bears Michael's name.

The park isn't the only place that celebrates Michael's legacy. In 2015, the Edmonton Public School Board honoured Michael's many community contributions by naming a new school after him.[10] In 2017, the Michael Phair School officially opened in Webber Green, 9407 211 Street.

Michael's contributions to the city in general, and to Edmonton's 2SLGBTQ+ community specifically, were also recognized when the Edmonton Pride Festival Society created the Michael Phair Award for individual contribution by a gay man. The University of Alberta's Institute for Sexual Minority Studies and Services (now know as the fYrefly Institute) also established the Michael Phair Leadership Award to recognize undergraduate students who have demonstrated leadership by giving back to their community. In February 2016, Michael was named chair of the University of Alberta's Board of Governors by Alberta's first NDP provincial government, and in 2022 Michael was appointed Chancellor of St. Stephen's College.

Today, Michael continues to be an exemplary activist and advocate. He is currently involved with Edmonton's Pride Seniors group, which was founded by Michael and his friend Sherry McKibben, who was notably Edmonton's first openly lesbian city councillor.[11] The Pride Seniors group is currently planning to develop a unique 2SLGBTQ+ seniors complex, which would become the first of its kind in Canada.

Michael continues to be active in Edmonton as a trusted advisor, friend, and community champion to so many who have come to know firsthand about his legacy of care and compassion. Our community is better and richer because of his many enduring contributions.

Gay Alliance Toward Equality

10169 104 STREET
(PHILLIPS LOFTS)

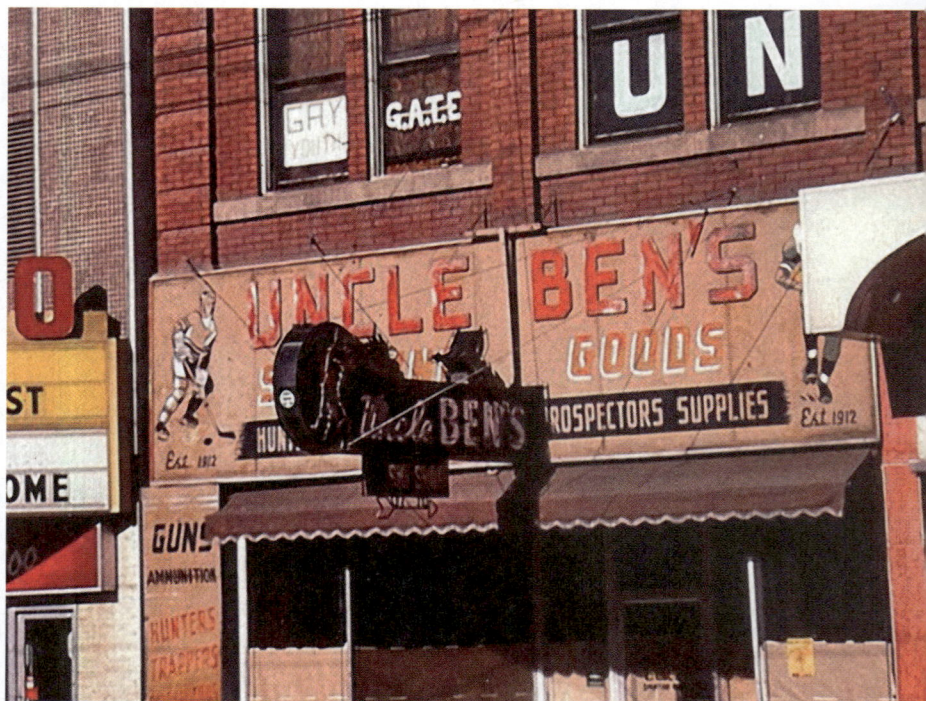

Gay Alliance Toward Equality (GATE) first began in Vancouver when Roedy Green organized like-minded Lotusland queers who wanted—and were willing to work toward—change in attitudes toward sexual minorities. As an organizing force, GATE moved parallel to the many streams of political activism that were in motion through the pivotal summer of 1969 and the gradual emergence of a more public and visible gay and lesbian community.[1]

In those early years, a primary focus for Roedy Green and GATE was political lobbying for more fair and equitable representation in Canadian society. GATE also provided an important social aspect for many gays and lesbians taking their very first steps into the public light, however. Michael Roberts, a contemporary of Green, decided Edmonton needed its own version of GATE.[2] Michael had Calgary roots, but founding a gay advocacy organization in Edmonton helped him discreetly protect his family back home.

In November of 1971, based within a small apartment in Edmonton, Michael established what would become the twin hallmarks of GATE: a discreet personal ad in the *Edmonton Journal* and a phone line where callers could receive information about the gay and lesbian community. These two elements were critical in helping to provide access to information and resources, or a sympathetic ear, for scores of 2SLGBTQ+ people, both locals and visitors. GATE also gave Edmonton's growing queer community a centralized place and a presence outside of the two gay nightclubs established in the early 1970s (Club '70 and Flashback, see page 216 and page 226).

In December 1971, to publicize GATE's arrival, Michael published an opinion letter in the *Edmonton Journal* and another in the *Gateway*, the University of Alberta's student newspaper. In writing to the *Edmonton Journal*, he stated,

▲ GALA Steering Committee picnic, Hawrelak Park, 1984
▼ GATE office, 1976

"We homosexuals have the right to be treated with the respect given to any human being and the right to full equality before the law."[3]

Between 1971 and 1972, Michael worked with GATE members Manus Sasonkin, a noted composer, conductor, and professor at the University of Alberta's Music Department, and Manus's partner, Jack Hurt, an accomplished musician who had played piano with the Edmonton Symphony, to set up the organization's founding constitution.[4] On June 28, 1972, GATE was incorporated, officially making it one of Edmonton's very first dedicated 2SLGBTQ+ community organizations.[5]

Also in 1972, GATE wrote a brief to the Alberta Legislature lobbying for the inclusion of sexual orientation as a protected ground in the province's new Individual's Rights Protection Act.[6] Michael Roberts told the Legislature that in failing to provide basic human rights protections for gays and lesbians, the government was denying civil liberties to almost 82,000 Albertans.[7]

As GATE began to grow, Michael realized that most of GATE's calls were coming from the university area, so he moved from the Sir John Franklin apartments to a house near the University of Alberta (11012 86 Avenue) in the spring of 1973, along with roommates Ken King and Bill Booth. This move allowed GATE to expand its services by creating room for informal counselling and a quasi-drop-in centre, which also became jokingly known as "Michael's living room."[8] Bill Booth, one of the earliest tenants in the GATE House, as it would become affectionately known, recalled that at first Michael was the only one allowed to answer the house phone. Eventually, he got burned out and others took turns responding to calls. That fall, all of the house phone calls started to be logged and informally notated, providing a detailed and fascinating look at the main concerns facing Prairie queers in the early 1970s. In 1974, phone line volunteers began receiving more formal training focussed on problem solving, empathetic understanding, and crisis-intervention skills to help prepare them for the kinds of calls and questions GATE most commonly received.

Perhaps unsurprisingly, most of the initial calls focussed on dating, cruising, and finding and connecting with other gays and lesbians. Club '70, which opened a year before Michael set up the phone line, could always be recommended as a popular club, as well as other unofficial meeting places, such as the taverns in a few of the larger downtown hotels, where queers and allies discretely gathered before the gay bars opened or late-night cruising on The Hill.

GATE House soon became a hive of activity, often with friends and lovers coming and going. GATE House lasted for about a year before GATE moved a short distance away and rented an upstairs office at 8825 109 Street in the Bruno Pizza building.[9] With this move, GATE evolved from a place where people just hung out, hooked up, and socialized to a more official office. Now suddenly money was needed to pay the office rent. As a result, GATE began reaching out more to the local community and hosting fundraising events to support its ongoing operations and advocacy. With this change, a community centre was born, which would eventually, through different incarnations, become what we know today as the Pride Centre of Edmonton.

In the fall of 1973, an attempt at developing a women's collective folded, and in 1974, some of those organizers brought their energy and efforts to GATE by focussing on areas of mutual interest and concern. When women started to become much more involved in GATE and its activities, it marked a turning point.[10] The office's proximity to the League for Socialist Action, which was just around the corner, also provided some intriguing opportunities to share resources, even connecting two lesbian activists as a couple. By now, Michael Roberts had moved away, and Bill Ives briefly served as the new chairperson before the position was taken over by Bob Radke in 1974.[11]

BILL BOOTH
GATE member

I first heard about GATE when I read an article by Michael Roberts in September 1971, saying he was starting GATE. The paper was being passed around the dormitory of Camrose College, accompanied by many rude comments.

I moved to Edmonton in the fall of 1972 to start classes at the University of Alberta, and it was there I finally worked up enough courage to phone the GATE telephone line. Michael answered my call, and I started the process of coming out and attended my first Saturday drop-in that November at Michael and Ken King's place in the Sir John Franklin apartment building.

Michael Roberts, Ken King, Robert Emery, and I moved into the GATE House on May 1, 1973. Michael moved to Toronto in July. By September, GATE had reorganized, and I became the social services director for the next four years. I remained a member of GATE until the spring of 1981 when I moved away from Edmonton for the summer.

To help raise money for their new office space, GATE held community fundraisers at Club '70 and eventually the Roost (see page 238). GATE would purchase the liquor licence for the evening, allowing the private clubs to stay open for an extra evening in the week. With the new office, the GATE phone line became increasingly popular by providing referrals to gay and lesbian-run businesses and groups while continuing to offer much-needed peer support. Don Meen, who had a social work background, held training sessions for peer counsellors and coached GATE's volunteer hosts to support conversations related to coming out, fears of being outed, relationship issues, and the impacts of internalized homophobia on mental health.

From its early focus on peer support, GATE grew its mandate to include broader causes such as addressing inequity in the age of consent laws, challenging immigration policy, and lobbying all levels of government to pay more attention to lesbian and gay issues. GATE was often very active during municipal, provincial, and federal elections, frequently canvassing candidates' opinions and attitudes on homosexuality and human rights.

By 1976, one third of GATE's membership were women.[12] By this time, GATE had moved across the river and set up shop downtown on 101 Street. Throughout the rest of the 1970s, GATE continued to take on a more significant political advocacy function, with the fight for basic human rights protections continuing to play a central role. As Radke recalls, in 1979, "We tried to get the support of the Human Rights Commission to get the government of Alberta to include sexual orientation as a prohibited ground for discrimination."[13] Another example of GATE's advocacy involved working with similar groups across Canada when in 1977 a CBC outlet in Halifax refused to carry a public service announcement by a local gay organization. In defence of the public backlash, a CBC representative in Alberta stated, "It is the considered CBC's view that Canadian society at the present time is not ready to condone homosexuality as socially acceptable."[14] This statement led to a national protest with pickets at CBC offices across Canada, including Edmonton.

GATE worked tirelessly to raise visibility and awareness throughout the city. Their efforts frequently included hosting educational workshops, participating in speaking engagements, and distributing posters and flyers in bars, clubs, and other venues around the city. In 1978, when Anita Bryant brought her anti-gay crusade to Edmonton, GATE members participated in the Coalition to Answer Anita Bryant, which included inclusive churches, women's organizations, communist groups, and a busload of activists from Calgary who all helped to stage a protest rally at the Alberta Legislature. More than three hundred people attended. The protestors chanted and marched to City Hall, where they held another rally.[15]

This political activity isn't to say that GATE was removed entirely from social events. Dances were still an essential fundraising activity, often serving as a popular alternative for those "tired of nothing but disco, disco, disco," as GATE stated in their May 1979 issue of *Communigay*, a community newsletter they published semi-regularly. GATE also held a weekly social night at the Roost. These Monday night events accounted for a sizable revenue stream until they were discontinued in August 1984.[16] Many people who didn't feel connected to the bar scene or organized religious or sporting groups used GATE as a friendly drop-in space to gather, meet others from the community, and socialize. GATE's growing gay and lesbian library was also a popular resource. In 1980, GATE moved to its most iconic location on 104 Street in the Philips Lofts building, just two blocks away from Flashback and the Roost.

In 1981, after police raided the Pisces Health Spa, the GATE call logs revealed a detailed, real-time portrait of the panic some community members were experiencing as they called seeking legal advice. Many asked what would happen to the Pisces membership list the police had seized and what steps could be taken to help defend the men arrested in the raid. Out of an abundance of caution, the GATE executive removed their own membership lists from their offices to reassure the community the police couldn't seize them.[17] GATE spokesperson Doug Whitfield helped launch the Privacy Defence Committee, which raised funds to support legal defence for those arrested in the spa raid; the committee also helped to manage the ensuing public media frenzy that erupted. GATE retained the legal services of Shelley Miller and Donna Hawley, making the lawyers available for any men who wanted to fight the charges, several of whom did.[18]

Part of the aftermath of the Pisces raid was also the creation of more organized Pride events, starting in 1982 with a Unity Pride Weekend of events. GATE was instrumental in political activities and helped to organize Pride activities before passing the torch to the newly created Gay and Lesbian Awareness Week Committee and the new GALA Civil Rights Committee (which was focussed more on direct political advocacy). These more formal committees fit with GATE's shift since the late 1970s, when the organization necessarily prioritized the social service aspects of its work.[19]

By the early 1980s, some of GATE's lesbian members had grown increasingly frustrated, stating, "They were doing all the work, but the men made all the decisions."[20] A few of these women left GATE to create Womonspace, an organization dedicated to women's issues that operated successfully for several decades (see page 178).

The 1980s had more struggles in store as the AIDS epidemic began to define the decade and the gay and lesbian community. In the spring of 1983, GATE presented a public lecture and discussion on the virus. In July 1984, just two weeks after Edmonton announced its first public case of AIDS, GATE began a community education and outreach program.[21] In May 1985, GATE proclaimed AIDS Awareness Month and sponsored a series of lectures, films, and forums to inform the public and

BOB RADKE
GATE member

I was "recruited" late in 1972 by my downstairs neighbour, Bill Ives, to join GATE. Bill became GATE's second chairperson in 1973. I became its third in 1974 and served in that position until 1979. In addition to serving as chairperson, I also assumed the role of director of civil rights.

In those early years, money was always a problem for GATE. We managed, often with great difficulty, to pay our rent. A transportation budget was unthinkable, and my own resources as a graduate student couldn't stretch that far either. Getting around to various out-of-town events where GATE needed to be represented involved considerable hitchhiking, some nights spent sleeping rough, and once, on the way to an Alberta Human Rights Commission event in Banff, being mugged along the way.

In the 1970s, the political environment wasn't very receptive to our aims, particularly in Alberta, but we achieved one important federal breakthrough. A nationally coordinated campaign succeeded in getting homosexuality removed from the Immigration Act as grounds for excluding immigrants and visitors. GATE did its part, submitting a brief to the federal commission studying immigration reform.

There was occasionally tension in the 1970s between GATE and some in our community who were uncomfortable with our high visibility. Following an article in the *Edmonton Journal*, which mentioned the locations of local gay clubs, we got some vigorous pushback. Mea culpa—I was the interviewee. I got a phone call from one of the Club '70 board members informing me that I was to be barred from the club. I took him at his word and found out decades later that no such decision had ever been made!

doctors about the disease.[22] Walter Cavalieri, a significant participant in both GATE and the newly created AIDS Network of Edmonton, formed an important bridge between the two groups. The connection between GATE and the AIDS Network of Edmonton resulted in pushback from Edmonton city council when, in 1985, the groups approached the city for funding; councillors Wickman and Leger expressed concerns about the linkage of the AIDS Network to a gay activist group.[23] Yet, with the creation of GALA in the early 1980s, GATE had begun to distance itself from political advocacy and lobbying efforts. This was necessary for GATE to receive the charitable status it needed to expand its crucial social service work, including the heavily used phone service.

In 1983, building upon some of its previous programming, GATE created a new program in partnership with McMan Youth Services called Gay Youth of Edmonton, which initially met biweekly and provided support for youth between the ages of sixteen and twenty.[24] This collaboration ended abruptly in January 1985 with a change in McMan's senior leadership.[25] McMan's board stated the youth group would no longer be supported and that the space was needed for other groups. GATE initiated a write-in protest against this decision while trying to secure new partnerships, funding, and meeting space.[26] The youth group soon found a new home with the Westwood Unitarian Society, with youth even participating in GALA '86 by hosting a Pride variety show. Youth groups would continue to be a staple of GATE programming, although the names would evolve over the years from the Gay and Lesbian Youth Group (GALYG) to Pink Triangle Youth (PTY) to Youth Understanding Youth (YUY). These name changes mirrored GATE's own evolution over the decades.

In 1988, GATE transformed into the Gay and Lesbian Community Centre of Edmonton (GLCCE). This name change reflected GATE's long-standing struggle to include women in its programming and mandate.[27] The dissolution of GATE, however, and the start of a new organization occurred for slightly more complicated reasons, mostly involving a lapse in official charitable status and the inability to provide audited financial statements for several years. Although GLCCE's main objectives stayed similar, much of GATE's programming continued uninterrupted, from the resource library, information line, and peer counselling to ongoing partnerships with the AIDS Network of Edmonton, GALYG, and GALA.

In 2004, GLCCE changed its name to become the Pride Centre of Edmonton, continuing to reflect the growing importance of greater inclusion of all members of the 2SLGBTQ+ community. Although physical locations and organizational names have changed many times over the years, GATE/GLCCE/PCE has been an essential resource in the 2SLGBTQ+ community for over fifty years. Not every Canadian city had an organization like GATE, making Edmonton's unique version and its steady growth all the more remarkable over the years, as both the hub and the heart of Edmonton's 2SLGBTQ+ community.

GATE LOCATIONS

1971 In December, GATE places its first ad in the *Edmonton Journal*

1972 In May, Michael Roberts and Ken King moved into the Sir John Franklin apartments at 11111 87 Ave, giving GATE its first unofficial location

1973 Michael Roberts moves across the river into a house with three roommates, which becomes known as GATE House, located at 11012 86 Avenue

1974 GATE opens its first official office at 8825 109 Street

1976 GATE moves into a downtown office at 10134 101 Street

1980 GATE moves into its most iconic location at 10169 104 Street, which today is the site of the Phillips Lofts

1987 GATE loses its charitable status but eventually re-establishes itself as the Gay and Lesbian Community Centre of Edmonton (GLCEE) located at 103, 10612 124 Street

1989 GLCEE moves to a new location at 9917 112 Street and celebrates its grand opening in May with MP Svend Robinson

1992/93 GLCEE moves to a new location at 104, 11745 Jasper Avenue

1995 GLCEE moves again to 10112 124 Street, which remains its home for several years

2002 GLCEE moves into the same building as Womonspace at 45, 9912 106 Street

2005 GLCEE changes its name to Pride Centre of Edmonton to be more inclusive of the diversity within the 2SLGBTQ+ community and is now located at 10010 109 Street

2006 Pride Centre of Edmonton moves out of the downtown core to 9540 111 Avenue

2011 A fire forces Pride Centre of Edmonton to find a new location near MacEwan University at 10618 105 Avenue (current location)

JEANNE PERREAULT
WITH MAUREEN MALLOY
GATE members

In 1969 I had just returned to Edmonton after a year in Chicago where I encountered the women's liberation movement, Black Power, consciousness raising, and the Lavender Menace. My American friend, Ginny Holmes, and I set up a women's co-op house in Garneau (we called it Syblyne House) and quickly discovered that men liked to be there—which clearly inhibited women's freedom of speech. We stopped welcoming men. We were joined by gifted and passionate women, notably Maureen Malloy, who helped with this piece. We were reading and writing, publishing, speechifying, spray-painting, being generally deeply earnest about what it took to make a revolution, obnoxious and righteous.

After trying on various names for ourselves (e.g.: WOW: Women Oriented Women, after Rita Mae Brown) we became Edmonton Lesbian Feminists (ELFs—please don't laugh) and Lesbian Separatists. Endless conversation, analyses, impassioned discussions with anyone we could pin down (including suburban women's book club events) ensued. Smashing patriarchy and its main agent of female oppression, monogamy, quickly wore us out. And you can imagine how the gay women from Club '70 or the crew drinking at the Corona Hotel on Jasper Ave felt about us and our feminist graffiti in the washrooms, and our asking the wrong women to dance with us (e.g., "I can't dance with you!" "Why not?" asked the adorable Maureen, about twenty-one years old. "We are both butch!" Well, that was interesting to us).

Within a couple of years we learned that not all women (including us) were fully committed to revolution, nor trustworthy. Broken up and broken-hearted, but still determined, we looked for other politically effective ways to make space for lesbians and noticed that some men were making gay political gestures that did not seem alien.

We discovered Gay Alliance Toward Equality—so bold an assertion then. The office, when I first discovered it, was a room on the second floor of an old office building on 109 Street. It felt very odd to be there, but somehow there was room for us. Don

Musback and Bill Ives became friends. We (that is, GATE) were committed to making ourselves known, to enable lesbians and gay men to find us. Maureen remembers taking the Greyhound up to Grande Prairie and regions with Don Musbach to speak with human rights groups about gay liberation and feminism, and we attended the second annual gay liberation conference in Winnipeg in '74.

We attempted to advertise our meetings in the *Edmonton Journal*'s classified section. They wouldn't accept our ads. We protested. We made posters, we talked endlessly. The sexual complexities of male gay liberation movements and women's parsing of porn, leftist values, etc. provided inexhaustible grist for us.

GATE was never a perfect fit, but many of the men were lovely—Bob Radke in particular was a force of stability, kindness, and common sense. At one point we made a presentation to Alberta (then) Progressive Conservatives in the Legislature—I'm not sure what we wanted them to do, specifically, but we made a great case. Our primary passion was feminism. Women's rights to abortion, access to birth control, freedom from violence, equal wages, etc. could not be GATE's centre of energy and I think the elements of political strategizing with which we were sympathetic could not hold our undivided attention.

More admirable women participated in GATE, but our own peculiar sticky revolutionary history and ongoing life—school, work, love—these caught our energies. I remain, five decades later, grateful for the open hands of the men who welcomed our bristly selves into GATE.

AIDS Network
of Edmonton

ORIGINAL LOCATION:
10233 98 STREET

CURRENT LOCATION:
9702 111 AVENUE

The HIV/AIDS pandemic is often described as one of the most significant and impactful events in all of queer history. There is no doubt that it spurred Edmonton's 2SLGBTQ+ community into action during a time of great uncertainty, intense emotion, and unparalleled grief and loss. There was also incredible resilience, however, which motivated a strong and enduring sense of community and togetherness. As one poignant example, many lesbian and bisexual women were on the frontlines of providing care to men who were dying and had no family support to rely upon. This was a remarkable time when the community came together to fight for its survival.

During the early 1980s, there was considerable hysteria around AIDS, a lot of it perpetuated by the media. Dr. Henri Toupin, a prominent neurologist and the owner of the Pisces Health Spa, was accused in the press of having AIDS, causing public hysteria and a moral panic among his patients.[1] The *Edmonton Sun* was later sued for two million dollars and forced to issue a public apology and retraction.[2] In other cases, the government failed to acknowledge and respond appropriately to the epidemic because it was thought to be killing the right people.

While other cities with large and visible 2SLGBTQ+ populations hosted "die-ins" and stormed health research facilities, Edmontonians responded to AIDS by forming small, community-oriented volunteer groups to support those living with the disease and to raise awareness about the epidemic. This sense of community and togetherness was vital because AIDS was used to justify homophobia worldwide. In Edmonton, people were rumoured to be walking around wearing T-shirts that read "AIDS Kills Fags Dead," invoking an advertising slogan of the era for insecticide. Those involved in combatting the AIDS epidemic were acutely aware that AIDS was being used

▲ AIDS/HIV Edmonton march
▼ Protesters holding banner: Alberta is not for all of us!

to justify violence and discrimination against the community and sought to hold space for those being targeted and stigmatized.

Historian Valerie Korinek argues that in the mid-1980s, when AIDS arrived in Edmonton, "there was an explosion of organizational development, activism, and attention paid to gay men (in particular), which stimulated health activism."[3] In fact, by 1985, "AIDS had arrived in all the prairie cities" and "dramatically transformed the organizational, activist, and queer communities" as "attention turned from liberationist goals to medical advocacy and support."[4] Several organizations emerged in Edmonton, including the AIDS Network of Edmonton, which was established in 1984 and later renamed HIV Edmonton in 1999.[5] In 1987, Kairos House was created by Catholic Social Services to provide accommodations and support for individuals living with HIV/AIDS.[6] Both HIV Edmonton and Kairos House still operate and provide essential services to this day.

The first publicly known AIDS patient in Edmonton was Ross Armstrong, who was diagnosed in 1984. After two years of living with the virus, Ross died on July 1, 1986.[7] Ross was known as a handsome and athletic competitive swimmer involved in Edmonton's early 2SLGBTQ+ sporting groups. He participated in the first-ever Gay Olympic Games in 1982.[8] When news of Armstrong's diagnosis reached educator Michael Phair, Michael joined forces with local volunteers to form an organization that could help those living with HIV/AIDS in Edmonton. The name AIDS Network of Edmonton was chosen because co-founders—including Liz Massiah and Walter Cavalieri—wanted to emphasize the organization's collaborative mandate and the fact that radical change would be possible only with multiple sectors of society on board, including the public school and health care systems.

With different backgrounds represented on the committee, and "with work coming in different provincial departments," the co-founders of the AIDS Network of Edmonton lacked an overarching plan for dealing with AIDS, but "all knew how to navigate the provincial system and press for policy change."[9] They also knew that it was essential to include the lived experience of people with AIDS in the organization and decision-making processes. People like Ross Armstrong played a significant role in raising awareness about AIDS in Edmonton.

Ross quickly emerged "as the public face of AIDS in Edmonton," an identity that came with a very high personal cost.[10] In an April 1986 article in the *Edmonton Journal*, Armstrong was referred to as the "City AIDS victim."[11] The obstacles Ross faced during his two-year battle with AIDS—and the bravery he demonstrated in the early years of the epidemic—eventually led HIV Edmonton to name the hub of their agency after him, the place where peer support and treatment information is available and where coffee and breakfast are regularly served.[12] The Ross Armstrong Centre continues to function as a critical resource for HIV-positive people and their allies.

One of the first tasks volunteers of the AIDS Network of Edmonton dealt with was the need to humanize the virus and the people affected by it. The newness of the virus, and uncertainty around it, had generated so much fear and stigma that people who were diagnosed often found themselves without any support. Many faced extreme discrimination; some were cast out and rejected by their own families. Network volunteers found themselves called upon more and more to assist with day-to-day tasks like buying groceries and planning memorials and funerals. This was emotionally draining work for all involved, but many lives were positively impacted by this vital work. As AIDS Network volunteers shared the stories and voices of people living with AIDS, media stereotypes were challenged by very real and local experiences. People with AIDS were not simply statistics; they were vibrant and dynamic community members, many of whom were dying in the prime of their lives.

DR. LARRY JEWELL
Past Board Chair, AIDS Network of Edmonton

I wish to dedicate this reflection to the memory of Donald Michalkow, a very dear friend lost to HIV. He is one of many, but for me, he is the very personal face of HIV/AIDS.

I came out as a gay man in 1967, received my medical degree from the University of Alberta in 1968, left for Toronto to pursue specialty training, and then returned home to Edmonton in 1975. At the onset of the HIV/AIDS epidemic, I realized that I wanted (and indeed was ethically obligated) to help since I had privileged access to medical colleagues whose involvement was essential. I joined the AIDS Network of Edmonton and soon became its second board chair (following Michael Phair). I served on the inaugural Provincial Advisory Committee on AIDS as an openly queer voice. The AIDS Network of Edmonton was the community that mobilized more quickly, compassionately, and effectively than other official or government agencies. This community response to HIV/AIDS, repeated in places large and small worldwide, created the modern queer community. We revealed ourselves as caring, powerful, and prepared to fight against what sometimes looked like insurmountable odds.

The many lives lost can perhaps be seen, in a certain sense, as a gift to today's community. We can never forget the names and faces of those we've lost, and we must remember the important lessons learned and use them well. Our fight is not over.

Barry, a gay man from a small northern Alberta community, recalled the way AIDS service networks, in their early days, had

41

to develop new methods of grieving.[13] Processes that would work in other circumstances—such as gathering together to share stories or having individual funerals—didn't work when people were dying as fast as they were. This reality forced organizations to grieve in semi-annual events where multiple losses were mourned together. Barry also recalled that often a time like Christmas would see an excessive number of deaths, making those losses loom heavier because of the festive nature of the season. Involvement in the field often made for a stark and defining moment in people's lives: there was the time before AIDS and the time after. The time after was one of urgency and immediacy. There was no certainty there would be a future.

David recalls the double whammy caused by the homophobia of people's friends and families and the stigma surrounding AIDS. This meant many—too many—people ended up dying alone. It fell upon friends and volunteer groups, such as the AIDS Network of Edmonton, to make sure this didn't happen. David also powerfully recalls the cumulative impact of so many deaths—not just the number, but the variability. Some people died slowly, with time to try to prepare, but others passed away fast and unexpectedly. Some chose to end their own lives rather than wait for the virus to kill them. The impact and the grief were realities that people outside the community often could not comprehend, contributing to further feelings of isolation and despair for volunteers and caregivers who could find genuine empathy and support only among one another.

Allison, a gay woman, found herself facing homophobia from medical professionals and colleagues when dealing with HIV-positive patients. She recalls patients berating her with questions, wanting to know why she was there and what she wanted. She remembers the parents of one man swooping in and removing their son from the hospital's care, ignoring

the wishes of his partner. Her experiences were raw and unjust—and were repeated time after time after time. Like many
volunteers, Allison found herself self-medicating with alcohol
and needing to seek counselling for herself to deal with the
mess of emotions this work dredged up.

Dennis, diagnosed in the early 1990s, recalls how the political landscape of the province affected him. This was the time
of the Delwin Vriend trials, which seemed to underscore how
little value the provincial government ascribed to 2SLGBTQ+
people. At the same time, there was doubt surrounding
whether the Alberta government would even cover the costs
of new HIV antiretrovirals. Dennis recalls there being coverage
only because of an unexpected surplus in budgetary funds.

Securing financial support and a suitable workspace would
prove to be an ongoing challenge for the AIDS Network of
Edmonton. The provincial and federal governments did not
actively address the concerns of people living with AIDS or
2SLGBTQ+ people more broadly in the 1980s, and funding for
such endeavours proved difficult to acquire. In 1984, the Imperial Sovereign Court of the Wild Rose (see page 46) raised eight
hundred dollars with a vibrant drag show and would go on to
raise additional funds for Kairos House well into the 2000s.[14]
That same year, the AIDS Network performed Lewis Carroll's
Alice in Wonderland as a community fundraiser in Victoria
Park. Michael Phair dressed as the Queen of Hearts, while
Ross Armstrong went as Alice in "tough drag." A cucumber
sandwich lunch accompanied the day-long performance, and
the AIDS Network raised close to five hundred dollars. In February 1985, after Phair had turned to the media seeking help
in finding a suitable office space, the City of Edmonton offered
to rent space in a two-storey brick building near the Winspear
Centre, which became the AIDS Network's first office.

The existence of the AIDS Network of Edmonton, which
provided education and promoted community volunteerism,
also served as a catalyst for making other important changes

possible, including in the arts community, healthcare, and beyond. Examples include the announcement of $6.5 million in funding by Minister Jim Dinning to help Albertans combat and prevent HIV, which included $130,000 to support the AIDS Network of Edmonton.[15] In 1988, Minister Dinning was honoured with the AIDS Network's first Community Leadership Award.[16]

Between 1986 and 1995, several plays, performances, and drag shows were held across Edmonton to raise money for the AIDS Network. Benefits were held at the Bonnie Doon Community Hall and local gay bars like Flashback (see page 226), the Roost (see page 238), and Boots 'N Saddle. At some of these events, Phair recalls cheekily handing out condoms to patrons of the city's gay bars, often with the quip: "Oh, this won't be big enough for you."[17]

The artistic community in Edmonton was greatly impacted by the HIV/AIDS epidemic, however, forever changing the city's cultural landscape. In 1988, Visual AIDS, an artist group based in New York City, started the Day Without Art: An International Day of Action and Mourning in Response to the AIDS Crisis. These movements quickly spread internationally, including to Edmonton. The Names Project AIDS Memorial Quilt came to Edmonton in 1990. Edmonton-based Brad Fraser's play *Unidentified Human Remains and the True Nature of Love*, which debuted in 1989, was the first to include an HIV-positive character.

Like many 2SLGBTQ+ community collectives in Edmonton, the AIDS Network was a small but mighty force. The group took on a great deal of critical work and punched well above its weight—pressuring the government on its inertia while turning the party at local clubs. They were a source of hope and light while doing a lot more behind the scenes than many people knew.

DR. BARBARA ROMANOWSKI

In 1981, a cluster of cases of "unusual pneumonia" in gay men living in Los Angeles was reported. A few years later, I saw my first case of HIV/AIDS in Edmonton. A young man who was returning home after becoming ill elsewhere in Canada, in order to be closer to his family. HIV/AIDS continued to claim many young lives—sons, brothers, uncles, lovers, husbands, and wives. It had a devastating toll on the lives of many.

The AIDS Network of Edmonton was always there for individuals with the infection and for their families. In the early days of the epidemic, it provided compassionate support, friendship, and a safe space. Volunteers offered transportation to medical appointments, shopping for groceries, and often spent time with individuals in their homes. As the epidemic expanded to other risk groups, the AIDS Network did not fail anyone, regardless of sexual orientation, risk activity, gender, or race. It played a critical role in educational activities both for those infected and for the public at large.

As treatments for HIV improved and the infection became "manageable," many individuals have become complacent and have forgotten the measures by which to prevent infection, whether it's safer sex, pre-exposure HIV therapy, or clean drug paraphernalia. Education and support remain vital, and the AIDS Network of Edmonton continues to play an important role.

Imperial Sovereign Court of the Wild Rose

10155 105 STREET
COAST PLAZA HOTEL
FORMERLY THE EXECUTIVE HOTEL

The Imperial Court of Wild Roses, later renamed the
Imperial Sovereign Court of the Wild Rose (ISCWR), began in
1976, when Paul Chisolm, known in drag as Millicent (Millie),
was crowned Empress I at the inaugural Coronation Ball held
at the downtown Edmonton Executive Hotel.[1] Millie, who also
reigned as Mz. Flashback I, was one of a group of about ten
people who, after attending a similar ball event in Vancouver, began work on forming an Edmonton chapter in what
would later become known as the International Court System,
founded by San Francisco activist and drag queen Jose Sarria.[2]
For nearly fifty years, and in dozens of cities, chapters of the
court system have hosted "coronations" in which new "monarchs" (aka emperors, empresses, and emprexes) are crowned.[3]

In August 1977, the ISCWR held its second Coronation Ball,
this time at the Chateau Lacombe. Organizers such as Emperor
II John Reid described the event to the *Edmonton Journal* as a
"private social affair that included dinner, dancing, skits, and
entertainment at local gay clubs."[4] The ball had an estimated
audience of five hundred people, including "men dressed in
formal evening attire, including top hats, white tuxedos with
tails, expensive three-piece suits and ruffled shirts," as well as
men in drag, "the dates of the men in formal attire."[5] *Edmonton
Journal* reporter Bob Remington noted that the hotel patrons
were "tolerant of the gays."[6]

Initially, the courts, including Edmonton's, were entertainment societies whose emphasis on fundraising focussed solely
on paying for the following year's ball. This focus changed in
1984. The impact of AIDS on 2SLGBTQ+ communities around the
world was devastating, and government indifference forced
communities to fund both research for a cure and compassionate care for those who were ignored and suffering from the
virus. The ISCWR, like many sister courts, rose to this occasion.

▲ Roost entrance at Coronation 27 (Kitten, Twiggy, Weena, Vicky)
▼ Drag Me Out to the Ballgame, June 2022

RON BYERS

Founding member,
Imperial Sovereign Court of the Wild Rose

As the Imperial Sovereign Court of the Wild Rose approaches its fiftieth anniversary, I look back over its history, which has had such an incredible impact in Edmonton, with pride. I still remember that first meeting we held back in 1976, when our small and very determined group became part of a growing International Court System composed of community-based LGBTQ+ organizations from all across North America.

It was only eight years after its formation that the ISCWR had its mission and purpose changed forever, when HIV/AIDS began taking the lives of our friends and loved ones in our city and other communities around the world, at a time when governments were often discriminatory and reticent to fund research, treatment, and education. It was the drag queens of the ISCWR who stepped up and began fundraising through performances, brunches, events, and other activities, which raised money to support community organizations like the AIDS Network of Edmonton, Kairos House, and so many other important causes.

Although the charitable beneficiaries have changed over the years, the ISCWR's mission has not. To date, over a million dollars has been raised and donated back to our community through the incredible efforts of this unique and wonderful organization. The mission of giving back is a true community legacy that we continue to honour and celebrate with much pride and gratitude.

In fact, the very first donation the AIDS Network of Edmonton's newly established Ross Armstrong Fund received came from the ISCWR.[7]

Over the years, many groups have benefitted from the fundraising efforts of the ISCWR. Each year, the selection of charities is left to the discretion of the newly elected emperor and empress. Some of these charities have included the Pride Centre of Edmonton, Elizabeth Fry Society, and diabetes, cancer, and Alzheimer's research. The ISCWR has also been a significant and long-time supporter of Camp fYrefly.[8] In 2021, the primary beneficiary of Emperor and Empress XLV, crowned during a virtual ball amid the Covid-19 pandemic, was the John M. Kerr Memorial Bursary. This bursary was founded in 1984 by Emperor VIII Rick and Empress VIII Mary Mess. Named in honour of John "Gramma" Kerr, the bursary is presented annually and has helped hundreds of 2SLGBTQ+ students with their post-secondary education.[9]

As one of Western Canada's longest-running 2SLGBTQ+ organizations, the ISCWR has witnessed significant change in the community. In fact, it has helped shape and define it. Initially, the ISCWR, like all chapters of the Imperial Court System, was focussed on drag, which meant, for many, gay men. The ISCWR helped transform the definition of drag, welcoming drag kings, such as Prince XIV Pepe, who was crowned as the Court's first female prince. The ISCWR also broke down barriers and stereotypes by inviting straight, cisgender women and men into the fold. The ISCWR even made history by crowning Canada's first Indigenous empress (Millie) and the first Black empress (Gracie Spoon).[10]

Another significant milestone in the ISCWR's history occurred during the reign of Emperor XXXIII Sundance Lonestar and Empress XXXIII Marni Gras. One of Marni's many goals as empress was to raise the public profile of the ISCWR outside of the 2SLGBTQ+ community. Part of this mission was accomplished with help from then MLA Rachel Notley. Marni,

KENYA DEWITT

Empress XLII,
Imperial Sovereign Court of the Wild Rose

I am not religious, but finding the Imperial Sovereign Court of the Wild Rose made me understand why people attend church, not necessarily for religion but for the community. By surrounding myself with like-minded people, for the first time I felt like I was home. I've often said the court saved me. The court gave me my chosen family and a sense of purpose. Through drag and servitude, I found myself—the version of myself I never fully allowed myself to be.

In 2017, I became the first cisgender (assigned female at birth) queen elected by my community to reign as Empress of Edmonton and all of northern Alberta. I always felt proud of my ascension, but until I learned that in previous years cisgender women were denied the opportunity to run as Empress, I knew this was not only an essential step forward for the organization but a massive moment for our community and future generations of monarchs and performers.

While there were several moments of my reign as Empress XLII that I will forever cherish, nothing compares to standing on stage at the end of a long year of fundraising and presenting a donation of thirty-five thousand dollars to the Elizabeth Fry Society—a charity near and dear to my heart.

Sundance, and other members of the ISCWR were introduced during a session of Alberta's Legislative Assembly. Marni was announced not only in full drag but also wearing her crown. Wearing a crown in the Legislature had been previously reserved for Her Majesty Queen Elizabeth II. The introduction of the ISCWR became an annual event and inspired courts in other cities to petition their own government legislatures for similar recognition of their good deeds.[11]

Over its long and storied history, the ISCWR has had to adapt to changing circumstances more than once. The ISCWR played a crucial role during the beginning of Edmonton's Pride movement. In 1982, the city held its first organized Pride festivities in the wake of increased activism and community outreach after the 1981 Pisces Health Spa raids (see page 84). Pride festivities did not include a march or a parade that year; however, several events occurred across the city and at nearby Camp Harris. Some ISCWR members sat on the Pride organizing committee along with individuals from GATE, Dignity Edmonton Dignité, Gay Fathers, the Privacy Defence Committee, and Womonspace.[12] ISCWR members such as Prince XLIV Harry Schnitzel have also spearheaded initiatives to help Edmonton's homeless population, with sock and clothing drives for Edmonton's CHEW project[13] and the spread of drop-off boxes to give food and water to those in need. More recently, the impact of the Covid-19 pandemic on traditional drag shows and venues created a need for the ISCWR to move toward virtual fundraising. Silent auctions and 50/50 draws tied to online entertainment enabled the Court to continue its long-standing mission of giving back to the community.

The ISCWR has recently had to pivot to address a growing decline in queer bars, clubs, and entertainment venues. The mainstream popularity of drag has made this transition easier because Edmonton has many spaces and pop-up events embracing drag as both art and entertainment. While the Court was previously limited to performances in places like gay

MARNI PANAS

Empress XXXIII & XXXVI,
Imperial Sovereign Court of the Wild Rose

On November 19, 2008, in recognition of the United Nations International Day of Tolerance, the Imperial Sovereign Court of the Wild Rose made history when I became the first person other than the British sovereign to be introduced to a legislature or parliament in Canada while wearing a crown. It almost didn't happen. When NDP Opposition House Leader Rachel Notley invited me, my Emperor, Sundance Lonestar, and other members of the ISCWR to the Alberta Legislature, I was informed that the only person who could wear a crown inside was Queen Elizabeth II. While I was prepared to remove my crown upon entering the gallery, I shared with security what this crown meant to Edmonton and Alberta's 2SLGBTQ+ community. Upon being notified of who I was and why I was there, the Speaker of the House gave special permission for me to enter while wearing my crown.

The Court has always played a significant role in my life as I came to learn and express who I truly am. This event remains one of my proudest moments as an empress and community leader. Introductions of current reigning monarchs have become an annual tradition at the Legislature and still only happen in Alberta.

bars and hotel conference rooms, ISCWR can now be found hosting sold-out drag brunches at a wide variety of pubs and restaurants and performing shows in parks, churches, and sporting venues.

When people talk about "found" or "chosen" family, the ISCWR provides a classic example of this kind of queer community. With chapters in more than eighty North American cities, the Imperial Court System is tied together by a shared history of noble and charitable deeds. In Edmonton, as in any city where a court society can be found, this results in a tight-knit family, with all the frictions and feuds that implies. After all, what would drag be without drama?

The true importance and depth of connection can perhaps be best described by Empress I Millicent herself, when she stepped down during the 1977 Coronation Ball at the Chateau Lacombe. In her final speech she said,

> I find it difficult to put into words the love and appreciation I owe many people who helped me during my year as first empress of the Imperial Court of the Wild Rose. It was a year of my life I will never regret and whose memories will stay with me till the end of eternity. It is also my wish to thank those people who helped in ruling over an empire which compares to none other. As my last request as Empress I, I ask only that you give my successors the same deep-felt love and warm appreciation you have given me. My continued support goes to these two people, and I hope yours as well. Once again, thank you, Edmonton. I will never forget you.[14]

Edmonton 2 Spirit Society

**PREVIOUS LOCATION:
10132 105 STREET
(ACROSS FROM BEAVER HILLS PARK)**

**NEW LOCATION:
106, 6770 129 AVENUE
AMISKWACÎY-WÂSKAHIKAN[1]
ᐊᒥᐢᑿᒌ·ᐵ·ᐧᐋᐢᑲᐦᐃᑲᐣ[2]**

"Beaver Hills House" is the nehiyawewin
itwewin (Cree word) for Edmonton.[2]

It is believed that Plains Cree Two Spirit (gay, lesbian, bisexual, transsexual, transgender, and intersex) people, much like Two Spirit people in other Indigenous Nations, were placed among them for specific purposes by the Creator and therefore were thought to be divine.[3] In Cree society, Two Spirit people were honoured and respected, often playing significant roles in people's lives.[4] Local Two Spirit Elder Edward Lavallee says, "They were often healers, shamans, mediators in marriage, and tribal disputes, keepers of their history and their lore, and taking part in and often leading in their social and spiritual ceremonies."[5] Historically, many Two Spirit people were members of ceremonial societies called wihtikancimuwin and performed at annual Sundance ceremonies; they continue these practices to the present day.[6]

Elder Lavallee shares that the entire Cree Nation, who practised Indigenous spirituality, once prayed to a powerful Two Spirit known as qweskincanshew; they believed this spirit would "turn things around for the good and well-being of all things on the earth."[7] Due to the adverse effects of Christianity and colonialism, qweskincanshew has nearly been forgotten.[8] This situation may reverse, however, as Two Spirit people rediscover their spirituality after centuries of oppression, marginalization, and colonization and reclaim their esteemed place in Indigenous societies, alongside 2SLGBTQ+ groups, and within Canadian society.[9]

Today, Two Spirit people are "working to be recognized, respected and engaged in an integral manner, within Indigenous communities and in society in general."[10] They are creating organizations to develop and mobilize the current movement toward self-discovery and recognition. They are promoting healing by creating healthy environments to discuss issues relevant their own well-being. Elder Edward Lavallee states,

59

▲ Elders Richard Jenkins (right) and Edward Lavallee (left), National Indigenous Peoples Day, Live with E2S, Beaver Hills Park, June 2021
▼ Edmonton 2 Spirit Society (E2S), downtown office (10132 105 Street)

"as their movement becomes stronger, they hope they will gain and retain their rightful roles."[11]

The Edmonton 2 Spirit Society (E2S) is an example of the contemporary Two Spirit movement, actively building recognition and respect for Two Spirit people both within Indigenous societies and in society at large. The society describes its goals as working "to re-establish and enhance our traditional roles and responsibilities as Two Spirit people in Indigenous communities while creating supportive environments within all societies for contemporary Two Spirit peoples."[12]

Rob Gurney, an E2S community member and volunteer, recalls challenges he encountered finding a sense of identity, belonging, and community before Two Spirit identity was recognized and before organizations like E2S emerged.[13] Reflecting on his youth, Rob says, "I had my own look. It was masculine and feminine, and I always knew that, but I couldn't identify it or what it was because I was raised in a small Christian town by my adoptive parents, who had the best of intentions. So, this wasn't something we talked about, but I knew something was going on."[14] As a child of the Sixties Scoop, Rob was raised by a Caucasian family and grew up with primarily Caucasian friends.[15] Throughout his youth and early adulthood, Rob says, "I didn't feel like I belonged with Indigenous or Caucasian. It was quite lonely a lot of the time."[16] Rob describes finding connection and a sense of belonging after first moving to Lethbridge while attending high school drama classes, then moving to Calgary and being introduced to drag through the bar scene.

After experiencing addiction and homelessness as a young adult, Rob found his place in Edmonton as one of the few Indigenous people at the leadership tables of larger not-for-profit organizations serving people working through food and housing insecurity. Even then, Rob recalls, "there was that same thing, that feeling of not really belonging anywhere. Then I started meeting more Indigenous people when I sobered up; that was nine years ago now. I had met a lot of people in the bar scene, but if you were in the bar scene, you were drinking, so that's who I knew."[17] Remembering the significance of E2S to his sense of identity, belonging, and connection with the community, Rob says,

> So E2S came along, and one of the members, Boyd, introduced me to the Two Spirit community and welcomed me and started teaching me about things. And I started meeting other people who were Indigenous and Two Spirited, and the word *Two Spirit* started coming out. And, I thought, finally … It was very emotional; I had an identity—it was— Oh my gosh, this is exactly who I am. I am not defined by my sexuality alone—I'm not these things that I have been told, I'm Two Spirited. It was so freeing, so empowering. It was such a beautiful way of knowing myself. It just made sense—I'm Two Spirited in every definition of the term. It was the most beautiful thing.[18]

Cheyenne Mihko Kihêw, speaking about E2S connecting to the Two Spirit community in Edmonton and beyond, states, "I think we [E2S] have done a really good job accessing our Elders and our Knowledge Carriers, but [as someone working at E2S] the learning has been invaluable for me too."[19] Cheyenne describes their journey learning about Two Spirit identities as a process of moving from binary notions to understanding the Cree Two Spirit teachings about eight genders.[20] Reflecting on these teachings, Cheyenne states, "I have an identity and it's not foggy anymore. Like, I can actually see who I am for once. I am not a woman and not a man; I'm like this in-between person, and two of the genders within those eight genders are not a man, not a woman, rather all genders in one, and the in-between person. So, it is really interesting for me to see myself in the teachings. It's just so affirming."[21]

E2S observes that Two Spirit groups were not established until the early twenty-first century, despite a long history

BROOKS ARCAND-PAUL
ᒍᐧᐱᐧᒍᐣ (SÎPÎYSIS)
MLA for Edmonton-West Henday

Growing up on the Alexander First Nation and attending school in nearby Morinville, identifying as Two Spirit was not something I had ever heard or thought possible. Whether because of internalized homophobia or racism, it was not something I'd ever really had a chance to consider. It wasn't until one evening, nîkawiy (my mom) and I were driving back from Bigstone Cree Nation that she mentioned I was her special Two Spirit son. It wasn't until a few years later that I started becoming curious about whether this was a term I could comfortably use, and it turned out it was!

Fast forward to today, and I am so proud of being a Two Spirit person and the first Two Spirit MLA in Alberta's history. Knowing that our Two Spirit kin have had a long history of respect in our Nations, but were temporarily displaced by European religious teachings and colonialism, reminds me of the importance of having our Two Spirit kin represented in every decision-making space available. From the federal level, with Two Spirit Member of Parliament Blake Desjarlais, to vital community organizations like the Edmonton 2 Spirit Society, our reified role in society will help us navigate these unprecedented and challenging times through our connection to our Nations, ceremonies, and traditional methods of governance.

of Two Spirit people living in the area. The society points to Indigenous peoples' oral histories, which demonstrate that Two Spirit people resided in amiskwacîy-wâskahikan embedded within Indigenous communities long before and since Edmonton was established in 1795.[22]

Tracing its own origins, E2S points to three foundational and interconnected Two Spirit groups, culminating in the formation of E2S in 2018.[23] Dale Ahenakew founded the first, the Aboriginal Two Spirit Working Group (ATSWG), created to support the local needs of Two Spirit people in Edmonton.[24] In 2002, ATSWG successfully co-hosted the International Two Spirit Peoples Gathering at the Nakoda Lodge in Morley, Alberta.[25] In the mid-2000s, Dale Ahenakew, Edward Lavallee, Roxanne Roan, and Warren Winnipeg, amongst others, incorporated ATSWG as the Two Spirit Circle of Edmonton Society.[26] This society actively addressed the needs of local Two Spirit people, networked within Indigenous communities, and created outreach programs to help educate the public.[27] Its impressive list of activities included co-hosting the first Canadian Forum on Two Spirit Peoples, HIV/AIDS, and Health (2003); creating public training programs about who Two Spirit people are and how to work with them (2004/2005); and holding ceremonies to delve into the cultural and historical teachings of Two Spirit people with the support of local Elders (2003–2006).[28]

In 2015, Dr. James Makokis and Ryan Buffalo established Two Spirit Edmonton (2SYEG). These founders significantly expanded the public profile of Two Spirit people by hosting floats in Edmonton's annual Pride parades and creating a strong social media presence, such as 2SYEG on Facebook.[29] Before the formation of 2SYEG, Makokis was the keynote speaker at a conference on Two Spirit identity hosted by the University of Alberta, the first such conference in Canada. At the conference, Makokis said that his own coming out was heavily influenced by the homophobia his father learned in Christian residential schools.[30] When Makokis stepped down from 2SYEG to attend to his expanding medical practice, Boyd Whiskeyjack took up the leadership and subsequently co-founded E2S in 2018 with Jeffery Chalifoux.

Since its incorporation, E2S has been busy supporting and building Edmonton's Two Spirit community through social, educational, ceremonial, and political events while also networking at national and international Two Spirit gatherings. Some of the social and community events that have been offered by E2S include weekly and monthly socials, movie nights, barbeques, potlucks, beading nights, community sharing circles, dinner drag and info, sober dance parties, and poetry reading fundraisers. The society has also supported Indigenous-inclusion focus groups, community naloxone training, and substance use support.[31]

One of the most significant events E2S participates in is the International Two Spirit Gathering. E2S is part of the International Council of Two Spirit Societies with groups throughout Turtle Island (North America). In 2020, E2S won the bid to host the International Two Spirit Gathering, but when Covid-19 hit, E2S quickly adopted online strategies. Recounting this shift, Cheyenne Mihko Kihêw recalls, "We did beading socials and ribbon skirt teachings, and we did some Covid-specific things like … an online session with Dr. James Makokis. We also had a nurse who is a community member in full drag talking about Covid and vaccines. Last year the Gathering shifted to a totally online virtual event."[32]

Rob Gurney recalls E2S holding spaces of community connection for its members by being inventive when physical gatherings were impossible. Rob fondly recounts receiving sweetgrass, with teachings about its medicinal properties, in the mail from E2S during the Covid-19 lockdowns, as a welcoming community outreach during this socially isolating time.

In August 2021, the thirty-fourth International Two Spirit Gathering was held in person. The Edmonton 2 Spirit Society hosted close to one hundred delegates from across Canada.

Activities included a sweat lodge, teachings from Two Spirit Elders from across the country, medicine picking, and a no-talent talent show. The Gathering also marked the first Annual Regional 2 Spirit Gathering hosted by E2S. Rob Gurney and Cheyenne Mihko Kihêw were inaugurated as Regional 2 Spirit Warriors, 2021, the first regional titleholders. This recognition reflects and celebrates their commitment and work on behalf of the Two Spirit communities of Beaver Hills.

Rob Gurney reflects, "It was an amazing Gathering. I made so many new friends, and that would have been enough to take with me. That being said, there was so much more. There was ceremony, eating together, a talent show, keeping the fire burning, prayer, powwow, collaborations, education, and lots of laughter. It was well done—a highlight of my summer."[33] Reflecting on the significance of E2S in his own life, like its impact E2S on the lives of many young people, Rob confides,

I'm a Sixties Scoop survivor, and I was raised very colo-nial, very Caucasian, and that was their intent to erase our identities, and they did a darned good job of it. A lot of us found our way in jail, we found our way in rehab, we found our way in trauma, and that's ongoing. But E2S takes that away for a lot of people growing up who don't have to do these things. E2S really is that connection, that in-between space, where you know we are going to teach you about your culture and traditions now, so you don't have to go through what our folks in residential schools and Sixties Scoop had to go through. It's hard to talk about because it's a real thing. So just to have a space where we can talk about it, and people who understand, is really important. I can't say enough good things about E2S and how it's helping our future generations.[34]

RICHARD JENKINS

Two Spirit Knowledge Keeper from
Moose Mountain or Moosewacis
(Moose Hills) area of Treaty 6 Territory

My earliest memories of growing up were of being in a city—the city of Edmonton or what Treaty 6 nehiyaw (Cree) folk call amisk-wacîy-wâskahikan —Beaver Hills House. I didn't know that name then but have come to learn it as the true and proper name of the place called Edmonton.

When I was young, I had no idea the amount of social change I would personally experience and be intimately involved in affecting my life in relation to my Indigenous, gender, and sexual identities. Looking back at my life from my current role as the Research and Data Oskapiew with the Edmonton 2 Spirit Society almost takes my breath away with delight and excitement about what has changed and what still lies ahead of my sixty-year-old self.

In settler terms, I "came out" as a gay Metis guy in 1982 when I was still nineteen while taking an applied problem-solving course called the Life Skills Program in "Edmonton." Fast forward to the fall of 2001 when a fellow Edmontonian approached me, Dale Ahenakew from the Ahtahtakoop First Nation in Saskatchewan, to assist him in his efforts through the Gay and Lesbian Community Centre of Edmonton to establish an Indigenous Two Spirit/Indigiqueer presence in Edmonton. That meeting would herald my "coming in" process back into an Indigenous gender and sexual identity called Two Spirit. From that moment, it would take another sixteen years and two iterations of Two Spirit+ organizations (Two Spirit Circle of Edmonton Society and 2 Spirit YEG) to land in my present role with the E2S. A process I liken to a return to home! In my mind, the E2S is a beacon of potential for all we still have yet to accomplish moving forward in this time of reconciliAction!

Metropolitan Community Church & Dignity Edmonton

FIRST LOCATION:
12530 110 AVENUE

FINAL LOCATION:
10086 MACDONALD DRIVE
(MCDOUGALL UNITED CHURCH BASEMENT)

BREA
WITHOUT
IS LIKE A
WITHO
SUNSHI

BETTER
LATENT
THAN
NEVER!

EDMONTO
WOMEN'S
COALITION

The Universal Fellowship of Metropolitan Community Churches (MCC) was founded in Los Angeles in 1968, one year before the infamous Stonewall Uprising, and has grown to include three hundred congregations represented in twenty-two countries.[1] Edmonton's chapter was established in 1977 by Reverend David Gunton, who was previously involved with MCC Toronto. The Edmonton group held its first meetings in the Unitarian Church at 12530 110 Avenue. While MCC Edmonton had several different reverends and deacons over its twenty-plus-year history, one of its long-standing members was Dr. Charles Bidwell. He served as a reverend and worked in various capacities with MCC Edmonton from 1978 onward.[2]

In 1978, Anita Bryant, a former beauty queen, born-again Christian singer, and spokesperson for the Florida Orange Juice Commission, embarked on a six-month Canadian tour sponsored by Renaissance International, which was home to the Canadian-based evangelical movement.[3] Her visit was billed as the Canada Christian Liberation Crusade and was designed to promote traditional family values and heterosexual marriage, all cloaked in a virulent anti-gay message.[4] In each Canadian city, Coalitions to Answer Anita Bryant formed and organized loud and vocal protests. The RCMP even sent undercover members to observe some of the protests and gather information on the so-called militant homosexuals.[5]

Bryant's visit to Edmonton was incredibly controversial and polarizing, with over six thousand people in attendance at the Edmonton Coliseum where she sang and spoke about Christian "love and acceptance."[6] Bryant was widely known across North America for her anti-gay sentiments and her attempts to block or overturn anti-discrimination ordinances for gay and lesbian communities in various U.S. cities, including most notably in her home state of Florida. Her virulently homophobic Save

▲ Protest in Edmonton for gay rights, 1970s
▼ McDougall United Church was the central downtown meeting place for MCC in the 1990s

FRANK TESTIN
Dignity member, 1985–2010

In the 1980s and '90s, Dignity members usually met at Tom's Deli or the Gas Pump for supper on Tuesday evenings, after most of us attended the five-thirty service at St. Joseph's Cathedral. Our conversations were always stimulating and often filled with much humour and laughter. We hosted monthly fundraising Sunday brunches in members' homes, and our Christmas pot-luck gatherings held in Unitarian churches attracted up to a hundred community members. We knew how to both work and play!

This was the time when Pope John Paul II ruled the Catholic Church with an iron fist, along with Cardinal Joseph Ratzinger, who came down hard on LGBTQ+ persons and dissident theologians. Often, I fumed at their ignorant pronouncements. When the Catholic Church abandoned us in October 1986 with the infamous Halloween letter, we organized our own spiritual gatherings in our homes, especially thanks to Dennis Benoit's leadership.

Sometimes, we collaborated with Integrity Edmonton, Lutherans Concerned, or Metropolitan Community Church to create a spiritual ritual, a few times hosted at All Saints Cathedral. It was vital that we were ecumenical; it didn't matter what your religion was. During those days, we also wrote many letters and organized parliamentary submissions advocating for human rights protections based on sexual orientation. For many years, we helped organize and actively participated in Pride Week, and I did my part by obtaining permits and reserving space in Rundle Park and Victoria Park for our Pride Games and potlucks.

I'm very proud that several Dignity members played an essential role in setting up and supporting the AIDS Network of Edmonton. Some of us were on staff and others served as volunteers during this dark, painful period of our community's history.

I am grateful for getting to know so many Dignity members and other LGBTQ+ persons at our community functions, especially in the 1980s and '90s. With the onset of HIV/AIDS and an unsympathetic Church, it was a difficult time to be LGBTQ+ and Catholic. Thank you all, as we have been and remain companions on this important journey.

Our Children crusade was based on the premise that "homo-sexuals cannot reproduce, so they must recruit." Bryant's campaign material often compared homosexuality to child abuse, pornography, and pedophilia. Bryant proclaimed that city anti-discrimination ordinances would force schools to "hire flaunting homosexuals to teach our children."[7]

The success of her campaign gave energy and impetus for the rebirth of the Religious Right, which made opposition to the 2SLGBTQ+ community central to its platform and fundrais-ing efforts across North America. Ironically, Bryant's crusade against homosexuality also gave momentum to the growing gay and lesbian movement, fuelled by the belief that "gay is good" and the rise of protests and Pride parades across North America, which sought not only to counter Bryant's anti-gay message but also to organize more broadly in the fight for human rights.

Bryant's notoriety increased when she actively campaigned for the California Briggs Initiative in 1978, which would have rendered public school employees' positive statements about homosexuality cause for termination. Bryant's rhetoric laid the foundation for many future "don't say gay" laws, includ-ing here in Alberta with Bill 44 and new legal requirements for parents to be notified anytime sexual orientation was discussed in schools.[8] Thanks to the efforts of activists like Harvey Milk and Sally Gearheart, the Briggs Initiative was defeated. Tragically, Harvey Milk was assassinated only a few short months later, on November 27, 1978.

Bryant's Christian revival tour arrived in Edmonton on April 29, 1978. It was met with significant opposition, including over three hundred protestors from both Edmonton and Calgary.[9] Media reports indicate that Bryant was provided with a police escort to her event at the Edmonton Coliseum. At the concert, one protestor chained themself to a hand railing, calling out, "You've got me in chains, Anita," for the duration of her entire three-hour performance. Meanwhile, another group of several hundred protestors, including a diverse coalition of members from MCC and Dignity Edmonton and various labour and women's groups, marched from the Alberta Legislature to downtown with various signs and placards which read, "God is a Lesbian" and "Anita: Get Out of My Gay Way."[10]

Many of the protest coalitions that formed across Canada in response to the Anita Bryant tour were significant, as gay and lesbian activists organized in large numbers, including some of the very first public gay rights protests in many Canadian cities. This community organizing would lay the foundation for future anti-right organizing in the 1980s to challenge the rising evangelical "family values" movement, which sought to block and roll back human rights protections and any progress towards 2SLGBTQ+ equality.[11]

In the 1980s, groups like MCC and Dignity Edmonton would take an increasingly visible and vocal role in supporting Edmonton's gay and lesbian community while seeking to build a more inclusive faith. This role would become particularly important with the arrival of the AIDS pandemic in Edmonton.

From the time of MCC Edmonton's inception, the priorities of gay men and lesbian women remained central to its mandate, with a panel discussion taking place on male and female stereotypes in September 1979, for example, and a workshop dedicated to the issues that lesbians face in the church at the annual conference in 1982.[12] In 1984, MCC Edmonton also supported the formation of the AIDS Network of Edmonton, holding grant money from the organization in trust until the new organization could obtain charitable status. MCC Edmonton also worked to support individuals with HIV/AIDS along with their friends and families by organizing memorial services for the deceased.[13] Later, MCC members volunteered to serve as visibly gay and lesbian Christians in the community by participating in Pride Week activities and often shared information on sexual orientation with religious groups, which included mainly United churches.[14]

In 1990, MCC moved to McDougall United Church's basement in the downtown core as the Unitarian Church of Edmonton's building, where they had been regularly meeting, was sold. In 1998, Reverend Bert and Evelyn Frey, from Garneau United Church, organized a Saturday conference on issues of spirituality and sexuality, which identified a critical community need. Members of the conference, led by Reverend Charles Bidwell and Phyllis Fleming from MCC Edmonton, went on to form the Diversity Conferences of Alberta Society (DCAS), which became an organization dedicated to working towards eliminating systemic discrimination based on sexual orientation and gender identity within faith communities.[15] The Freys were unexpected allies who were very active in the United Church and worked for 2SLGBTQ+ rights both within and outside the church community from the 1970s onward.[16]

Beginning in 1998, DCAS started to grow and held several important conferences at MacEwan University (then Grant MacEwan Community College), with presentations ranging from Indigenous spirituality, internalized homophobia, coming out, suicide awareness, HIV/AIDS, laws on homosexuality, educational reforms, and spiritual pathways and journeys.[17] DCAS strived to include the full spectrum of 2SLGBTQ+ identities with featured sessions on bisexuality with Todd Janes and transgender issues featuring Reverend Mickey Wilson, who founded the Lambda Christian Community Church in Edmonton.[18] Other presenters included Lyle Millang, a local member of Lutherans Concerned North America, and Lorna Murray, who was involved with both Womonspace and Integrity, which promoted 2SLGBTQ+ inclusion within the Anglican Church.

Due to declining attendance, MCC Edmonton finally closed its doors in 2001. Many former members began attending a new and growing group of affirming United churches throughout the city and surrounding area, however.[19]

REVEREND MICKEY WILSON

My personal history as a queer and trans person working as a leader in faith communities began in rural Alberta in 1984. I watched my church split in 1988 over the United Church's decision to remove sexual orientation as a barrier to ordination for its gay and lesbian members. I went on to Baptist college and seminary and eventually left because of my sexual orientation.

While attending MCC Edmonton and working as a worship leader, I was appointed as a missioner to Inner City Pastoral Ministries in Edmonton's inner city in 1992. I spent a number of years there as a pastoral associate, helping with worship and lunch leadership and eventually served on the board. Part of my work there was making connections with unhoused queer and trans people. In 1994, a small group began meeting in a living room to worship. I was asked to lead and pastor this small group, most of whom were from conservative faith backgrounds and could not find a safe, affirming faith community. Over the next few years, that small group became a thriving faith community of more than sixty people. I had the privilege of leading that group for about fifteen years. During that time, I was blessed to work with many denominations and groups, such as the Diversity Conferences of Alberta Society, with the same goal of creating safe and affirming houses of worship.

The story of Lambda Christian Community Church and other queer- and trans-centred churches and faith groups in Edmonton has played a crucial role in fostering inclusivity and acceptance within the religious landscape. By embracing, serving, and supporting the queer and trans community, these churches challenged traditional norms and contributed to the broader movement for equality. Lambda Christian Community Church in particular served as a haven for individuals who experienced marginalization and exclusion from the conservative religious institutions that had been their church homes.

These churches contributed to the social fabric of Edmonton by providing a space where individuals could express their spirituality without fear of judgement based on their sexual orientation or gender identity. This inclusivity was part of a ripple effect, influencing the broader religious community to become more welcoming and open-minded. The impact extended far beyond the church walls, reaching families, friends, and local communities.

By actively engaging with social issues, these churches and those who led them promoted dialogue and understanding between different groups, fostering greater compassion within the local religious circles and beyond, even at national and international levels. The influence of Lambda Christian Community Church and similar congregations can be measured not only in the number of attendees but also in the positive shifts in attitudes toward diversity and acceptance in religious communities and beyond.

I still serve in part-time ministry in Edmonton to this day. The religious landscape has seen considerable change, and there are more welcoming spaces. But exclusion and spiritual trauma are still the experiences of a great many people. Out queer and trans voices from the pew and the pulpit are still needed, and I am always proud to put on the collar and speak our truth.

Another essential local 2SLGBTQ+ faith group was Dignity Edmonton Dignité, which was incorporated in 1980 and became part of the Dignity Canada Dignité national network.[20] Dignity Edmonton was founded with the belief that "gay Catholics are members of Christ's mystical body, numbered among the people of God."[21] Objectives included working for the development of sexual theology in the Catholic Church, striving for social justice and acceptance in society, and reinforcing gay Catholics' sense of self and dignity as members of both the gay/lesbian community and the Catholic Church. Dignity's main areas of activity included spiritual development, education, social involvement, feminist issues, and hosting social events.[22] Membership, which included a subscription to a local and national newsletter, was twenty-five dollars a year for students, seniors, and unemployed persons, and thirty-five dollars a year for others.

In the 1980s and 1990s, twenty to thirty Dignity members would regularly meet on Tuesdays to attend Mass at St. Joseph's Basilica and would often gather afterwards for dinner at various neighbourhood restaurants, including Tom's Deli on Jasper Avenue and the Gas Pump on 114 Street, which frequently included a trip to Boots 'N Saddle to end the night.[23] Sunday brunches were also popular and regularly held at members' homes as a social activity and fundraiser. Dignity members were encouraged to bring at least one guest to meetings and events.[24] Monthly chapter meetings were held at the Catholic Social Services building on 99 Street, which generally included guest speakers such as politicians, healthcare professionals, artists, theologians, and ordinary folks sharing their personal stories.[25]

Once a month, on a Sunday evening, Dignity members would organize a liturgical service presided over by an invited priest at Paul Kane House in Oliver. This service became more difficult, however, when the Vatican released its infamous 1986 Halloween letter on the pastoral care of homosexual persons.[26]

Dignity Edmonton frequently sponsored larger events around Christmas and New Year's, which typically involved a church service and shared meal, attracting eighty to one hundred participants.[27] These events were often held at the Westwood Unitarian Congregation. Once or twice a year, during Lent, Dignity would host a one-day retreat held at the Ursuline Convent or their cottage on Lac Ste. Anne, west of the city.

Dignity also promoted active involvement in other 2SLGBTQ+ community events in the city, such as dances hosted by Womonspace and events organized by the Gay Alliance Toward Equality (GATE).[28] Dignity was also very involved in early Pride Week events, including hosting an ecumenical service with MCC on the Sunday of Pride Week, which would often be held at Rundle Park or occasionally at Victoria Park. Dignity members would frequently help post Pride Week posters around the city and hand out copies of the GATE newsletter at local 2SLGBTQ+ bars and clubs.

In May 1982, Dignity Edmonton hosted the first Dignity Canada Dignité national convention at the Hotel Macdonald. The convention featured several workshops, assemblies, and a special Mass, which addressed topics such as gay freedom and gospel values, being a woman in the Church, sexual ethics, and freedom and authority in the Church.[29] Reports from the conference, however, highlighted the difficulties that members faced in finding a unified stance on homosexuality within the Catholic Church. Father Thomas Gallagher, from St. Joseph's College in Edmonton, stated that it would most likely not be possible for groups such as Dignity to receive formal acceptance from the Church since the Church believed homosexuality to be inherently disordered and "wrong." The endorsement of organizations such as Dignity would mean the Church would essentially condone homosexuality, which it was unwilling to do.[30] Such comments and reactions from the Catholic community were common.

REVEREND DR. NANCY L. STEEVES
Southminster-Steinhauer United Church

In 1988, the United Church of Canada (UCC) committed to affirm and include persons of all gender identities and sexual orientations in its membership and within all areas of leadership. Eleven years later, Southminster-Steinhauer United Church (SSUC) in Edmonton became the first UCC congregation in Alberta to intentionally and proudly identify as an inclusive spiritual community that not only welcomed but affirmed and celebrated members of the 2SLGBTQI+ community. In 2003, I was invited to become their minister as an out, partnered lesbian woman and for the following two decades was privileged to be part of living into that commitment to advocacy and inclusion. Twenty-two years earlier, at the time of my ordination, I could not have even dreamed of such openness and acceptance, nor could I have imagined a congregation that would joyously host and celebrate my marriage in 2006.

Following his retirement as pastor of Metropolitan Community Church in Edmonton, the Reverend Dr. Charles Bidwell returned to SSUC as a member and played a significant role in the congregation's continuing journey into its affirming identity. SSUC advocated for the inclusion of sexual orientation in human rights legislation and equal marriage, hosted educational events, diversity conferences, and supported numerous UCC congregations across the province in becoming affirming spiritual communities.

SSUC has proudly marched in Pride parades, is a committed supporter of Camp fYrefly (a leadership retreat for queer and trans youth), has hosted Rainbow Connection (a program to provide safe space for queer and questioning youth), and established Camp Dragonfly (a summer camp for trans+, gender-creative, and gender-diverse children). History has taught us that the protection of vulnerable minorities will never be assured for all time but will always need our vigilance. Thanks to the pioneering work of so many, the affirming commitment to ensuring safe and inclusive spiritual communities continues, but now with the support of the majority, not the minority, of UCC congregations in our city.

To help raise awareness and visibility, Dignity Edmonton sought to take out an advertisement in the *Western Catholic Standard*, published by the Archdiocese of Edmonton. The ad was rejected and described as a "moral matter" that "wasn't appropriate for [their] readership." Dignity would frequently write to Archbishop Joseph MacNeil, with no response, and to local parish priests asking them to share information about Dignity and their events.[31]

Bill Curtin, who was the vice-chair of the Edmonton chapter of Dignity at the time, said that clergy would frequently encourage gay people to try to train themselves to be heterosexual, including by marrying someone of the opposite gender. Those like Curtin, who chose to live openly gay, were often outcast by their parish.[32] A letter to the editor of the *Western Catholic Reporter* written in response to Curtin's remarks highlighted the marginalization of gay Catholics as it stressed that homosexuality was just as much a sin as fornication and that clergy who had counselled Curtin in the past were correct to suggest prayer and redemption.

In June 1984, Michael Phair appealed to Edmonton's 2SLGBTQ+ community for help in establishing a local AIDS organization.[33] Three Dignity Edmonton members, Barry Breau, Tom Gale, and Bernard Dousse, joined Michael and others to help set up the new organization, which would become known as the AIDS Network of Edmonton (page 34). Barry later became its first executive director, and Tom and Bernard were among the first volunteers to organize activities and support for people with AIDS.

Dignity also collaborated with Integrity Edmonton and hosted combined church services and seder meals at All Saints Anglican Cathedral. Over the years, Dignity amassed what it called "the largest and best Gay Issue Library in the City" at member Roger's house, with members encouraged to call Roger to schedule a visit to peruse and borrow books.[34]

Through all of its many efforts, Dignity Edmonton argued that the Church needed to accept members of the gay and lesbian community and treat them with love and respect. This advocacy frequently included preparing submissions and writing briefs to the provincial legislature and federal parliamentary committees, which sought input into human rights legislation. Typically, Dignity's position was at odds with those of the Alberta Catholic hierarchy and the Canadian Conference of Catholic Bishops. Christians have a duty, Dignity members argued, to take special care to include and protect marginalized members of society, including gay and lesbian people.[35] Over many years, Dignity Edmonton developed a collective voice and a strong sense that they were representing the beliefs of most Catholics—whether straight or 2SLGBTQ+— and that the Catholic bishops were the ones out of touch with their members.

PART 2

Fighting Back: Pride and Protest

Pisces Health Spa

10508 109 STREET

For centuries, bathhouses have served as safe gathering places for gay and bisexual men to find intimacy and build community. Although there are many variations in design and layout, most bathhouses have a combination of public and private areas, with video lounges for both television and adult films and a "wet area" featuring amenities such as hot tubs, steam rooms, and showers. In these confines, men find companionship that is both social and sexual, the baths being a safe space to meet, relative to public places like parks, tea rooms, and other cruising grounds like The Hill in Edmonton (see page 298).[1]

As far back as 1492, public baths existed in places like Florence and Granada; even then they were subject to government intervention.[2] Police raided the Bains de Gymnase in Paris in 1876; six men were prosecuted for an "offence against public decency," while the manager and employees were arrested for "facilitating pederasty."[3] New York City's Ariston Hotel Baths were raided in 1903, with seven of the twenty-six men being arrested and receiving prison sentences ranging up to twenty years for sodomy.[4]

Gay and bisexual men in Edmonton have been frequenting baths since at least the 1940s. Although not a dedicated gay space, the Georgia Baths was known to turn a blind eye to the activities of its patrons. In the 1970s, as the 2SLGBTQ+ community began to grow in size and visibility, new bathhouses opened, including many that didn't shy away from catering explicitly to the gay and bisexual community. The Gymini baths opened downtown before relocating to the space vacated by the legendary gay nightclub Flashback (see page 226) in 1979.[5] The most (in)famous of Edmonton bathhouses, though, was the Pisces.

▲ Pisces Health Spa membership card
▼ Pisces Health Spa original location, present day (10508 109 Street)

The Pisces Health Spa, often described as the nicest bathhouse on the Prairies, was open for two years before the police raid that launched it into infamy.[6] Even before Pisces opened its doors, there was tension between the police and bathhouse operators and patrons across Canada. Montreal underwent Operation Cleanup to prepare for the 1976 Olympics, which included raiding city bathhouses four times over eighteen months.[7] Bathhouses in Montreal, Ottawa, and Toronto were raided by police semi-regularly in the late 1970s, culminating in the Toronto Police Service's Operation Soap in 1981, which saw four bathhouses simultaneously raided in one night, followed by a flurry of intense public backlash and community outrage.[8]

Two facts made Edmonton's bathhouse raid unique in Canada. The first was that the so-called immoral activities at Pisces had been brought to the attention of the Edmonton Police Service (EPS) by an individual complainant. Fred Griffis, a twenty-four-year-old gay man, is reported to have brought concerns about the activities happening in the Spa to the EPS.[9] Jim Dardis, a detective with the EPS Morality Control Unit, acknowledged the police were familiar with Pisces but had received no prior complaints or concerns. In fact, lawyers for the Pisces owners had sent a letter to the EPS notifying police of the Spa's opening. To this day, the motivations for EPS interest in and surveillance of Pisces remain unknown. What is clear, however, is that the police enlisted Griffis to work for them as what newspapers later referred to as a "gay spy."[10] Griffis is reported to have visited Pisces three times, providing EPS with enough information to launch an intensive months-long investigation of its own.

The second fact was the ability of the EPS to build on the tactics and experiences learned through Operation Soap in Toronto.[11] Starting in early February 1981, EPS members began to go undercover in an effort to infiltrate the Spa, making note of not just sexual activities they witnessed but also private conversations they overheard. While pairs of detectives recorded the activities inside the Spa in almost pornographic detail, their colleagues lurked in a nearby business where they noted licence plates and recorded people coming and going from Pisces.[12]

The investigation culminated in the early morning hours of Saturday, May 30, 1981, when dozens of police officers, including members of the RCMP, gathered to raid the Spa. A pair of detectives, who were undercover inside the Spa, let their colleagues in and then turned up the music to cover the sound of splintering doors as the police swarmed through the building, arresting everyone they could find, some people still naked in the showers.

The raid had been methodically planned, right down to which rooms each pair of officers was assigned to secure, arresting whomever they found inside. The entire raid was recorded with both photographic and video cameras. Patrons were photographed exactly as they were found, even if naked. They were then told to get dressed, photographed again holding name cards, and marched out of the Spa into waiting police vans. The men arrested were unsure what would happen next. Several asked whether they were being sent to jail. Others worried the police would call their employers and family members. Their anxiety and fear were palpable.

The raid had been so methodically organized that not only were two Crown Prosecutors present at the Spa (which was highly unusual), but courthouse staff were also alerted and on site, ready to process the "found-ins" at a special five a.m. court hearing. Michael Phair, one of the found-ins, recalled the fear and uncertainty the found-ins felt that night, as one by one they were taken in for questioning, no defence lawyers present. Another found-in reported the deep sense of stigma and shame he felt as the police treated the found-ins like criminals.

At sunrise, they were given their court dates and released into a fog of shame and uncertainty for their lives and futures. When they were released from the courthouse into the early

SHELLEY L. MILLER, Q.C.

Even with only three years of law practice before undertaking the defence of the majority charged as Pisces Spa found-ins, I knew the normal criminal law procedures in Edmonton courtrooms in these cases were being thrown askew. Not only were the prosecutors doubled up but a disproportionate number of police witnesses lined up for a minor charge that would normally be withdrawn. Then the hostile atmosphere established at the start of proceedings expanded in intensity throughout and the collective outrage turned toward me personally. I was advancing routine cross-examination and traditional legal argument to defend the charge listed in the Criminal Code, but the mood on the bench and in the courtroom made it clear that what was on trial was the issue of male homosexuality itself.

The darkest recollection? Witnessing how the rule of law could be contorted by allowing the frightened passions of one group with legislated powers to inflame adjacent groups with greater powers, and over weeks a growing frenzy could extinguish checks and balances meant to prevent unharnessed excesses.

The brightest recollection? Despite awareness that the punishment never fit the crime, my clients showed me, with their unfailing courage, grace, and bittersweet humour, the finest examples of true manliness.

morning sunshine, the men of Pisces somberly marched procession-like back to their parked cars. Whispers started to spread and the group immediately began to organize. They planned to meet later that night at the Roost. It was time to fight back.

Fifty-six men were initially charged in the raid with the offence of being found in a common bawdy house (hence a "found-in"), contrary to Section 193(2)(b) of the Criminal Code of Canada. Simultaneous to the raid, Pisces owners Dr. Henri Toupin and his partner Eric Stein and Spa manager John Kerr were awakened, detained at their personal residences, and charged with being keepers of a common bawdy house.[13] With more than sixty people originally charged and arrested, the Pisces raid is believed to be one of the largest mass arrests in Alberta's history.

Word about the raid spread quickly throughout the local gay and lesbian community, and the response was immediate. The Gay Alliance Towards Equality (GATE) became the central body to help organize and focus community resistance. Flashback, Theatre 3, and the Roost all stepped up to provide spaces for the men to meet with lawyers, plan their defence, and raise funds.[14] Sadly, response from Edmonton's media was also immediate. Names of found-ins began appearing in the local newspaper and on television, along with reports that the police had seized the Pisces membership list, which contained more than two thousand names.[15] This public revelation added even more anxiety and fear to the community. Would those names also be released? Would other Spa members be charged? Who would be targeted next? Was it even safe to walk the streets? The media's actions fanned the flames of homophobia and hatred.

Often in past raids, shame and fear had been enough to keep public outcry at a minimum; the men arrested just wanted the matter to quietly go away so they could resume their lives. Increasingly, this was no longer the case, and Edmonton wasn't going to be an exception. The community galvanized and organized. The Privacy Defence Committee (PDC) was formed to help fight the charges against the found-ins, including fundraising events to help pay for legal representation for those arrested.[16] There also was considerable public backlash to the police raid, and not just from the gay community. A large protest outside of City Hall, led by members of the heterosexual community, drew attention to the injustice, with calls to better direct police resources on issues that mattered rather than targeting the behaviours of consenting adults and violating their privacy.[17] Doug Whitfield, civil rights director for GATE, stated that this was a war that gays would not lose.[18] Michael Phair, now chair of the PDC, emphasized that the raid "broke the myth that if gays were quiet and didn't flaunt it, we'd be left alone."[19]

In the end, more than thirty found-ins pleaded not guilty, requiring more than thirty trials before a series of judges.[20] Not guilty pleas were entered on June 30 and, with unprecedented speed, the trials were set for August, with one scheduled every two days. This schedule left lawyers with very little time to prepare, but nevertheless, the men of Pisces would not go down without a fight. Little did they know the next fight would be against the homophobia of the court.

The proposal to fight the charges laid was quickly derailed. That plan relied heavily on proving Pisces was not the common bawdy house it was alleged to be. To everyone's surprise, however, the Spa owners and manager pled guilty to the criminal charges against them only days after the raid, making the legal case against the found-ins much more challenging. GATE's Whitfield and national activist George Hislop condemned the owners' actions, suggesting they were "abandoning" Spa members by pleading guilty.[21] Hislop knew what he was talking about: he'd previously been charged with keeping a common bawdy house as part of Toronto's bathhouse raids in 1978, in which almost three hundred men were arrested; most were eventually found not guilty.

While the police undertook the raid and gathered evidence, the Crown Prosecutor's office stood ready to prosecute the criminal charges. Leading the prosecution's attack was William (Morrie) Ferries, who was known for his flamboyance and gained even more notoriety for his homophobia. At the trial of the first found-in, Ferries described the Spa as a place for "depraved" and "pathetic individuals" to "rut like animals."[22] He pursued the prosecution of the found-ins with a seemingly gleeful obsession. There can be no doubt that the Crown was a willing participant in the persecution of the men of Pisces and the devastation that followed in its wake.

Of the fifty-six found-ins arrested, almost all were found guilty. The average fine was $250, with an accompanying criminal record, although some appealed and went to trial. Michael Phair was one of the few who fought back; in the end, he won his appeal and received an unconditional discharge. Most others were not so fortunate.

The majority of the men arrested have never spoken on the public record about their experience.[23] Many simply disappeared, and a few short years later, as the AIDS pandemic arrived in Edmonton, several died.

Pisces co-owner Dr. Henri Toupin was suspended for six months by the Alberta College of Physicians and Surgeons for what they described as conduct unbecoming of a member of the profession and ordered to pay all legal costs of the hearing. Dr. Toupin was treated shamefully by the local media, including accusations that he had HIV, later retracted by the *Edmonton Sun* upon threat of legal action. In addition to having criminal records, Toupin, Stein, and Kerr were issued $45,000 in fines that ranged in severity: Pisces Health Spa Ltd. ($20,000), Toupin ($10,000), Stein ($5,000), and Kerr ($10,000). These fines were more than ten times the amount issued in any previous bawdy house case in Canada.[24] Upon appeal, the fines were reduced, but the record of convictions remained.[25]

Toupin never reopened the Spa and passed away a few years later. Although there were reports of a Pisces II opening under new management in the same location, it didn't appear to last long.

Looking back on the Pisces raid, PDC member Philip Knight commented on the fear, depression, and suicidal thoughts many of those charged endured in the weeks and months following the raid.[26] Many of the men arrested were from small towns; some had children and families; others worked as clergy, as teachers, or in government. As a result of the raid, Knight stated, "Most have just disappeared from the gay community ... Some have left town."[27] Knight asked publicly, "The raid clogged up the courts for months, cost a lot of money, and for what? It wrecked some people's lives ... What did the raid accomplish other than to cause fear and anger?"[28]

One positive element did emerge from the raid. The outrage over the injustice of police actions galvanized many members of Edmonton's 2SLGBTQ+ community who became more visible, vocal, and organized. This new consciousness would be a significant factor that contributed to Edmonton's first organized Pride events in 1982. Soon thereafter, a new organization called Gay and Lesbian Awareness (GALA) formed to continue building on this legacy. GALA would not only organize Pride festivities for the next decade, but also fight actively for the human and civil rights of 2SLGBTQ+ Edmontonians well into the late 1990s.

In 2019, Edmonton police chief Dale McFee issued an apology to the city's 2SLGBTQ+ community, acknowledging the history of harm, persecution, and devastation caused by police actions like the raid.[29] Notably, Pisces Health Spa was never mentioned by name in the apology. Chief McFee stated, "Our actions caused pain. They eroded trust. They created fear. They caused members of the public and our service alike to feel unsafe on their own streets, in their workplaces and even their homes."[30] Shelley Miller, a lawyer who defended many of the men arrested at the Pisces raid, was on hand to hear the Chief's historic apology. She can still recall the homophobia from the police and court of the day and its impact on everyone involved.

Michael Phair, the most vocal and well-known found-in (see page 6), later said there was no going back after Pisces. He would go on to become an influential community leader involved in helping to support countless 2SLGBTQ+ community organizations and causes, and later be elected to five terms on Edmonton's city council. In homage to John Lennon's song "Imagine," Michael Phair shared this variation with the community at the time of the Pisces raid in 1981.

Imagine a world where men love men
and women love women
Where all human beings are respected
and loved
Some people think that it can't be done
and that I'm foolish to try
but imagine if it were true![31]

Forty years later, the men of Pisces have not been and will not be forgotten.

MICHAEL PHAIR

Around midnight, suddenly, out of the corner of my eye, I saw police running down the hallway while we were in the TV room. A police officer yelled, "This is a raid. Stay where you are!" It was June 1, 1981.

I relive this moment of the Pisces Bathhouse Raid often—and it still generates fear, angst, and surprise. I remember thinking, *What will happen to me and the other fifty-plus men in Pisces?*

What followed the police raid included photos of each of us arrested as found-ins, court summons were handed out at two a.m., with everyone put into police vans to take us all to the Court House, where a judge was waiting to interrogate us in the courtroom. And this was only the beginning of months upon months of sensationalized media reports, court cases, guilty verdicts, and fines.

Although I had heard about similar police raids in Toronto and Montreal, I was very dismayed that I had not paid close enough attention to what was happening. I had no idea about the charges or the consequences of being found guilty and the "criminal offence" that followed. I felt quite ill-informed, stupid, and angry with myself. I wanted to learn more and fight back. A day later, I got involved with others in the queer community, helping to organize a defence against the police charges. We initially focussed on finding legal support and raising money to defend the found-ins. Within myself I discovered the courage and drive to speak publicly about the raids and push for equal rights for gay and lesbian Edmontonians. For me, there was no turning back. I came out publicly and was determined to help make things better for "us."

Legislative Assembly of Alberta

9820 107 STREET

The Alberta Legislature building has been a critical site of 2SLGBTQ+ activism in Edmonton over the last several decades, from early protests and marches and the famous image of Delwin Vriend kissing his boyfriend after his win in Vriend v. Alberta (1998) to the recent protests in support of Gay–Straight Alliances (GSAs) and trans rights. Because provinces govern education and health care and possess their own human rights codes, 2SLGBTQ+ rights have often hinged on how much provincial governments have been willing to give our community and how far communities have been willing to go to fight for our own rights. This point is especially true in Alberta, where Delwin Vriend had to take the province to the Supreme Court of Canada just to have sexual orientation added to the Individual's Rights Protection Act (IRPA).[1]

The fight for human rights recognition has been the battleground for more than five decades of 2SLGBTQ+ activism in Alberta. The IRPA was introduced in 1972, just after the Progressive Conservatives formed government in the 1971 election, seizing power from the ultra-conservative Social Credit party. Predating the Canadian Charter of Rights and Freedoms by nearly a decade, the IRPA stated, "It is recognized in Alberta as a fundamental principle and as a matter of policy that all persons are equal in dignity and rights without regard to race, religious beliefs, colour, gender, physical disability, mental disability, age, ancestry or place of origin." Nowhere did the IRPA explicitly include sexual orientation as a protected ground against discrimination, and therein lay the struggle of the next quarter-century.

Almost immediately after the IRPA was introduced, Edmonton's Gay Alliance Towards Equality (GATE), under the leadership of its founder Michael Roberts, began to lobby for the inclusion of sexual orientation. In just a few years, GATE and

▲ Michael Phair on the grounds of the Legislature
▼ Delwin Vriend with Murray Billett

JANIS IRWIN

MLA for Edmonton-Highlands-Norwood

When I was first elected to the Alberta Legislature in 2019, I learned I was the only "out" MLA in the thirtieth Legislature. But I wasn't the first openly gay or queer MLA in our province's history. Our first "out" MLAs were elected in 2015—not nearly early enough. I was honoured to continue to walk the path they had started and that of other queer politicians who blazed the trail in our province, like Michael Phair and Sherry McKibben. In 2023, I am so proud that in Alberta's thirty-first Legislature, I am joined by many more queer MLAs, including Alberta's first Two Spirit MLA, Brooks Arcand-Paul, who represents Edmonton-West Henday.

When I was first elected, I assumed the United Conservative Party would know better than to attack 2SLGBTQ+ rights in Alberta. Unfortunately, I was soon proven wrong. We were horrified when the UCP restricted students' access to GSAs and continued to attack vulnerable Albertans. Equipped with the stories and voices of students, teachers, parents, and countless Albertans, we rallied, spoke out, and pushed back.

I want 2SLGBTQ+ Albertans to know at this challenging moment when queer and trans rights are again under attack, our queer MLAs, and the entire Alberta New Democratic Party caucus, stand with them. We will keep fighting back, and we'll keep fighting for a better and more socially just province. We'll also keep celebrating Alberta's 2SLGBTQ+ communities in all their beautiful diversity. We won't forget where we've been, and we'll keep focussed on where we still need to go.

Alberta's 2SLGBTQ+ population would meet their first major obstacle in the form of then Labour Minister Les Young. In 1979, GATE, now under the leadership of Bob Radke, was again presenting to the Alberta Human Rights Commission. The chairman of the commission was Bob Lundgrian, an Edmonton lawyer who was notably, at the time, opposed to human rights protections for gays and lesbians. Young defended his selection of Lundgrian, stating, "Homosexuals must expect discrimination if they make their sexual preference obvious."[2]

When asked about protections for gays and lesbians in the areas of work and accommodation, Minister Young emphatically replied, "Why would the government enact legislation for a minority that would allow the public display in a workplace of a sexual orientation which as a generality is not accepted?"[3] Douglas Goold, an *Edmonton Journal* editorial writer, with whom Young engaged in a televised debate, countered that the "government's role is not only to reflect but to lead public opinion."[4] The Alberta Human Rights Commission's outright refusal to bring this issue forward to the Alberta Legislature created what Reverend Philip Speranza of the Metropolitan Community Church called "a constant climate of fear" for Alberta's 2SLGBTQ+ population.[5]

In 1981, the police raid on the Pisces Health Spa further illuminated the need for equal protection under the law. In the years following the raid, a new organization called Gay and Lesbian Awareness (GALA) was formed to help organize and orchestrate activism against the Alberta government's unwillingness to amend the IRPA. GALA's activism managed to sway many Human Rights Commission members, but the Commission could only make recommendations; actual changes to government legislation had to come from the Legislative Assembly.

In January 1985, the Alberta Human Rights Commission proposed an amendment to IRPA to include gays and lesbians. Representatives from GALA, including Michael Phair, met with then Minister of Labour Les Young and other MLAs about employment discrimination against gays and lesbians, then met with members of the press to discuss the issue.[6] This amendment never came to fruition, but meetings like this are emblematic of the tireless fight for justice that activists like Michael Roberts, Bob Radke, Michael Phair, Maureen Irwin, Liz Massiah, Murray Billett, and many others fought for on behalf of the 2SLGBTQ+ community.

Fear around AIDS affected the fight for equal rights. Employers, ignorant of how AIDS was spread, wanted the ability to fire people. In 1987 GALA representative Tom Edge said, "The fact that you make it difficult to fire a person because of their sexual preference does not mean the disease is going to spread."[7] Edge pointed out examples of the discrimination being faced by Alberta's gays and lesbians, including a man being fired after an anonymous report that he was gay, and landlords not renting to two single men they assumed were a gay couple.[8] What was the response of then Labour Minister Ian Reid? In March 1988, Reid said that IRPA was "intended mainly to prevent discrimination against visible minorities" and he knew of "no outward physical characteristics of homosexuals."[9]

Slowly, though, the tide was turning. A 1985 Gallup poll showed that seventy percent of Canadians agreed that discrimination based on sexual orientation should be illegal.[10] This growing support was gradually taking hold within the Alberta government. In 1989, Elaine McCoy "became the first minister responsible for the province's Human Rights Act ever to support laws protecting sexual orientation."[11] She promised to take the question of sexual orientation inclusion to the Conservative caucus despite objections from colleagues, like then Agriculture Minister Ernie Isley, who couldn't "think of any reason why we'd want to develop special legislation to cover what is a behavioural activity."[12]

The ensuing debate in the Legislature showed just how far there still was to go. New Democrat MLA William Roberts, who had courted the gay and lesbian vote in Edmonton-Centre to get elected, was kicked out of the Assembly—the first time in thirty-eight years this power was used—when he saw the government stifling debate on the proposed amendment to include sexual orientation as a protected ground against discrimination.[13] Just a year after vowing her support, McCoy faced such virulent resistance that she said it might be another eight to ten years before gays and lesbians could see themselves protected under the IRPA.[14] Her timeline, as it turned out, was dead-on.

In 1991, lab instructor Delwin Vriend was fired from his position at the King's College (now the King's University) in Edmonton after the College discovered he was gay.[15] Vriend attempted to file a complaint with the Alberta Human Rights Commission but was denied because sexual orientation was not protected under human rights legislation at the time. With the support of a legal team, which included Douglas Stollery and Sheila Greckol, Vriend took the Commission to court.[16]

In a 1994 Provincial Court ruling, Justice Anne Russell determined that Vriend's termination "violated anti-discrimination protections of the Individual Rights Protection Act (IRPA), which she interpreted to include protection from discrimination on the basis of sexual orientation."[17] Russell noted that the IRPA did not specifically prohibit such discrimination; Russell read it in, however, to enable the legislation to comply with Section 15 of the Charter.

Provincial Justice Minister Ken Rostad ordered his department to challenge the decision, in effect continuing a legal battle to win the right to discriminate openly against gay, lesbian, and bisexual Albertans. Then Labor Minister Stockwell Day flat out said that "No one is fired because they're a homosexual," arguing that religious institutions "should be able to ban gays."[18] Shockingly, the majority of the Alberta Court of Appeal overturned Russell's decision in 1996.

Alberta's 2SLGBTQ+ population mobilized, led by GALA, with support from the Delwin Vriend Defense Fund, to challenge

DELWIN VRIEND

Reflecting back on my own journey and that of so many others, I am struck by how we've had to consistently struggle and fight against those who want to enforce their idea of how we should live, love, and think. It pains me to see the gradual and very purposeful repeal of the rights and responsibilities we have gained over many years of struggle and activism. We simply cannot afford to let our guard down in this increasingly hostile right-wing environment. We must continue to work to ensure that those who still have their dignity and humanity blocked by bigots can become full and valued members of our society. Our government and the institutions and corporations that are complicit with it continue to permit and encourage discrimination, and we cannot allow them to continue on the path they are on. I thank all of you who have and continue to work for justice for all Albertans. Keep up the good fight! I'm with you.

this ruling and to fight the growing number of groups springing up to defend the right to discriminate openly against 2SLGBTQ+ people. In anticipation of Vriend winning at the Supreme Court of Canada, these groups, including one that had support from former Alberta Premier Peter Lougheed, began to petition Alberta's government to invoke the notwithstanding clause, an overriding power written into the Charter.

In the 1998 Vriend v. Alberta decision, the Supreme Court ruled that Alberta's failure to provide anti-discrimination protections for gays and lesbians was indeed unconstitutional. Sexual orientation, the Court said, must be read into Alberta's human rights legislation. After seven years, Vriend had achieved victory, but a question remained: would the Klein government invoke the notwithstanding clause, circumventing Canada's highest court ruling?[19] The answer, simply, was no.[20] This decision was not only a symbolic victory for the 2SLGBTQ+ community, but also had real-world implications, meaning that it was now possible for gay, lesbian, and bisexual Albertans to start filing discrimination complaints at the Alberta Human Rights Commission.[21]

The Vriend decision has been ranked as one of the most important decisions in the history of the Supreme Court of Canada for its impact on equality rights across the country. It would set a precedent that would later impact same-sex pension, adoption, and inheritance rights and ultimately pave the way for the legalization of same-sex marriage.[22] To say the Vriend decision was monumental to the 2SLGBTQ+ community across Canada would be an understatement.

Only a few years later, still under the Klein government, the spectre of the notwithstanding clause returned. In 2002, the Ontario Superior Court ruled that barring gays and lesbians from marrying was a violation of constitutional rights. While Klein had conceded defeat in Vriend v. Alberta, he insisted his government would use the notwithstanding clause should any court try to legalize same-sex marriage in Alberta. Indeed, two years earlier, Innovation and Science Minister Victor Doerksen had "put forth a private members bill that led to an amendment to the Marriage Act to entrench the definition of marriage as a union between a man and a woman."[23] By 2005, when same-sex marriage was finally legalized, Klein called for a national referendum on the issue, an idea looked on favourably by then Member of Parliament for Calgary Southeast Jason Kenney.[24] In the end, though, marriage equality became law, with Edmonton's Keenan Carley and Robert Bradford becoming the first same-sex couple to receive a legal marriage licence in Alberta.[25]

In July 1997, then Alberta Family and Social Services Minister Stockwell Day instituted a policy banning gays and lesbians from becoming foster parents. A legal challenge was launched by a woman known as Ms. T, who had been considered an exemplary foster parent for seventeen years and had fostered more than seventy children. When the ministry learned she had ended her heterosexual marriage and entered into a lesbian relationship, officials refused to place any more children with her, citing her "non-traditional" family structure.[26] In justifying this decision, Minister Day stated the government would place foster and adoptive children only with "natural" families, saying these children needed the "most normative societal situation possible."[27]

A provincial election and cabinet shuffle replaced Day with Social Services Minister Lyle Oberg, who continued to defend the policy and insisted all placements were made in the "best interests of the child." In April 1999, the Alberta government surprisingly reversed its decision and announced it would now allow private adoptions and foster care placements for same-sex couples.[28] Oberg, however, was quick to declare this wasn't an about-face or a softening of the government's position on 2SLGBTQ+ rights. It was more of a "defensive ploy" to prevent the court from changing the legal definition of spouse and being forced to grant even more rights to "homosexuals."[29]

Despite these policy changes, there were still many obstacles to overcome. In 2007, after years of facing both subtle and overt forms of discrimination, Blair Croft and Lance Anderson of Edmonton became one of the first same-sex couples to adopt a child legally through the provincial government.[30] Their perseverance and success not only challenged and changed attitudes; it also paved the way for many other 2SLGBTQ+ families to adopt publicly.

Schisms in Alberta politics almost always seemed to return to 2SLGBTQ+ issues. While Premier Alison Redford was affirming queer and trans Albertans by participating in Edmonton's 2012 Pride festivities—the first sitting premier to do so—those further on the right of the political spectrum, like members of the Wildrose Party, were drawing connections between Lady Gaga's "Born This Way" (an 2SLGBTQ+ pride anthem released in 2011) and "homosexuals" being damned to an eternity in a "Lake of Fire."[31] The Wildrose Party had previously run on a campaign platform that promised to abolish the Alberta Human Rights Commission.

Redford's surprising election marked a significant change in the way the provincial government treated the 2SLGBTQ+ community. For the first time, the community was invited into the Alberta Legislature for a proactive dialogue about 2SLGBTQ+ rights. This invitation set the stage for several changes under the Redford government, which included new resources on homophobic bullying, recognition of Gay–Straight Alliances, and updates to Alberta's Vital Statistics Act to allow changes to the sex listed on birth certificates. Redford also became the first premier in Alberta's history to raise the Pride flag over the Alberta Legislature building, and she also hosted the Premier's Pride Brunch in Support of Camp fYrefly.

After Redford's short term in office, 2SLGBTQ+ progress continued to march forward. Under Premier Dave Hancock, the homophobic preamble in the Marriage Act was repealed.

DOUGLAS STOLLERY, C.M., K.C.

I started as a student at the University of Alberta in the early 1970s. Over the course of my degree, I didn't meet a single person at university—student, faculty, or staff—whom I knew to be openly gay or lesbian. Of course, it wasn't because there were no gay men or lesbians at the university. Instead, everyone was in the closet. In the face of rampant discrimination against members of the 2SLGBTQ+ community, that was the only way to protect your safety and future employment prospects. For me, and I expect for many others, the closet was a dark and lonely place.

Over the years, across most of the country, human rights laws came to be extended to include protections against sexual orientation discrimination. But not in Alberta. As a matter of public policy, the Alberta government refused to recognize the human rights and inherent dignity of members of the 2SLGBTQ+ community. This refusal served to reinforce the existing discrimination against the community. For many, the closet doors remained firmly closed.

Delwin Vriend had the courage to challenge this overt discrimination by the Alberta government. It was my privilege to serve as a member of the legal team that worked on his case, which ultimately led to recognition by the Supreme Court of Canada of the inherent dignity of all persons, including members of the 2SLGBTQ+ community. With this landmark decision, the closet doors slowly began to open in Alberta.

Looking back over the past twenty-five years, much progress has been made, but our human rights are not entirely secure. We still have work to do to build a province that is truly welcoming, inclusive, and accepting of everyone.

Thanks to concerted pressure from allies like Liberal MLAs Kent Hehr and Laurie Blakeman, Conservative MLA Sandra Jansen, and Deputy Premier Thomas Lukaszuk, Bill 10 was introduced under the Prentice government, legislating enhanced supports and protections for Gay–Straight Alliances and Queer–Straight Alliances. For the very first time, there were strong and visible 2SLGBTQ+ allies in all political parties.

The 2015 election of the New Democratic Party (NDP) under Rachel Notley was a watershed moment and brought sweeping changes in 2SLGBTQ+ representation and visibility. For the first time, several out and proud 2SLGBTQ+ members were elected, including Michael Connelly, Estefan Cortes-Vargas, and Ricardo Miranda, who would become the first 2SLGBTQ+ person to hold ministerial office when he was appointed as the Minister of Culture and Tourism. Cortes-Vargas would later come out as the first nonbinary member to hold political office in Alberta.

The NDP government continued to propel 2SLGBTQ+ equality forward by introducing a number of important changes, including amendments to Alberta's Human Rights Act to add gender identity and gender expression as protected grounds against discrimination. The NDP government also sought to improve school policy requirements and enhance protections for 2SLGBTQ+ students and staff by introducing Bill 24, An Act to Protect Gay–Straight Alliances. This bill brought immediate opposition from Jason Kenney's United Conservative Party (UCP), the new conservative hydra that had grown out of the merger of the Progressive Conservatives and the Wildrose Party. The crux of Bill 24 centred around the parental notification requirements of school-based clubs such as GSAS.[32] So opposed was the UCP to Bill 24 that the bill was one of the first items on the chopping block after their ascension to a government in 2019.[33] Such responses continued the historical lack of allyship and support from conservative parties in Alberta.

On May 30, 2023, Alberta's political landscape underwent yet another monumental shift with the re-election of the UCP under the leadership of Danielle Smith, former leader of the Wildrose Party. There was some hope, however, as the NDP managed to win the largest opposition in Alberta's history.

Less than a year after the UCP was elected, the "Lake of Fire" was back and burning hotter than ever as Premier Smith introduced a series of unprecedented policy announcements attacking trans youth and 2SLGBTQ+ human rights. Smith's anti-2SLGBTQ+ legislation included preventing students from using chosen names and pronouns related to gender identity at school without parental consent; banning all trans participants from competing in female mature sports; requiring parents to opt their children "in" rather than "opt out" of any planned discussions or presentations about sexual orientation, gender identity, or human sexuality in K-12 schools; requiring that all third-party teaching materials on sexual orientation, gender identity, and human sexuality used in schools receive advance approval from the Ministry of Education; prohibiting all gender-affirmation surgeries (top and bottom) for minors; and restricting access to puberty-delaying and cross-sex hormones for minors.[34] These government announcements seemed to be inspired by similar moves in Republican states like Florida, Texas, and Alabama.

Smith's anti-2SLGBTQ+ legislation was widely denounced by medical professionals, social workers, teachers, unions, legal experts, and the 2SLGBTQ+ community with the critique that the policies were not based on credible research or scientific evidence but right-wing ideology.[35] Despite this disavowal, at the time of writing, Smith seems to be moving forward with full knowledge that the only way these policies would be legal in Canada is if she invokes the Charter's notwithstanding clause to legislate these changes, in violation of Alberta's human rights legislation and the equality provisions enshrined within Section 15 of the Charter. As a result of this blatant discrimination, Pride festivals across Alberta banned the UCP from participating: "You may not join our celebrations in June when you plan to attack us in September. Queer rights should not be a political decision. Trans rights are human rights."[36]

Throughout Alberta's history 2SLGBTQ+ human rights have seldom been given, but have had to be fought for. In the 1970s and 1980s, when members of GATE and GALA appealed to the Alberta Human Rights Commission, they did so very much on their own. They found few allies on the floor of the Legislature and had equally few in the press or general public. The hard work and determination of those early advocates created a legal shift, one concurrent with a changing social mindset that can be attributed perhaps to each and every 2SLGBTQ+ Albertan who came out to anyone in their lives. Long-time GALA and Equal Alberta member Murray Billett often says, "Discrimination hinders coming out; coming out hinders discrimination." This statement is as true on the streets of communities as it is on the Legislature floor.

There is still much work to do to protect 2SLGBTQ+ Albertans, especially racialized queer, trans, and Two Spirit youth. Still, with growing numbers of loud and proud voices inside our community and increasing numbers of allies from outside our community, we can continue to hold current and future governments accountable until we become truly equal in dignity and rights.

Edmonton
City Hall

1 SIR WINSTON CHURCHILL SQUARE

City Hall has always been an important symbol of progress and inclusion. It has also been a site of pain, protest, and pride for Edmonton's 2SLGBTQ+ community. What happens at City Hall matters, not just politically but also symbolically.

One of the earliest protests in support of the city's gay and lesbian community happened in 1981 as both heterosexual and queer citizens united on the steps of City Hall against the heavy-handed police raid of the Pisces Health Spa (see page 84), which protestors claimed was an assault not just on gay men, but an infringement on every citizen's right to privacy.

For decades, the doors to City Hall were closed to members of Edmonton's gay and lesbian community. Things began to change in the early 1990s, however, with the election of the city's first gay and lesbian councillors and a growing visibility and recognition of Edmonton's 2SLGBTQ+ community with Pride celebrations and events happening throughout the year.

Before the 1990s, allies in City Hall existed but were frequently outnumbered by those who mocked or outright loathed 2SLGBTQ+ people—as seen by the struggles in the mid- and late 1980s to have a Pride day proclaimed, for example. But change was coming not just in Edmonton but across Canada. Following Svend Robinson's coming out as the first openly gay member of Parliament in 1988, a host of other 2SLGBTQ+ politicians followed suit. In 1992, Michael Phair (see page 6) became the first openly gay city councillor in Edmonton, and the following year, then Mayor Jan Reimer declared June 26 to be Gay and Lesbian Pride Day before leading the annual Pride march down Whyte Avenue.[1] In 1994, Sherry McKibben won a council seat in a by-election and became the first openly lesbian city councillor in Edmonton's history. McKibben beat out seventeen contenders to win a council seat, bolstered by her previous work at the Boyle McCauley Health Centre.[2]

▲ First Mayor's Pride Brunch: QC Gu, Michael Phair, Laurie Blakeman, Sam, Jill Delarue, Carl Swanson, Emily Johnson, Mayor Stephen Mandel
▼ City Hall, present day

JEFF WINKELAAR
GALA Member, 1984–86

Pride today is quite different than those early days in the 1980s. From 1984 to 1986, GALA requested Edmonton's city council to proclaim a Gay and Lesbian Awareness Day. While it was voted down every year, the devil in the details of the request was revealing, a bit comical on the surface, and somewhat pathetic in retrospect. In 1984, we met with several city councillors to introduce the need for a proclamation and our reasoning behind the request. With one exception, we received either a chilly or an openly hostile response, even from so-called liberal council members. Olivia Butti was disgusted and refused to meet with us. Julian Kinisky did, but it was a short session, and we left after receiving a finger-wagging rant and lecture. Percy Wickman, an advocate for the disabled community who later became a Liberal Party MLA, was openly hostile at our meeting and suggested that we were somehow adulterating his own minority interests.

While I know in retrospect that Jan Reimer came around in future years, and did indeed declare Gay and Lesbian Awareness Day when she became mayor in 1992, she was not helpful in those early days and raised questions about homosexuality being linked to overpopulation. On the flip side, thankfully, there was Councillor Ed Ewasiuk, who supported the passage of our motion the very first year it was presented and in all subsequent years.

On the day we first addressed City Hall, about fifteen GALA members and friends filled Council Chambers only to quickly be met with the snickering derision of Mayor Lawrence Decore and most city councillors. When the proclamation request was defeated by a vote of twelve to one, we walked out in concert with explicit expressions of disgust on our faces. While city council's reaction was negative and even a bit disconcerting or alarming, we adopted a thick-skinned attitude. We had at least garnered some good media coverage and took it as a stepping stone to future successes! Those were the days when Pride was indeed a protest!

When McKibben joined Phair on city council, that made two openly gay and lesbian councillors, a rare feat in Canada at the time.

When Mayor Reimer declared June 26, 1993, to be Edmonton's first official Gay and Lesbian Pride Day, there was much debate about the proclamation, especially after Reimer decided to march in the annual parade. On June 8, 1993, the *Edmonton Journal* published letters from across Alberta complaining about the proclamation. One person wrote they were "embarrassed" to be an Edmontonian, while others decried the move as undemocratic and out of touch.[3] Thankfully, the proclamation was not reversed, as had happened in Calgary two years prior. The Pride march that year concluded in Old Strathcona's McIntyre Park with an impassioned speech by Phair about the importance of human rights. Delwin Vriend, then fighting his anti-gay discrimination suit, was in attendance.[4]

It wasn't long after Vriend's termination that the City of Edmonton stepped up, at the request of the staff union, and implemented its own policy against discrimination on the basis of sexual orientation.[5] Vriend took this as proof that public opinion was shifting in support of human rights and inclusion.[6] As a further step forward, in 1998 City of Edmonton employees were given same-sex benefits.[7]

In 2004, the year after then Mayor Bill Smith was forced, under the pressure of a human rights complaint, to proclaim Pride Week, a group of anti-gay protestors took to the steps of City Hall to ensure this wouldn't be repeated. Twelve members of the so-called Better Canada Coalition presented a petition with one thousand signatures in support of banning Pride proclamations as well as any future Pride parades. The petition fell well short of the 66,611 signatures required to be officially recognized, however.[8]

City Hall has also been the site of many important 2SLGBTQ+ events over the years, both sanctioned and not. Edmonton's

JAN REIMER

Mayor of Edmonton, 1989–1995

Proclamations were most times considered a ho-hum affair delegated to the mayor—that is, until the reaction and drama that surrounded Edmonton's first Gay Pride Proclamation. When I look back at that time on city council, there were many good memories, like the leadership, strength, and kindness from people like Michael Phair, Sherry McKibben, Maureen Irwin, and Murray Billett. They were all amazing individuals who contributed so much to the community in so many important ways. But there were also bad memories, like the extreme reactions and homophobic vitriol that surfaced. This was particularly hard on my staff, who answered the phone hearing intolerant diatribes, which today are magnified through social media or worse.

It's been seventy-five years since the founding of the Universal Declaration of Human Rights, and it is still an uphill battle on many fronts. Working with Michael and Sherry during their time on city council, we had united voices in making Edmonton a more livable, humane, and compassionate place. And their example in doing this important work is so needed today. Human rights are foundational for safe, livable cities and can never be taken for granted or ignored.

most famous drag queen, Darrin Hagen, had his photo taken in a legendary mermaid outfit in front of the City Hall fountain. In *The Edmonton Queen*, Hagen's 1997 memoir, he recounts doing a go-go dance and falling into a snowbank at City Hall; the memoir also recalls Darrin choreographing the "first-ever water ballet in the City Hall reflecting pool."[9] In May 1998, 2SLGBTQ+ choirs gathered together at City Hall as part of the Canadian GALA Choruses Festival, the largest gathering of queer-identified choruses in Canadian history.[10] City Hall was also the site for more somber moments, such as 1999's candlelight vigil marking those lost to HIV and AIDS.

After the clock on 2SLGBTQ+ progress rolled back under Mayor Bill Smith, the light and rainbows returned to City Hall with the election of Stephen Mandel in 2004. Mayor Mandel was arguably one of the most pro-2SLGBTQ+ leaders in Edmonton's history.[11] He not only frequently attended Edmonton's Pride Festival and 2SLGBTQ+ events, but was also immensely proud to host the first Mayor's Pride Brunch in Support of Camp fYrefly. As a Jewish person, Mandel would often say that he understood the impacts of discrimination and wanted to create a city that included everyone. Mayor Mandel was instrumental in the creation of the Edmonton Police Service's Hate and Bias Crime Unit, which quickly became an essential resource for 2SLGBTQ+ and other vulnerable communities.

After Mandel's retirement in 2013, city councillor Don Iveson was elected mayor, and the torch of 2SLGBTQ+ progress was kept ablaze. Iveson remained a staunch supporter of diversity, human rights, and 2SLGBTQ+ inclusion during his two terms as mayor. He was a vocal ally and frequent participant at many 2SLGBTQ+ events and could often be seen having a beer at a Fruit Loop dance party, proudly marching in the Pride parade, and leading important conversations about inclusion at City Hall.

SANDI STETSON

Pride Festival Coordinator, 2006–2011

I first became involved in 2006, when the Edmonton Pride Week Society hired me as their very first festival coordinator, just a few months before Pride was scheduled to take place. I was told that if they didn't hire someone to help organize the festival, Pride wouldn't happen that year. They also told me that I would have to raise enough money to cover my salary! It was daunting, but I was excited to take on the challenge.

Over the five years I was involved in Pride, I had the amazing privilege of working alongside Ken MacDonald, the board chair, and many other amazing board members and volunteers. Each year, the Festival continued to grow. In 2008, we participated in the World Pride Conference in Vancouver and brought back many important learnings, passion, and enthusiasm to create our own fabulous Pride events! Pride wasn't just an event. It was a movement.

Pride was very impactful in my life. I learned and grew so much, and it was so incredibly rewarding to be involved with so many amazing people, many of whom I count as friends. Pride in Edmonton was always something very poignant and powerful.

By 2006, the annual Pride Awards were held at City Hall and a rainbow pride flag was proudly flying over the building. Rainbow crosswalks even began appearing on city streets. With these visible symbols of inclusion, it was evident to 2SLGBTQ+ Edmontonians just how far we had come as a community since the homophobic days of the past. However, there were still municipal battles to fight. It wouldn't be until December 2019, thanks to the leadership of Councillor Aaron Paquette, the city's first Indigenous councillor since the 1970s, that a bylaw prohibiting the practice, promotion, and advertising of "conversion therapy" was passed unanimously by city council. This vital legislation became a model for similar bylaws in municipalities across the country.[12]

If you look closely at the trademark pyramids of City Hall, you just might catch a glimpse of a rainbow reflected into the hallowed hallways and be reminded of the champions who have blazed a trail towards inclusion and the rights and privileges we all enjoy today. We can proudly say that our City Hall now welcomes everyone.

STEPHEN MANDEL
Mayor of Edmonton, 2004–2013

During the city's 2004 municipal election, the issue of Edmonton's Pride Parade and 2SLGBTQ+ rights was raised, but the discussion was never very heated. As the city's newly elected mayor, I believed the vast majority of Edmontonians had realized the time had come to respect the rights of all people. However, there was still controversy about the Pride Week proclamation. Pride was part of Edmonton's summer events schedule, so why wouldn't I recognize the event's significance by acknowledging it through a proclamation!? I didn't realize that members of the 2SLGBTQ+ community had, for many years, felt alienated and disenfranchised. Edmonton was not, in fact, a "city" that was welcoming to them. I learned this firsthand through interactions with individuals who came and thanked us, often very emotionally, for city council's support. These actions proved to me that I was naïve. Much work still needed to be done. Putting politics aside, I was asked to be the Pride Parade's Grand Marshal, which was an honour and a great experience. I recall how the streets were lined with people of all ages. I had a ball. The parade culminated at Churchill Square, where the crowds gathered, and the party continued for quite a while.

Almost immediately after I was sworn in as mayor, Michael Phair approached me about hosting the Mayor's Pride Brunch with funds supporting Camp fYrefly. As we all know, Michael was and always will be a passionate advocate, but he felt that Pride had to be about more than just a party. He believed that a brunch led by the mayor, with a clear community purpose, would help meet that goal. It sounded like a great idea to me! The wheels were set in motion. The first brunch was held at the Norwood Legion. The crowd was not large, but the event was now on its way. Over the next several years, the brunch grew to sell out at the Chateau Lacombe Hotel. The event was very moving as we heard story after story about how the camp helped children find community and develop a better understanding of themselves. I have to admit the stories brought tears of joy to my eyes. The maturity of the presenters was amazing. You have to give a lot of credit to those who organized and worked at Camp fYrefly. They were the unsung stars.

Another area which for many years had created some community conflict was the police. In reality, a vast majority of the police were not in conflict with the 2SLGBTQ+ community, but a greater understanding was clearly needed. In the nominating process for the Police Commission, we put forward Murray Billett as a very competent individual who was selected to serve. He served a full six-year term with an exemplary record. He helped to foster mutual respect and understanding, which built upon the long-standing work of the Edmonton Police Service's 2SLGBTQ+ community liaison committee, which started back in 1992!

Over the years, there have been many wonderful community events that [my wife] Lynn and I have attended, many of which continue today. I learned through my time on city council that the 2SLGBTQ+ community is just like so many other communities. Some issues drew them together, while other topics caused some challenges. However, when the issue concerns human rights, we all must unanimously support each other. This is what makes Edmonton such a great and wonderful community.

Edmonton Courthouse

OLD LOCATION:
100 STREET AND 102A AVENUE[1]

CURRENT LOCATION:
1A SIR WINSTON
CHURCHILL SQUARE (ESTABLISHED IN 1972)

Court House, Edmonton, Alta.

The relationship between the 2SLGBTQ+ community and the Canadian legal system has been marked by an often fraught and complex history of discrimination, prejudice, and persecution.[2] In the past, 2SLGBTQ+ people were arrested and incarcerated simply for loving someone of the same sex. Our government and courts have often not been kind and imposed some of the harshest sentences based on the belief that homosexuality was a crime against nature. The Canadian government once sought to actively purge 2SLGBTQ+ people from the armed forces, RCMP, and federal civil service under the false belief that homosexuality represented a threat to national security.[3]

In Edmonton, several criminal cases were brought against members of the 2SLGBTQ+ community, often stemming from moralistic, colonial-era laws governing sex, gender, and sexuality. Edmonton's 2SLGBTQ+ community has also been central to legal battles for equality rights at the provincial and federal levels. The Supreme Court of Canada's ruling in Vriend v. Alberta (1998), for example, read sexual orientation into the Alberta Human Rights Code after Delwin Vriend was fired from the King's College in 1991 for being gay (see page 105).[4] Some historical cases, like the bawdy house charges brought against patrons of the Pisces Health Spa in 1981 (see page 84), are becoming more well-known.[5] Others, like the prosecution of two exotic dancers in 1975 for immoral theatrical performance, are still buried in the legal archives.[6]

The persecution of gay men has a long and complex history in Edmonton, with early reports of men being charged with gross indecency at seasonal mining camps dating back to 1880. Charges such as gross indecency, sodomy, and vagrancy have long been used to target and persecute gay men explicitly and, in at least one case, a Black woman in Yellowknife.[7]

▲ Edmonton Court House, 1912
▼ Original Courthouse Location, present day (100 102A Avenue)

Historical records from the Northwest Mounted Police indicate charges of indecency and sodomy as early as 1905 in the new provinces of Alberta and Saskatchewan. In several cases, gay men were designated as dangerous sexual offenders or sexual psychopaths for no reason other than having intimate relationships with someone of the same sex.

In 1942, the RCMP and Edmonton city police investigated ten men connected to Edmonton's Strand Theatre, eventually laying thirty-seven charges of gross indecency, which resulted in nine men being convicted, six of whom served jail terms (see page 158).[8] As journalist turned senator Paula Simons reported, the police "seized private love letters as evidence" and used the fact that one of the men had ordered a book by Oscar Wilde as evidence of "criminal perversion."[9] There was some speculation as to whether the accused men could receive a fair trial, as the charges "would naturally make all decent people in Edmonton apprehensive and disgusted."[10] In 2015, Edmonton author and playwright Darrin Hagen wrote, produced, and directed *Witch Hunt at the Strand* based on these events, using court records to recreate the overt homophobia and hysteria of the time.

Gross indecency charges against gay men were the subject of widespread media attention throughout the 1940s and 1950s in Canada.[11] Police were particularly cunning when it came to eliciting confessions from those accused of gross indecency. In fact, in 1948, an appeal was allowed on a gross indecency charge in Edmonton after a judge found that a confession to a police officer by a man who had slept with another man was inadmissible on numerous counts.[12] The 1940s and 1950s also saw renewed interest in obscenity laws and pornographic materials available at newsstands, including anything gay related.[13] The panic over indecent literature in Canada reached Edmonton in 1966 when the *Edmonton Journal* ran a story about a dinner held by the Edmonton chapter of Youth for Christ, where the organization's national president, Wes Aarum, decried "clerics" who were said to be "encouraging teenagers to live in sin" by exposing them to homosexuality, "twilight pornography," and "skin magazines"; he also bemoaned restricted adult films which were becoming more "sex orientated."[14]

In 1965, a Calgary man named Everett George Klippert became the last person in Canada to be arrested, tried, and imprisoned for gross indecency before the partial decriminalization of homosexual acts in 1969.[15] Klippert was deemed "a criminal sexual psychopath" by the courts and incarcerated indefinitely until his release in 1971. Klippert's release from prison was mainly due to the significant media attention drawn to his unjust imprisonment.[16] After his release, Klippert married a woman and lived quietly in Edmonton until his death in 1996.

In December 1967, the federal government introduced sweeping changes to the Criminal Code of Canada on issues related to sex and gender, including homosexuality, abortion, and divorce. Bill c-150, which received royal assent on June 27, 1969—coincidentally, the same day as the Stonewall Riots in New York City— partially legalized same-sex sexual intercourse for consenting adults over twenty-one and for all married persons regardless of age.[17] These laws were changed again in 1987 when the charge of gross indecency was finally removed from the Criminal Code and buggery was changed to more specifically refer to anal intercourse. Bill c-150 was far from perfect, however; the national hype surrounding the 1969 criminal reforms has recently been criticized by some queer historians as being overzealous. The changes actually "recriminalized" homosexuality insofar as the omnibus bill allowed only consenting adults to engage in anal intercourse in "private" with no more than two persons present, leaving group sex, public sex, and even bathhouses wide open for criminal persecution.[18]

Nevertheless, the first national recognition of legal rights for 2SLGBTQ+ Canadians was important and awakened a new societal consciousness, one that would insist on visibility

JUSTICE JULIE C. LLOYD
Alberta Court of Justice

Section 15 of the Charter of Rights and Freedoms states, "Every individual is equal before and under the law and has the right to the equal protection and benefit of the law without discrimination ...." These words did not describe the reality of queer folk in Alberta. The laws mostly excluded gay, lesbian, and bisexual folks, and discrimination was an everyday experience. As a young lawyer and a lesbian, I was skeptical that section 15 would make enough of a difference in our lives. The Charter was designed to change statutes, not hearts and minds.

As courts began to consider these challenges and write decisions, Canadians began to see and understand things differently. Canadians saw that equality is a deeply held and cherished Canadian value. Canadians understood that treating people unfairly because of false and harmful stereotypes was wrong and saw that the moral issue was never homosexuality; the moral issue was always discrimination.

In a few short years, not only did hundreds of statutes get changed, but, to my surprise, many Canadians' hearts and minds were changed, too, and this country became a kinder and more just place for us all.

and further equality under the law. This was a watershed moment, and there would be no looking back. In some cases, it seemed like 2SLGBTQ+ equality moved two steps forward and one step backwards. Government policies and laws were almost always fraught with contradictions and half measures, the long-standing gay blood ban being but one modern example.[19]

The 1970s, 1980s, and 1990s saw several legal ups and downs for the 2SLGBTQ+ community. Large bathhouse raids occurred in Montreal, Toronto, Edmonton, and Calgary as late as 2002. The Edmonton Police Service even had its own specialized investigations team called the Morality Control Unit, which investigated, sometimes with questionable tactics, what it believed to be vice crimes, which often included anything deemed to offend the moral standards of the community, including prostitution, pornography, gambling, lewdness, obscenity, and anything to do with homosexuality.

In 1975, two exotic dancers dressed in drag simulated live sex at Chez Pierre's cabaret in downtown Edmonton and were arrested for immoral theatrical performance, a rare charge in the Criminal Code's "corruption of morals" section. After an appeal and retrial, both performers were convicted.[20] Then, in January 1980, Edmonton police confiscated the pornographic horror-comedy *Dracula Sucks* from the Jasper Cinema Centre even though the provincial censorship board had approved it.[21] The cinema's ownership group appealed the conviction to the Supreme Court of Canada, which ordered a retrial on the basis that the Alberta judge erred in law by confusing his own personal distaste for the film with the supposedly more objective "community standards test."[22]

Police harassment and targeting of the 2SLGBTQ+ community was a common occurrence, with gay men a frequent target.[23] In 1976, two young men were charged and arrested for the crime of kissing in a parked car at 5 a.m. in Queen Elizabeth Park.[24] There was, of course, the raid on the Pisces Health

Spa in 1981, and then, over a period of a month in the summer of 1988, almost twenty men were charged with committing indecent acts based on covert police operations in Victoria Park, Government House Park, and the washrooms at Borden Park. Complaints from the city parks department were alleged to have prompted the investigations.[25] Constable Stew Dickie, a member of the city park patrol, said he estimated four hundred gay men "occasionally or often [visited parks] for sex in public washrooms, on park trails, and in secluded areas off the trails."[26]

When a so-called flood of complaints began a new investigation in 1992, police went undercover as they had during the Pisces Spa raid.[27] This Victoria Park dragnet resulted in multiple men being charged, not only for indecent acts but also for sexual assault. Assault charges were laid when police officers claimed they had been groped while undercover. Accusations of entrapment and community outrage over these questionable tactics were significant factors in establishing the Edmonton Police Service's Gay and Lesbian Liaison Committee in 1992, and eventually most charges were dropped. However, reputational damage was done when the *Edmonton Journal* published the names of the men arrested in the park raids, mirroring their actions of more than a decade earlier during the Pisces Health Spa raid and ensuing sensationalized media coverage.[28] Apparently, no lessons had been learned.

Edmonton's Law Courts were often the first line of defence against police harassment, questionable tactics, and trumped-up charges. The courthouse was also a place where media attention shone a powerful spotlight on both the charges and the accused—often with dubious ethics and devastating results. As the years passed, the media's portrayal changed, reflecting a growing public awareness and acceptance of 2SLGBTQ+ people in the city. This change was thanks mainly to members of the 2SLGBTQ+ community who stepped forward to help educate, advocate, and hold the police, courts, and media accountable. Still, yet more work remains to be accomplished. The fight for justice is far from over, especially for racialized, trans, and Two Spirit members of our community.

Edmonton Police Service

9620 103A AVENUE

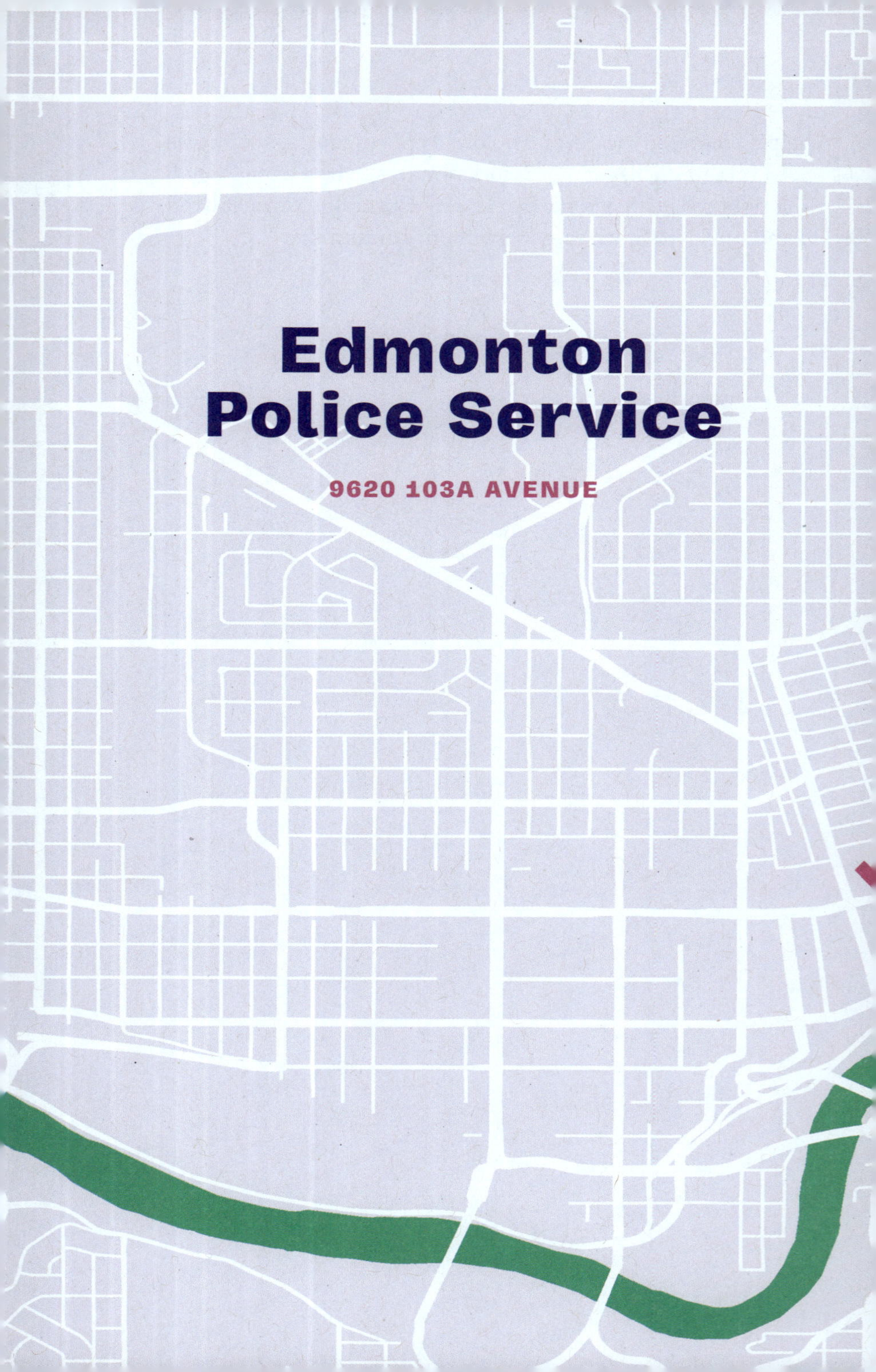

The 1981 raid on the Pisces Health Spa (see page 84) may be the best-known police action directed against Edmonton's 2SLGBTQ+ community, but it was by no means the first such instance of police intimidation, overreach, and oppression in Edmonton. Sadly, it also wouldn't be the last.

Law enforcement often marches in lockstep with the politicians and politics of the day. This point is particularly true when we look back on Alberta's history in the 1930s and 1940s. In 1935, on the heels of the Great Depression, a Baptist evangelical minister named William Aberhart, leading the Social Credit party, swept to power with an election platform that included a promise to "repair the morality" of the province. Premier Aberhart, often known as Bible Bill, would lay the foundation for Alberta's socially conservative ethos, including a damaging history of eugenics, racism, and homophobia. Aberhart's election resulted in calls to step up the policing of morality within the province. There was a legal basis for this policing, of course. In 1890, the Government of Canada passed a gross indecency amendment that criminalized any sexual activity between two men, an amendment that law enforcement would use to persecute gay men well into the 1980s and beyond.[1]

Between April 1, 1942, and March 31, 1943, thirty-seven charges of gross indecency and indecent acts were laid in Alberta, coinciding with Premier Aberhart's correspondence with the RCMP and enforcement of his Christian fundamentalist principles.[2] This witch hunt would correspond with the infamous 1942 same-sex trials, the culmination of a coordinated effort between the RCMP and the Edmonton Police Service (EPS) that resulted in the arrest of ten men, nine of whom were convicted at trial.[3] Six of the men served time in jail.

▲ Liaison Committee marches in Pride Parade
▼ Edmonton Police Headquarters, present day (9620 103A Avenue)

This investigation was likely sparked by a 1941 personal ad published in the *Edmonton Journal*, which read simply, "Young man from Vancouver, wants friends." Wilfred Collier answered Donald MacCullum's ad and later admitted they had intimate relations, which resulted in a jail sentence of two years minus a day, for a "single act of consenting intimacy with another adult male in private." The subsequent police interrogation of MacCullum led to further investigations, including one into Donald Sebastien, a teenage male sex worker, whom the police coerced into giving testimony implicating others. The theory behind these police investigations was simple: once they could identify someone as a homosexual, that person was, by definition, already a criminal. Personal correspondence, such as romantic letters, was often seized as evidence.

The homophobia entrenched in both the police investigations and the subsequent trials was mirrored both in the highest echelons of the provincial government and in the sensational media coverage the trials received. For example, the *Edmonton Journal* ran a front-page story highlighting Justice Ives's claims the accused men were running a "ring of bestiality."[4] This wasn't just about moral regulation but also indicative of insidious homophobia and widespread fear of homosexuality. Such moral panic would become a defining feature of police and judicial systems for decades to come.[5]

Not even a private bedroom was safe. In 1955, Edmonton police broke into a house and arrested two men for engaging in same-sex relations. A neighbour is reported to have complained to the police after overhearing their "bestial love-making." James McCurdy and Marvin Friestad were arrested, and Friestad was sentenced to a year in prison based on his confession.[6]

The year 1969 is memorable for the partial decriminalization of homosexuality in Canada and the Stonewall Uprising in New York City, which occurred in response to ongoing police brutality and the raid of a local gay bar. While Stonewall is often cited as a spark that ignited the modern 2SLGBTQ+ rights movement, its impact on Canada's and, in particular, Edmonton's 2SLGBTQ+ communities is much harder to trace. Indeed, the early 1970s witnessed Edmonton's gay and lesbian community come together more visibly, with the opening of gay bars like Club '70 (see page 216) and with the formation of organizations like Gay Alliance Towards Equality (GATE; see page 18). But Edmonton GATE members claimed that police harassment was a significant factor in many people's decisions to remain closeted.

In December 1977, two young men were arrested when seen kissing in a parked car in Queen Elizabeth Park at 5 a.m.[7] While in police custody, the young men reported being subjected to verbal harassment. The police even called their employers to inform them of the gross indecency charges. Thankfully, neither employer showed much concern.

Very real fears around police attitudes towards sexual minorities often contributed to victims of gay bashings not coming forward to report the attacks. In 1979, several individuals were beaten by a group of men around Alberta College in the downtown, which was a part of the cruising strip known as The Hill (see page 298). In 1980, Craig Morris, a former manager of Audreys Books, reported he'd been attacked four times in the previous three years.[8] John McNally, an EPS constable tasked with patrolling the downtown beat, said that gays and lesbians "deserve the same protection anyone else gets, [but] they don't report it [violence] often enough."[9] Male sex workers from The Hill also reported a rise in violence in the late 1970s and stated, "The police give us no protection from gay-beaters. They protect the women working on 106th street, but if something happens here, it takes forever for the police to show up."[10]

Canada may not have had one specific Stonewall moment, but many consider the bathhouse raids to have produced a similar effect in Canadian cities.[11] Montreal saw action taken

MURRAY G. BILLETT

As a young family man struggling to come out, I learned that living in the closet is both wrong and exhausting. Many mentors have taught me that a life of risk, regret, deceit, denial, and obligation is profoundly unhealthy. Still, too many forget that queer people exist in every profession, race, religion, and country in the world. These early life lessons were instructive in my activism in the community and within policing.

These were all essential lessons I shared in 1992 as one of the founding members of the Edmonton Police Service's Gay and Lesbian Liaison Committee. Subsequently, in 2002, my appointment as Edmonton's first "out" gay police commissioner created headline news. A very challenging yet rewarding time for myself, family, community.

The advancement of equality rights in policing happened through the perseverance and dedication of many allies and activists. Through this relentless activism, police and politicians recognized that Edmonton is changing and that these changes affect how our city and community must be policed and supported.

Ultimately, we need to understand that the police are people, and people are the police. Over time, EPS has been getting better at reflecting this reality. The big lesson I continue to remind myself and others is that discrimination hinders coming out and coming out hinders discrimination.

against gay baths in 1976 as the city "cleaned up" for the Olympics. Police raided Toronto's bathhouses in 1981 as part of Operation Soap, a metaphor once again linked to moral cleansing. In Edmonton, the Pisces Health Spa was raided by EPS, with support from the RCMP, on May 30, 1981.

Sheila Greckol, one of the defence attorneys for the patrons charged, was surprised by many of the tactics used by police, including the large number of officers involved (forty-five from EPS and ten RCMP), the late-night time of the raid, the use of video cameras in the investigation, and a lack of regard for the rights of the men arrested, including the absence of legal counsel.[12] The raid predated the Canadian Charter of Rights and Freedoms, but Anne McLellan, then Associate Dean of Law at the University of Alberta, noted that little changed in the legal system after the Charter was adopted: the Charter contained no provision for the rights of gays and lesbians.[13] Philip Knight, a member of the Privacy Defence Committee, which was formed to support those arrested in the Pisces raid, later wondered why the police even bothered to raid the spa: "What did the raid accomplish other than to cause fear and anger?"[14] A formal apology from Edmonton Police Service to the 2SLGBTQ+ community wouldn't happen until 2019. By the time of that apology, the relationship between the police and the 2SLGBTQ+ community had changed significantly from one of persecution to mutual cooperation.

One significant and unanticipated feat the Pisces Health Spa raid accomplished was to galvanize the 2SLGBTQ+ community in an attempt to fight back. The 1970s and 1980s brought an increase in both visibility and advocacy. While part of this action stemmed from community mobilization in response to the AIDS crisis (and government denial and inaction), another derived from ongoing injustices the 2SLGBTQ+ community continued to experience. Edmonton's 2SLGBTQ+ community had to organize and demand changes to government policies and legislation to counter state and societal oppression.

A crucial part of this strategy was accomplished through visibility (e.g., Pride events, rallies, and celebrations) and by demanding accountability in the form of community safety and human rights protections. Organizations like GALA, Metropolitan Community Church and Dignity Edmonton (see page 68), and various sports groups increased their memberships and became much more active in advocating for 2SLGBTQ+ inclusion and human rights. A vital part of this activism also meant changing the relationship between the 2SLGBTQ+ community and the police.

In 1992, GALA's activism resulted in the official formation of a Gay and Lesbian Liaison Committee, the first such committee in the history of EPS and one of a few in Canada.[15] The increased visibility of the 2SLGBTQ+ community that accompanied the growth of Edmonton's Pride parades in the early 1990s necessitated the development of a closer and ongoing relationship with the police. GALA's Liz Massiah noted that "this committee is a recognition that we deserve equality, not only when we're working within the police service, but also when we have concerns particular to our community."[16]

The newly created liaison committee initially involved three 2SLGBTQ+ community members and two EPS officers, Staff Sergeant Joe Rodgers and Constable Cathy Johnson. The committee's purpose was to address ongoing harassment and help de-escalate other issues affecting the 2SLGBTQ+ community. The committee was also designed to ensure that "homosexuality will not be used as a barrier to advancement" within the police service.[17] An informal committee, which had been meeting for a year before the formal creation of the liaison committee, had already identified several key issues of concern, including the need to address "systemic barriers in the recruiting and promotion of homosexual officers."[18]

Edmonton was only the third city in Canada to establish a formal gay and lesbian police liaison committee. Similar groups had been formed in Toronto and Montreal, both of which had also experienced bathhouse raids in the early 1980s. Edmonton's Gay and Lesbian Liaison Committee was designed to be proactive and not only focus on historical misdeeds but also issues of current and future concern.[19] The need for such a focus had never been more apparent.

In the fall of 1992, six men were arrested as part of an undercover operation in Victoria Park and Government House Park. These areas had long been known as public cruising grounds for gay, bisexual, and closeted men. Brenda Spielman, an EPS spokesperson, said the investigation was launched after complaints about "indecent acts" occurring in wooded park areas. She said attempts had been made to curtail the issues, including pamphlets distributed on cars and increased patrols, but undercover officers were sent in when alleged incidents continued. These officers reported having their groins fondled, and charges of sexual assault were laid.[20] City Councillor Michael Phair expressed his concern over the fact that there had been no consultation with the 2SLGBTQ+ community before the operation had begun. Just as with the Pisces Health Spa raid, the question was raised: what were the police trying to achieve?[21] Answering this question and others was one of the main reasons that the Gay and Lesbian Liaison Committee was created.

Over its first few years in existence, the police liaison committee grew to include twelve members. When the downtown police headquarters became home to a unique art installation depicting gay bashing, Superintendent Colin Vann emphasized the need for empathy regarding hate crimes targeting the 2SLGBTQ+ community. The painting was part of a larger project that had installations at Latitude 53 gallery and local hospitals.[22] Spencer Harrison, the artist, said that "in our society, especially within Alberta, it's more acceptable to be a gay-basher than it is to be a gay person" and hoped his artwork would help illustrate this reality to the police service.[23]

In 1999, with support from the liaison committee, the EPS launched an anti-gay-bashing campaign, which featured posters stating, "Being gay is not a crime. Gay bashing is."[24] The campaign included 180 posters on about a quarter of city buses and was supported by $1,000 in donations to fund the campaign. Fred Dicker, the co-chair of the liaison committee, stated he hoped the campaign would "give some people pause to think about their prejudices and prompt others to report assaults."[25]

The liaison committee also played a vital role in keeping the police focussed on issues affecting Edmonton's 2SLGBTQ+ communities, even at times when the tone coming from the provincial government was very different. In 2005, with the national discourse surrounding marriage equality at its peak, and the provincial discourse from the Klein government expressing strong opposition (including threats of using the Charter's notwithstanding clause), entrenched political homophobia did what it always does: gave the green light for homophobes to attack. During the 2005 Pride festival, the newly created the hate crimes unit investigated an increase in gay-bashing incidents.[26]

The EPS Hate and Bias Crime Unit included Constable Stephen Camp, one of the unit's co-founders, who devised a unique way for police recruits to experience firsthand the type of attitudes and biases that 2SLGBTQ+ Edmontonians faced every day. Volunteer male recruits were asked to walk down Whyte Avenue doing one simple yet radical act: holding each other's hands. Recruits reported feeling unsafe and afraid. This activity was an innovative way for future police officers to make an emotional connection to what so many 2SLGBTQ+ people experienced on the streets of Edmonton every day.[27] This sensitivity training was so successful that a story ran in *The Advocate* magazine, and the Atlanta Police Service adopted the exercise as part of its own training.[28]

Danielle Campbell was the first openly 2SLGBTQ+ recruit in the history of EPS when she applied and was accepted on June 5, 1989. However, EPS made Campbell undergo two additional steps before being hired. First, she was required to undergo a psychological assessment with a psychiatrist, in addition to the standard written psychological test all recruits had to take. The second requirement was an in-person meeting with a senior officer who made Campbell pray with him.[29] Despite these barriers, Campbell went on to have a lengthy and successful career, including serving as deputy chief. Campbell's courage and perseverance helped pave the way for many other 2SLGBTQ+ police officers to apply and find success as members of EPS. Notably, EPS became one of the first police services in Canada to openly welcome transgender members in its ranks.

Another historical moment occurred in 2004 when Murray Billett was appointed to the Edmonton Police Commission. Billett had been involved with GALA and the early days of the gay and lesbian police liaison committee. This community work made him a natural appointee. On the commission, he could advocate for a more robust police response to hate crimes to protect minority communities.[30] When he left the commission in 2009, it was with a sense that some things still needed to change, including better handling of calls involving people with mental health and addiction issues, as well as more credible civilian oversight.[31]

Over the years, the police liaison committee included many other 2SLGBTQ+ community activists and advocates such as Fred Dicker, Liz Massiah, Rob Wells, Steven Townsend, Candas Dorsey, Pam and Karen Hoffman, Kristopher Wells, Chevi Rabbit, and Marni Panas. One of the committee's goals was to promote open dialogue and build bridges between the police and the 2SLGBTQ+ community, and one of the key bridges involved the annual Pride parade. Police presence at Pride festivities had long been a necessary reality. In the early years, police were there to de-escalate situations between protesters and parade participants. In later years, as the parade grew, their presence was required by municipal event guidelines. By the late 2000s, EPS was not just at the parade; its members were marching in it, encouraged by their own 2SLGBTQ+ members, including Danielle Campbell, marching in uniform.[32] EPS members also participated in the Gay Cup, an annual Pride softball game against members of the 2SLGBTQ+ community.

EPS viewed participation in Pride as a way to strengthen the relationship with the communities it served.[33] Activities included hosting the Edmonton Police Chief's Pride Reception, which the liaison committee sponsored to help build relationships of trust and respect within the 2SLGBTQ+ community. In 2009, Chief Michael J. Boyd received the inaugural Sexual Minorities Liaison Committee Pride Award in recognition of his efforts to help build a more 2SLGBTQ+-inclusive and responsive police service.

While some saw the participation of the police in Pride as a sign of progress, this wasn't a universal sentiment. In Edmonton, as in other cities, cries went out to minimize or entirely remove police participation from the Pride festival. A 2017 ban on uniforms in Toronto's Pride parade was mirrored in Edmonton's 2018 Pride festivities. Plain-clothes officers still participated, a step Superintendent Brad Doucette cited as "an excellent opportunity for our members and the community to continue building and strengthening relationships without the barrier that the uniform sometimes represents."[34] Police vehicles, lights, and sirens had been banned the year previously. After a protest disrupted the 2018 parade, EPS withdrew its participation, citing the need to respect the community's wishes.[35] In the end, the 2019 Pride parade was cancelled by the Edmonton Pride Festival Society, along with other planned events, due to pushback from some members of the Two Spirit, trans, and racialized community. (Other contested issues included increasing corporate sponsorship and the lack of participation from trans and racialized groups in Pride planning and activities.)

Clearly, important work remains to be accomplished. Today, after more than twenty-five years in partnership with the police, Edmonton's Sexual and Gender Minorities Community Liaison Committee continues to help promote dialogue, support training, and build mutual trust and respect between the police and the 2SLGBTQ+ community. Other groups in the community want no part of the police and believe the community can address its own needs without police involvement. Many communities across North America are dealing with these tensions and actively building new models of community care and safety, especially as hate crimes targeting the 2SLGBTQ+ community continue to increase.

The Strand and Pantages Theatre

10209 JASPER AVENUE

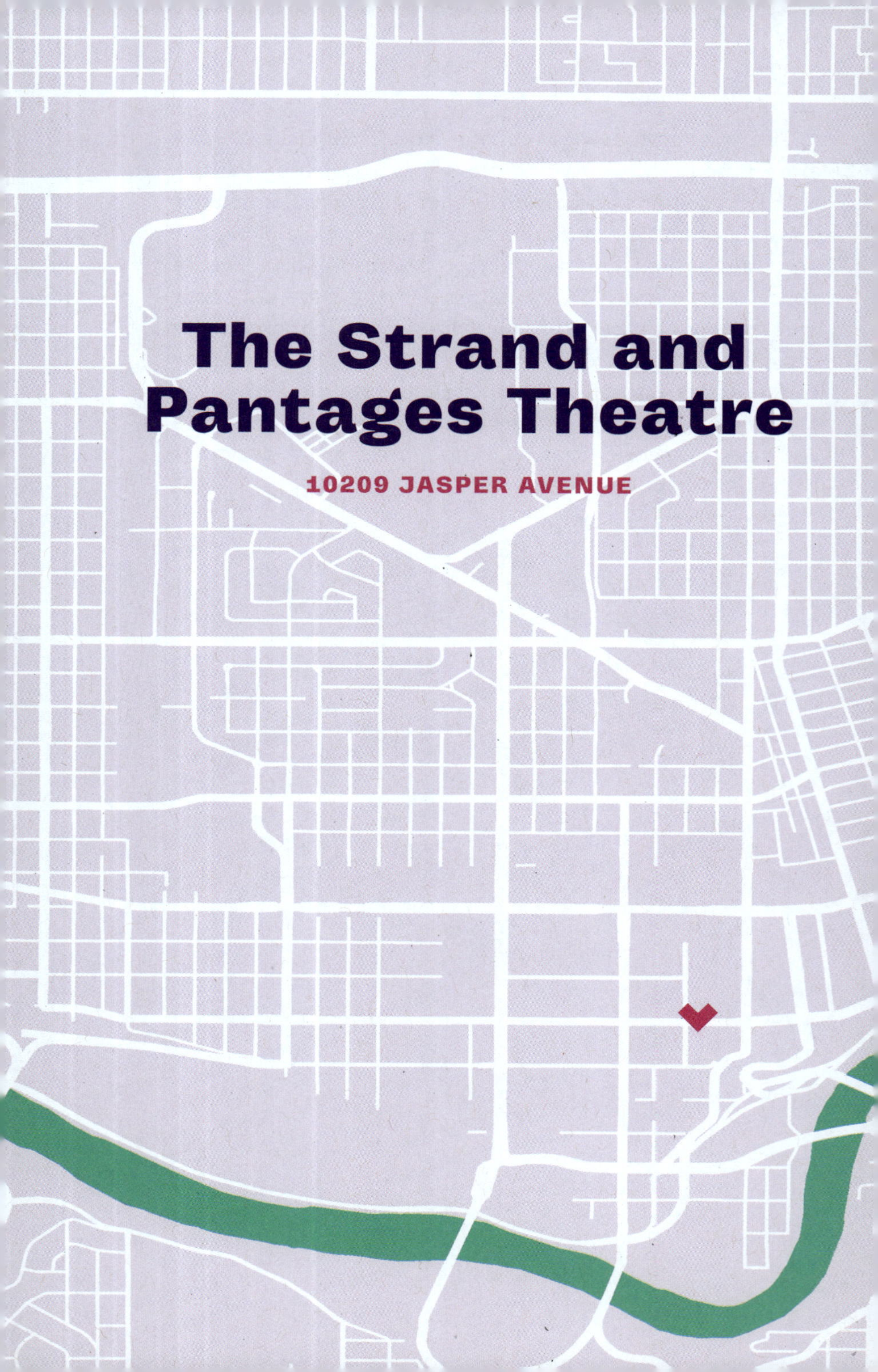

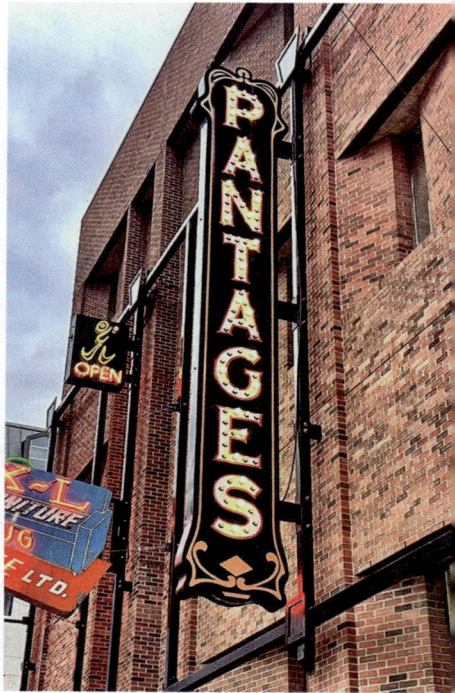

Home to the oldest and largest Fringe festival in North America, Edmonton came by its reputation as a theatre town honestly. Early in the last century, the city boasted a wide variety of dedicated performance halls and theatre spaces in the downtown core. One of these historic venues had roots in the Klondike Gold Rush and would later be at the centre of a gay sex scandal that set the city's theatre community ablaze.[1]

In 1898, Alexander Pantages, a man small in stature but large in ambition, made his way to Dawson City to find his fortune. Like so many others, he arrived in the aftermath, just in time to see the gold rush fade. But he did manage to find a way to good fortune by making the acquaintance of Kathleen Eloise Rockwell, also known as "Klondike Kate," a burlesque dancer who had headed north seeking her own kind of luck.

On her way to Yukon, Kate was refused entry by the North-West Mounted Police, who attempted to regulate a lawless frontier, control the traffic of liquor, and keep out any undesirable or unwanted visitors such as those who would "mine the miners," which often included thieves, gamblers, murderers, and "ladies of ultimate accessibility."[2] Undeterred by the rules or the famous Yukon rapids, Kate disguised herself as a man and jumped on the men's-only scow's deck and made her way to Dawson City.

Both wandering souls, Kate and Alexander became lovers and business partners who turned out to be a formidable team. Both had a taste for show business and a con. They were noted not only for watering down the champagne but also for cheating miners out of their gold. Together, they bought a struggling theatre and rechristened it the Orpheum.[3] Although small in scale, the theatre raked in an astonishing eight thousand dollars a day at its peak, largely from the throngs of miners who came to witness *The Yukon Flame*, a provocative burlesque

▲ Strand Theatre, 1978 / Pantages Sign, present day (10330 104 Street)
▼ The Strand original location, present day (10209 Jasper Avenue)

show Kate had created that used hundreds of yards of bright red fabric to reveal just enough to drive audiences into a frenzy.[4] Kate was also known for her kindness and generosity, which led her to receive the title Queen of the Klondike.

After amassing and losing an extraordinary fortune (reported to be more than five hundred thousand dollars), Alexander Pantages moved back to the United States and eventually returned home to Seattle, where he built the first Pantages Theatre. While in Seattle, he secretly married Lois Mendenhall, a talented young musician from California. After he disclosed the marriage to Kate via a letter, Kate sued Pantages for breaking his promise to marry her and settled out of court for twenty-five thousand dollars, an astonishing amount of money at the time.[5] Kate eventually made her way back to the U.S. and settled in Oregon, where she became a pioneering homesteader and avid rockhound who never lost her glamour or charm.[6]

Pantages continued his quest for riches, cashed in on his reputation as a purveyor of successful touring houses, and began to build theatres, each more elaborate than the last. To bring his vision to life, he commissioned a young Scottish-born architect, B. Marcus Priteca. Priteca designed his first Pantages Theatre in San Francisco, followed by two more in Seattle. A fourth followed in 1908 in Vancouver. They developed a long-lasting partnership designing thirty theatres, each built ornately to make a grand cultural statement, much like churches. By 1926, Pantages owned or controlled seventy-four theatres throughout Canada and the United States, making his the most prominent theatre chain in North America.

For those struggling to make ends meet, an afternoon at the theatre was a form of escapism, and at the height of his success, Pantages was reported to have earned between twenty and thirty million dollars, equivalent to hundreds of millions in today's dollars. For someone who grew up poor and illiterate, Pantages typified the American rags-to-riches success story.

Like any good American tragedy, however, a scandal soon followed to bring down his empire.[7]

As part of his growing theatre network, Pantages sought to further expand across Canada. After figuring out how successfully and profitably to program the live acts that toured up and down the west coast, Pantages sought to move eastwards. To connect his growing network he needed a Prairie outpost that would bridge the long gap between Vancouver and Winnipeg. Thus he set his sights on the wilds of Edmonton.

To achieve his vision, Pantages entered into partnership with George Brown, an Edmonton-based developer. Pantages shrewdly refused to foot the entire bill for a new theatre, which was initially proposed to include a ten-storey office tower. Brown convinced Edmonton city council to lend fifty thousand dollars toward the project. Beyond the first two storeys, the office tower never materialized, but the elaborate theatre was built in 1913 at the cost of $125,000 (about $4,000,000 today).[8]

The building and theatre had two different architects. Edmonton architect Edward Collis Hopkins created the understated two-storey brick frontage, while Priteca designed the actual theatre.[9] On the side of the building, on the wall facing Jasper Avenue, painted letters read *PANTAGES: Unequalled Vaudeville*. This bold announcement heralded the start of a grand theatre experience in Edmonton. Notably, the northeast corner of the building featured what would become another landmark institution: Edmonton's first cafeteria, the American Dairy Lunch, which operated until it became Ciro's in 1955.[10]

On May 12, 1913, the Pantages opened to a spectacular debut.[11] Thousands of Edmontonians rushed through the main entrance, albeit forty-five minutes later than the advertised launch, as final construction was still being completed moments before the doors opened. So many people showed up that the doorman, Charles Wilson, couldn't verify who had tickets and who didn't. It was his first night on the job, a duty he would perform for decades through the building's many incarnations.

What the opening-night audience witnessed was a remarkable sight. Priteca had created a Neo-Greek fantasia, seating 1600 patrons. Lush and ornate, the theatre featured imported Italian and Grecian marble, Chinese silk wall panels, hand-painted murals, and heavy draperies trimmed in elaborate embroidery. The opening performance went on until midnight and was followed by a banquet that continued into the early hours of the morning. The *Edmonton Bulletin* referred to the Pantages as "the handsomest theatre in Western Canada." The *Edmonton Journal* described the theatre as "[t]he most Northerly High Class Vaudeville Playhouse in North America."[12] It was a sensation.

Over the next decade, the Pantages hosted the brightest lights of vaudeville—including the Marx Brothers, Sophie Tucker, Will Rogers, Buster Keaton, Eddy Foy, Harry Lauder, and Stan Laurel (of Laurel and Hardy fame)—as performers made their way to Edmonton as part of a regular western tour. Joy Yule brought his newborn son on stage, marking the debut of the Hollywood star who would eventually be known as Mickey Rooney.[13]

A seismic cultural shift was already in the making, however. The new film industry was forcing the vaudeville circuit to adapt, and old performing theatres and roadhouses transitioned to movie houses. Fortunes were also shifting in the show business world. Eventually, the Pantages was the only theatre in Edmonton still offering vaudeville, as the rest of the entertainment houses had installed movie screens and changed their names. For a time, films and live performers shared the same bill. But eventually, the cost of touring live performers to audiences who preferred to be dazzled by the new medium of film was too prohibitive, and the touring circuit fell into disrepair, then stopped altogether.

In 1921, there were disagreements between Brown and Pantages. There was no programming at all on the Pantages stage in July of that year. Pantages offered this advice to

Brown: "Declare bankruptcy." He pulled his touring circuit, deleting Edmonton as a stop on the national tour, the lifeblood of entertainment houses across the country. It took Brown only a few months to make the transition permanent, and the mighty Pantages Theatre reopened as a movie house called the Metropolitan.[14]

The stock market crash of 1929–30 and the onset of the Great Depression accelerated the demise of vaudeville roadshows. When touring ended, the "Western Road" closed permanently. There was a bright side, however, as community theatre gained renewed interest and attention. The Edmonton Little Theatre launched in 1929 with a mandate to nurture local theatrical talent, and thus, Edmonton's second life as a theatre town began.[15]

At the beginning of the Depression, the Metropolitan closed completely. In 1931, it was purchased by Alex Entwhistle, updated for sound movies, and renamed the Strand Cinema, part of a national chain of movie houses.[16] The theatre was also used in other ways, often providing a prominent and stately gathering space. In addition, the stage was frequently shared by arts organizations like Edmonton Little Theatre, Empire Opera Company, and Civic Opera Company, becoming essential to the downtown performing arts community.

The offices in the corner building were filled with local businesses, including lawyers and dentists. Notably, the building also contained rehearsal spaces where theatre could be created and acting classes were taught, and one small apartment housed the family of the doorman, Charles Wilson.

In 1931, Edmonton Little Theatre held its first drama class, with its first production opening on the old Pantages stage. *Liliom* by Ferenc Molnar was directed by a woman who would leave an indelible impression on Edmonton's theatre history: Elizabeth Sterling Haynes, who went on to co-found the Banff School of Fine Arts. A decade later, Haynes would become an unwitting bystander in one of the biggest scandals to rock Edmonton's theatre community.

In 1935, newly elected Premier William "Bible Bill" Aberhart attempted to steer Alberta into a sort of Prairie theocracy. From 1936 to 1940, Bible Bill tore up the airwaves in full-throttle fire and brimstone with prophecies broadcast province-wide and beyond. From the centre stage of the Strand he would rail against the evils of modern society in front of a live audience. Topics frequently included the war, Jews, declining morality, and Alberta's role in Confederation.[17]

In 1942, a scandal that one judge referred to salaciously as a "ring of bestiality" shocked Edmonton's arts community and became the talk of the city.[18] Harvey Kagna, the former president of the Edmonton Little Theatre company and a playwright and makeup artist, was charged with more than a dozen accounts of gross indecency, a charge that could mean almost anything the prosecutor wanted. In this case, it referred to Kagna's sexual relationships with other men, many of them in the arts community. Kagna was also a close friend and confidant of Elizabeth Sterling Haynes and her husband, Nelson.

Caught in what was reported as one of the most extensive dragnet operations targeting gay men in Western Canada were actor/playwright Jimmy Richardson; Atha Andrewe, a virtuoso conductor who served as the artistic director of the Empire Opera Company; and Wilfred Collier, a former employee at the provincial Department of Education.[19] The police interrogated the men and pressured them to turn against each other and name their partners. Charges were eventually brought against at least ten men, nine of whom were convicted, their prison sentences ranging from one and a half to three years. Anyone identified as homosexual was by definition a criminal and an immediate object of police attention and potential prosecution. The ensuing media frenzy and judicial overreach resulted in dozens of charges of gross indecency.[20] News coverage of the arrests and subsequent trials published the names of the accused and even their home addresses.[21]

Kagna, age thirty-seven, was initially charged with twelve criminal offences and sentenced to three years in the penitentiary. Andrewe fled the country but was later extradited from Mexico and sentenced to two years in prison. By the time the dust settled, several men's lives and reputations had been destroyed. "I have nothing further to live for," Kagna is alleged to have told police at the time of his arrest. "I have disgraced my family and I don't care what happens to me. The only thing left for me to do is to do away with myself, and jump off the High Level Bridge."[22] Before sentencing Kagna, Justice Ives addressed the accused, stating, "I do not know how many other young men there are in the city who have been debauched by you and your confreres, the older men. I have no doubt there are a number."[23] It would take decades for the theatre community to recover, and to this day many are reluctant to talk about the scandal.

In 1945, seeking to distance itself from the Kagna scandal, the Edmonton Little Theatre renamed itself the Edmonton Community Theatre. By the 1950s, Edmonton's theatre community was burgeoning, thanks partly to the post-war boom and people with new ideas who started to arrive in Edmonton. Importantly, the new people had no connections to the strife and scandals of the past.

The Strand underwent its own resurgence when it was renovated in 1953, purchased by the Famous Players chain in 1956, and then bought out by First Northern Building Corporation in 1959.[24] Theatre pioneer Margaret Mooney remembers studying acting with Edmonton theatre legend Elizabeth Sterling Haynes in the Strand's second-floor offices from 1949 to 1955. She also recalls being consigned to construct and gather props for the first Walterdale melodrama, *Tempted, Tried and True*, presented on the Strand stage in 1965.

It's impossible to say when the Strand became known as a place for gay men to connect, but in the pre-gay-bar years, when downtown was the place for 2SLGBTQ+ people to meet,

DARRIN HAGEN

When I staged the first version of my play about the same-sex trials of 1942, I didn't expect there would be anyone alive who would be affected by telling the story. But Edmonton is a small town. And people have deep roots here. As I emerged from a performance of *Witch Hunt at the Strand*, I was approached by a descendant of one of the men whose long-distance love letters to a gay Edmonton actor became the very evidence that resulted in his friend's charges and imprisonment for gross indecency. This family opened their archives and shared even more letters, and were instrumental in piecing together some of the lives that were shattered by the injustices of the 1942 scandal, many of them deeply involved in Edmonton's theatre community.

As I dug deeper, I found families who were completely surprised to learn what their ancestors had endured at the hands of the justice system. As the web widened, I learned that a friend of mine was attached to the case through her father. Another friend learned from his father that one of these men was his great-uncle—the one that no one ever spoke of.

I was saddened to see that in some cases, even eighty years after the original scandal had occurred, there was still secrecy. And silence. And in some cases—shame.

one of the locations where gay and bisexual men could find each other was in the flickering half-light of second-run movies that showed at the old theatre. Even as late as 1971, the Strand was well-known in the gay community as a place to cruise and connect, specifically in the notorious back row. It was common enough knowledge within the gay community that it even merited inclusion in an infamous underground publication called "A Guide for the Naive Homosexual."[25] The Strand was listed with a short and frank description: "A lively back row, but is definitely not recommended except for the most brazen and desperate of people."[26]

In 1976, the fading theatre was declared a Provincial Historic Resource. On December 30, 1978, the final showing of Elliott Gould in *The Silent Partner* was the last performance on the fifty-six-year-old stage.[27] Despite being distinguished as a landmark of historical significance, it was demolished to make way for the IPL tower, which was later named after Enbridge Inc., which built Alberta's first oil pipeline to Wisconsin.[28]

A replica of the marquee from the original Pantages Theatre still shines brightly on display as part of the Neon Sign Museum on 104 Street. If objects could talk, it might tell one hell of a story.

Centennial Plaza

9904, 9924 101A AVENUE

When most people think of a Pride festival, the image that comes to mind is a lengthy parade filled with colourful floats riding down a street lined with tens of thousands of spectators. This has undoubtedly been the case for many of Edmonton's Pride celebrations over the past thirty-plus years, but there was a time when the way we celebrated Pride looked very different.

In 1989, Centennial Plaza became the site of "the first openly gay rally [held] in Edmonton in eight years or more."[1] This was the culmination of two weeks of events organized throughout the city to promote gay and lesbian awareness after several months of debate within city council, and in the local media, as to whether there was a need to formally recognize a Gay and Lesbian Awareness Day in Edmonton.

The year 1989 was, of course, not the first year Pride events were held in Edmonton. Even before the 1981 police raid of the Pisces Health Spa, local 2SLGBTQ+ venues and groups such as GATE and Dignity Edmonton had celebrated Pride with various activities, often held at Camp Harris, located just west of the city.[2] These events usually occurred quietly inside the local 2SLGBTQ+ community, without much fanfare or mainstream media attention. After the 1981 raid, the media spotlight began to follow gay and lesbian community advocates who were fighting back against oppression and advocating for equal rights in all aspects of society.

In 1982, several community organizations (including GATE, Dignity Edmonton, Roughnecks, Flashback, and the Imperial Sovereign Court of the Wild Rose) came together to organize a more public weekend of events in what is considered Edmonton's first organized Pride celebration. In the early years of Pride, events often centred around arts, film, sports, music, and picnics that were primarily aimed at the 2SLGBTQ+ community.

▲ Lesbian and Gay Day, 1990
▼ Proud attendees at 1989 programming at Centennial Plaza

One featured Pride event included a benefit concert by comedian Robin Tyler, who quipped about her upcoming show that "people don't have to be gay to come on Sunday night ... they just have to be happy."[3] During that first Pride weekend in 1982, an estimated five hundred people participated in a variety of events organized around the theme of gay pride through unity.

Activists noted that this "unity weekend" created an important sense of community and fostered a very real feeling of gay pride.[4] The following year, Scott McConnell, an organizer of the 1983 festival, noted that the Pride festival was also a "chance to work with the straight community and become more unified."[5] Kathy Baker, the organizer of a Pride-themed film night, hoped the week would show that gays and lesbians have similar community and social needs, and that it would help break down some of the stereotypes still associated with gay and lesbian people.

By 1984, community advocates had created a new group separate from GATE, with a more explicit focus on supporting community visibility and engaging in political advocacy. This group was called Gay and Lesbian Awareness (GALA) and would spearhead Edmonton's 2SLGBTQ+ Pride festivities for the next decade and beyond.

The creation of GALA added a greater political emphasis to Pride events, which would continue for subsequent years. Almost immediately, GALA began to petition City Hall for official civic recognition. Councillor Ed Ewasiuk was in favour of declaring Wednesday, June 27, 1984 as Gay and Lesbian Awareness Day, but Mayor Laurence Decore and other city councillors were bluntly opposed. The year's festivities proceeded regardless of the lack of City support, with an afternoon of events at Rundle Park, which included a children's concert, and an ecumenical service and a dance to end the week.[6] GALA's 1985 proclamation request was also rejected by city council, with one person stating Mayor Decore's ongoing unwillingness to proclaim the day was like saying, "endorsing them is like endorsing leprosy."[7]

One of the major events of the 1985 festival was a screening of the Academy Award-winning film *The Times of Harvey Milk*. This documentary highlighted the life of San Francisco's first openly gay elected official and premiered at the Princess Theatre as part of GALA's Pride Week programming, which also included a jazz night, a chorus night with Edmonton Vocal Minority, a wine and cheese social hosted by Womonspace, and a barbecue and dance organized by GATE.[8] The packed calendar of community events didn't have any impact on city council, however.

By 1989, little progress had been made in GALA's attempts to secure an official Pride proclamation from city council. When the 1989 request was rejected once again, GALA's response was to host a satirical "Edmontonchuk Silly Council" meeting and issue their own mock proclamation.[9] Two provincial government NDP MLA opposition members joined local performers in staging the entertaining protest, which included a drag performer and a lampooning of City Councillor Julian Kinisky, who had made news headlines by declaring he would move to Australia if council granted the request for a gay day.[10] Slowly, more council members began to speak in favour of recognizing Gay and Lesbian Awareness Day, including councillors Jan Reimer and Brian Mason, who was previously president of the Edmonton Voters' Association. That same year, British Columbia MP Svend Robinson, Canada's first publicly out member of Parliament, travelled to Edmonton to join in the Pride Week celebrations, which included opening Edmonton's new Gay and Lesbian Community Centre. Pride '89 also featured a session entitled "Racism, Racial Difference, and Identity," described as a workshop for people of colour, mixed ancestry, and white allies.

Forward momentum continued to build. Only a few months after GALA '89, Jan Reimer was elected mayor. For the first time, Edmonton's 2SLGBTQ+ community had a strong ally in the

Mayor's Office, and when it came time for the 1990 Pride festival, she was on hand to participate, along with Glen Murray, a recently elected out gay alderman from Winnipeg. In addition to GALA, prominent community groups like the Imperial Sovereign Court of the Wild Rose (see page 46) and the Gay and Lesbian Community Centre of Edmonton (GLCCE) played essential roles in this year's festivities, including co-sponsoring the community Pride dance that ended the week of celebration.

One key feature still missing from Pride events was a parade. In the early 1990s, GALA decided it was time to address that critical absence. This decision required relocating out of downtown, and a new home for the Pride festival was found along Whyte Avenue at McIntyre Park. Edmonton's first official Pride parade featured a short route that included two blocks on Whyte Avenue. The 1991 parade featured about thirty participants, some of whom wore paper bags over their heads to hide their identities; it was led by Michael Phair and Maureen Irwin, who also did most of the organizing and cleanup. The Pride parade and celebrations also served as an important rallying point to support Delwin Vriend (see page 105).

In 1992, MP Svend Robinson returned to speak to the assembled Pride festival crowd, whose growing excitement had been somewhat deflated by a blindside from City Hall. Although city council had finally agreed to proclaim a Gay Pride Day, the motion required "sign off" from the mayor, who was away on vacation. The responsibility for signing the proclamation was left to acting Mayor Sheila McKay, who refused.[11] This blatant rejection didn't stop the celebration. Not even recent incidents of gay bashing or homophobic hecklers along the parade route could dampen the community's enthusiasm, heightened by Michael Phair's recent announcement that he would be running for city council that fall. GALA reps were thrilled with the turnout for the 1992 parade, which they estimated at around two hundred people. With both increasing visibility and vocal resistance from protestors, the Edmonton Police Service was invited to future parades to help direct traffic and provide protection along the parade route.[12]

In 1993 the theme was A Family of Pride. Pride parade attendance was bolstered by the first official Pride proclamation from city council. Mayor Jan Reimer had attended previously, but this year, her participation was accompanied by a special message: every person should be treated with dignity and respect, and the City of Edmonton would recognize that "gays and lesbians exist in this city." The proclamation was met by mixed reviews from Edmontonians. Some citizens claimed that city council had no business "endorsing such a lifestyle."[13] Newly elected alderman Michael Phair countered by stating that gays and lesbians are "a vital part of the city."[14]

Pride festivities on Whyte Avenue continued to grow despite the 1995 mayoral election, which saw Bill Smith defeat Jan Reimer, resulting in the 2SLGBTQ+ community losing an important ally. Mayor Smith refused requests for a Pride proclamation, a position that would continue for almost the entirety of his tenure as mayor. It seemed like progress was moving backwards until 2003, when the Edmonton Pride Week Society issued the threat of a human rights complaint. With mounting pressure from community leaders such as Murray Billett, Mayor Smith finally proclaimed Gay and Lesbian Awareness Day despite his personal and religious objections. In response to the Pride proclamation after many years of steadfast refusals, local drag queen Kitten Kaboodle (Scott Campbell) highlighted the significance of the city's recognition: "It gives us the sense we're part of the community and not ostracized."[15]

Pride returned to the heart of the city in 1998 when GALA changed the date of celebrations from June to the May long weekend to coincide with the Canadian GALA Choruses Festival. Chorus festival participants pushed the number of Pride attendees to new records. However, the parade was cancelled due to a lack of funding.[16] This was a time long before corporate sponsors, and GALA had no way to pay for the

BILL LEE
GALA Steering Committee Member

I came out in 1984 at age thirty-six. As part of my coming-out process, I joined the GALA Steering Committee. Our committee was mostly focussed on organizing community Pride events, although we didn't call it Pride then, it was just GALA (Gay and Lesbian Awareness). At the time, the GALA Committee consisted of Barry Breau, Liz Massiah, Jeff Winkelaar, John Doyle, Lorna Murray, and me. GALA served as the focal point for all of Edmonton's various gay and lesbian groups who wanted to be part of early community Pride celebrations. Soon after, GALA grew and became more politically active, with a major focus on community visibility and advocating for basic human rights protections.

rising costs associated with the Pride parade, which included security, closing city streets, and erecting barricades. Instead of a parade, a Pride rally was held in Churchill Square, echoing Pride events from years earlier that had taken place just a block south at Centennial Plaza. Hosting the Pride rally right outside of City Hall was both symbolic and significant.

Mayor Smith's ongoing refusal to proclaim Pride Day didn't change after Delwin Vriend's 1998 Supreme Court victory, and Edmonton's 2SLGBTQ+ community was growing less willing to accept blatant homophobia. Pride 1999 started with a march to City Hall as the community proclaimed the week for themselves.[17] This year also saw the Pride parade return, starting at Grant Notley Park, where it remained until 2015. Over the years, routes varied slightly, going down 100 Avenue or Jasper Avenue and often ending at Oliver Park. After 2004, the parade route changed to finish in Churchill Square, right at the footsteps of City Hall. No matter the location, Edmonton Pride parades often ended with colourful entertainment, beer gardens, and business and community fairs. These events were usually held in partnership with local community groups like the Imperial Sovereign Court of the Wild Rose, Northern Chaps, Edmonton Rainbow Business Association (ERBA), Dignity Edmonton, Metropolitan Community Church, and public sector unions.

By the late 1990s, GALA itself dissolved, and its Pride planning branch transformed into the newly established Edmonton Pride Festival Society (EPFS). While GALA had also been a political advocacy group, EPFS had as its sole mandate the production and promotion of the Pride festival. With the start of the new millennium, the roots of Edmonton's Pride festival were firmly established, and would continue to grow and flourish each year. Political support from all levels of government was also growing.

Stephen Mandel was the first mayor to participate formally in the Pride parade and did so for many years. Edmonton-Centre Member of Parliament and federal Justice Minister Anne McLellan joined the Pride festivities in 2001 and marched in the parade with a colourful rainbow umbrella.[18] Just over a decade later, in 2012, Alison Redford would become the first sitting premier to attend Pride.[19] Redford also became the first premier in Alberta's history to raise the rainbow pride flag over the Alberta Legislature as part of worldwide protests against the Olympics being held in Sochi, Russia, and its anti-2SLGBTQ+ human rights abuses.[20] In 2015, then federal Liberal leader and future Prime Minister Justin Trudeau marched in Edmonton's Pride parade alongside Premier Rachel Notley, who had long been an ally of the 2SLGBTQ+ community.[21] Another milestone occurred when Andrew Ference became the first Edmonton Oiler hockey player, and first team captain of any major professional team sport in North America, to march in a Pride parade.[22]

By the end of the 1990s, participation in the Pride parades had broken the 10,000-attendance mark. The early 2000s saw the Pride parade continue to grow by leaps and bounds, with attendance quickly doubling and then tripling as public support for the 2SLGBTQ+ community increased. This rapid growth led to the need for new events focussed on family, with a growing number of visible and vocal 2SLGBTQ+ parents and a lot more "out and proud" 2SLGBTQ+ children and youth now participating. Other new events included the Mayor's Pride Brunch, which began at the Norwood Royal Canadian Legion hall and grew into a fundraiser for Camp fYrefly. Another highlight was the newly established Edmonton Pride Run and Walk, which started in 2015 to raise funds for student bursaries at the University of Alberta and to date has raised more than fifty thousand dollars.

In 2015, the thirty-fifth anniversary of Edmonton's Pride Festival was marked, including the official launch of the Edmonton Queer History Project and a specially curated exhibition at the Art Gallery of Alberta.[23] Rising popularity and growth also helped EPFS work with other festivals in Edmonton, such as KDays, where they hosted a unique Pride

Socks fundraiser and held a special Pride Day. For the first time, Edmonton's Fringe Festival also participated in the 2017 Pride Parade.[24] Pride was seemingly celebrated everywhere in Edmonton, from the Legislature grounds to the suburbs.

With growth and rising corporate involvement, however, came increasing critiques, although these were not unique to Edmonton. The meaning of "Pride" was increasingly called into question, with voices speaking out against military and police participation, increasing corporate sponsorship, and the lack of visibility and representation of Two Spirit, trans, and racialized communities. A 2015 attempt to incorporate a Women and Trans Festival and March as part of the Pride festival was initially successful, but that success could not be repeated in subsequent years.[25] The presence of the Edmonton Police Service had long been a part of Pride festival activities, including providing security, directing traffic, and hosting events such as the Edmonton Police Chief's Pride Reception. Likewise, the Canadian Armed Forces had been represented in the Pride parade, and in 2013 raised the rainbow flag at the Namao base, marking the first time this had happened at any military base in Canada.[26]

In 2018, concerns over the ongoing presence of police and military resulted in the Pride parade, now back in Old Strathcona, being disrupted by a protest. Similar protests had been occurring at Pride events across North America. In 2016, Black Lives Matter in Toronto stopped the Pride parade, demanding an end to police participation because of ongoing mistreatment of Black and racialized communities, and called for greater representation of Black, Indigenous, and trans voices in festival operations. These same demands were echoed in the Edmonton protest, resulting in EPFS agreeing to more community consultation before hosting Pride the following year. On April 10, 2019, EPFS sent a letter stating its calendar of events for the year would be cancelled; EPFS later dissolved completely.[27]

WARREN HURT
Pride Festival volunteer

I was privileged to serve on the Pride Festival organizing committee for a number of years. One vivid memory that stands out was the Pride celebration the year following the historic Vriend v. Alberta decision by the Supreme Court of Canada. I remember the newfound enthusiasm and sense of confidence in the queer community. We were an energetic group of volunteers who enjoyed the opportunity to make Pride Week even bigger and better.

The community energy was palpable. The parade started downtown at Grant Notley Park, overlooking the majestic river valley. I recall the weather being unseasonably cold with steady rain. However, the parade was full of joyful participants, and went ahead undaunted, much like the renewed spirit of our community.

However, this didn't spell the end of Pride activities. Evolution Wonderlounge and Fruit Loop proceeded with street festivals, and Shades of Colour and Rarica Now, two of the groups involved in the 2018 Edmonton protests, hosted a rally to commemorate the fiftieth anniversary of New York City's Stonewall Uprising. Other groups also hosted events during June, and smaller communities around Edmonton, such as St. Albert, Spruce Grove, and Fort Saskatchewan, also hosted vibrant Pride celebrations.[28]

The Covid pandemic forced further changes to Pride. Instead of gathering in person for community celebrations, Pride went online with events organized by Fruit Loop and other community groups. Thanks to the resiliency of our community, we learned the importance of Pride: it could not be cancelled.

In 2022, Pride activities returned with Fruit Loop hosting a three-day family-friendly festival at Grindstone just off Whyte Avenue in early June and the newly formed Edmonton Pride Fest hosting a two-day pride event in Churchill Square at the end of the month. Several of Edmonton's major sports teams also held Pride events, including the Stingers, Oil Kings, and Riverhawks. The Edmonton Oilers launched the inaugural Pride Cup in the Ice District plaza. In 2023, there were more than one hundred Pride events in Edmonton and surrounding communities, including Pride Fest, which moved its major celebration to August. It was truly a Summer of Pride with a record number of events occurring throughout June, July, and August.

While it is still uncertain what form future Pride festivals and parades in Edmonton will take, one thing remains certain: Pride will always find a way. Throughout its history, Pride has started, stopped, and faced ongoing challenges as part of its evolution, purpose, and meaning. From its earliest roots in protest and the celebration of diverse identities and communities, Pride has been and will remain an essential part of Edmonton's history.

PART 3

Creating Space and Place: Lesbian Herstory

Womonspace

9930 106 STREET

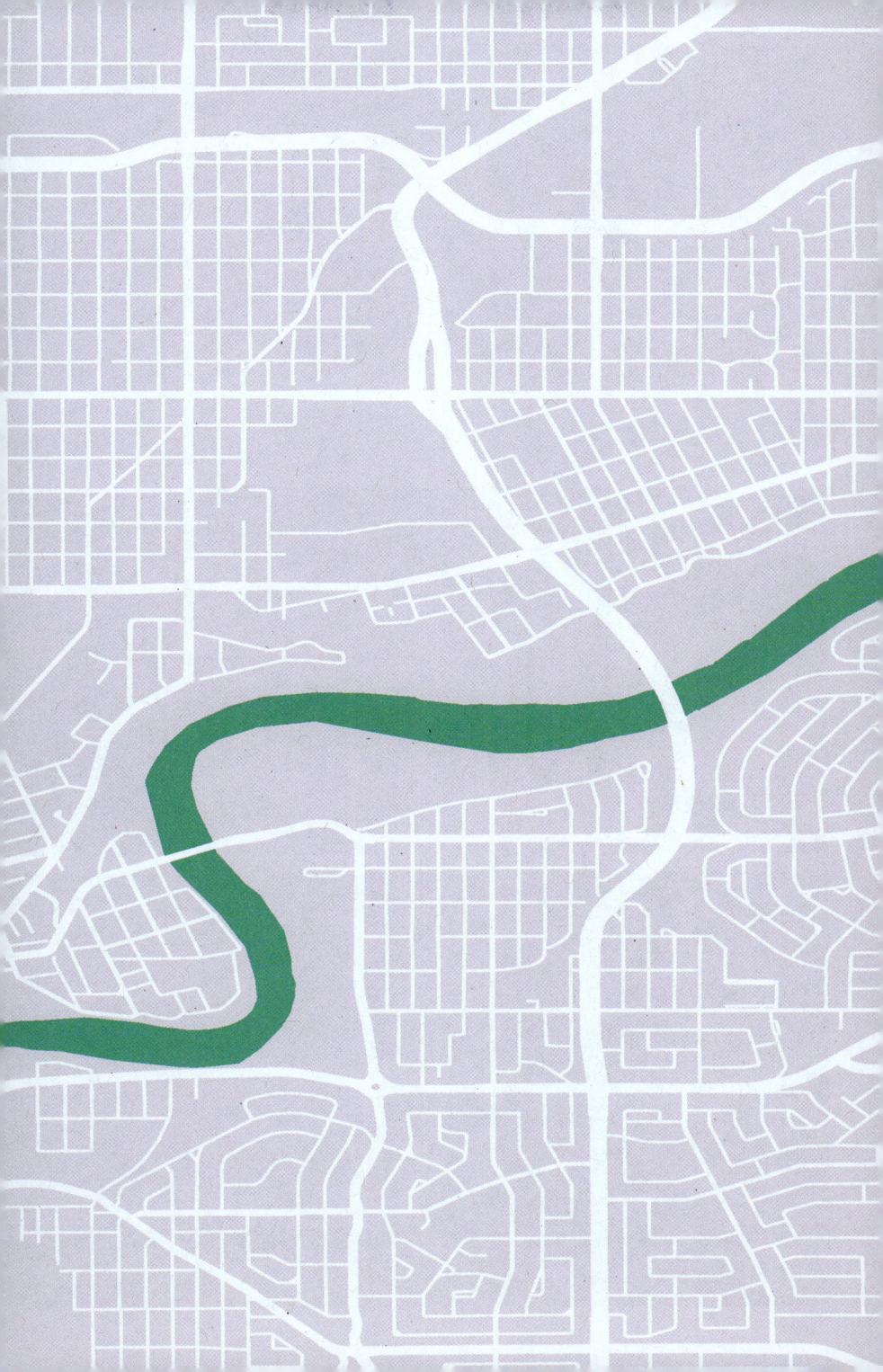

womonspace
Membership Card

Membership No. 1055
Expires end of 10/2000

Membership cards must be presented at dances and events to be eligible for reduced rates.

womonspace

Womonspace was the longest-running social, recreational, and educational society created by lesbians for lesbians in Edmonton and surrounding areas; it can arguably be called one of Edmonton's most successful and impactful 2SLGBTQ+ organizations for its contribution to building Edmonton's lesbian community over its thirty-seven-year run.[1] Initial planning for Womonspace began in 1981 when two women, Jeanne R. and Ann E., who were counsellors at Gay Alliance Toward Equality (GATE; see page 18), decided to create a safe, positive recreational space for lesbians in response to repeated complaints that there was nothing for women to do in Edmonton.[2]

With financial support and guidance from GATE, Jeanne and Ann held the first women's dance in September 1981 at Odd Fellows Hall.[3] While organizing that first dance and conversing with other women, Jeanne and Ann realized there was more than enough expertise to create and run a lesbian organization.[4] In January 1982, Ann and Jeanne, along with Linda, Cherene, Darlene, Shirl, and Candy, formed Womonspace and agreed to serve as its founding executive committee until formal elections could be held. With this process Womonspace was born.[5] Initial activities included organizing coffee house–type drop-ins, camping trips, and women-only dances. The organizing group also worked to sponsor the *Word Is Out* newsletter and helped to support an Edmonton Lesbian Collective working to help establish a women's centre, called Every Woman's Place (EWP). Womonspace's first office and resource library was housed within EWP, which was located in the Oliver area.[6]

Womonspace grew organically in response to its board's interests, needs, talents, and membership, which was composed entirely of committed volunteers. In 1982, along with being

▲ Womonspace membership card
◀ Womonspace banner being carried in a Pride Parade
▼ Womonspace one-time location, present day (9930 106 Street)

COLLEEN SUTHERLAND
Former Womonspace board president

Womonspace was founded as a recreational and social group for lesbians in the Edmonton area. We produced a regular newsletter and organized many popular community dances, silent auctions, picnics, camping trips, golf tournaments, game nights, car rallies, and gym nights.

From 2006 to 2011, I spent five dedicated years as president (and previously membership director) to the Womonspace board. During my time on the board, our focus was on establishing rapport between lesbians of Edmonton and the greater community, which included new connections and collaborations with TD Bank, HIV Edmonton, Camp fYrefly, the Pride Centre of Edmonton, Edmonton Pride Festival Society, and Western Canadian Pride Festival. These were exciting times for both Womonspace and our community!

incorporated as a non-profit society, Womonspace received
its first liquor licence. Offering licensed dances enabled
Womonspace to become financially independent of GATE and
raise funds for subsequent Womonspace dances and a host
of recreational, social, and educational activities.[7] Over the
years, Womonspace grew to offer a wide variety of activities,
including pool and golf tournaments, cards and games nights,
gym nights, ski trips, camping trips, self-defence classes, softball teams, hayrides, roller skating, film nights, and safer-sex
workshops.[8]

To inform its membership of activities and news, and poten-
tially expand its membership, Womonspace started a monthly
newsletter called *Womonspace News* in October 1982. Lindy
Pratch, a long-time contributor and an editor of *Womonspace
News*, recalls, "Copies were mailed to members in discreet
envelopes. Additional free copies were distributed around the
city in lesbian-friendly locations" (i.e., bookstores, coffee shops,
and the Gay and Lesbian Community Centre), with additional
copies left at the dances for members and guests.[9]

An inaugural issue of *Womonspace News* hints at the
absence of recreational and social spaces for lesbians in
Edmonton before the creation of the Womonspace organization. Karen writes, "Up until last year, lesbians here had only
one place to go to socialize; Flashback on Tuesday nights. Our
purpose at Womonspace is to add to that singular outlet with
a variety of other social activities just for women."[10] Lindy
recalls the turmoil and challenges of negotiating Edmonton's
bar scene, remembering that many Edmonton clubs, including Flashback (see page 226), the Roost (see page 238), and
Boots 'N Saddle, were private member clubs. These clubs used
membership policies to restrict who was coming through the
doors, and at times, lesbians were denied access.[11] For a time,
both the Roost and Flashback held separate Ladies' Nights
and Men's Nights.[12] Because Ladies' Nights tended to fall
midweek, Womonspace members approached Flashback to

inquire about the possibility of holding a women's night on the weekends. They were told that a women's night would be unfair to other patrons, but a few months later, the bar dedicated Friday nights as Men's Night, angering some of the Womonspace members.[13]

Beyond such managerial decisions, club patrons were not always welcoming to lesbians. Lindy describes instances at Flashback on weekends when lesbians were called names and manhandled by straight and gay men, who did not believe they should be there.[14] Boots 'N Saddle denied access to women, citing fights between lesbians and damage to property as reasons.[15] Coreen Douglas and Kathy Baker from Womonspace sent an open letter to the Boots 'N Saddle management suggesting if a "cruise bar" for men was desired, why not just declare it as such.[16] Womonspace offered Edmonton's lesbian community a welcome and much-needed alternative; as Lindy recollects, "Once a month we had our own space with Womonspace, so that was good."[17]

Recounting the history of Womonspace, Lindy says, "those regular monthly dances really did feel like we were knitting together a community. Instead of a gathering of maybe five or ten women that would go to a house party, there would be a larger group of 100 or 150 women that were at a dance, so there was more of a sense of 'we're not alone,' and we can be ourselves in the space and enjoy ourselves."[18] If one recalls some of the challenges faced by lesbians in Edmonton in the 1980s, Womonspace represented to many a safe harbour, a place to relax and be themselves, when such spaces in the public sphere were very limited.[19]

Along with the monthly dances, *Womonspace News* offered Edmonton's lesbians a space to learn about community events and activities in the city and beyond. In the days before the Internet and social media, *Womonspace News* provided members with an important forum to learn with and from each other by sharing poetry, art, book reviews, thoughts on lesbian spirituality, and stories of lesbian experiences (e.g., lesbian ageing, coming out later in life, disabilities, and challenges).[20]

Heated debates sometimes arose and were borne out within the pages of the newsletter. When political views inevitably became part of editorials and letters to editors, upheavals resulted. Some highly contested topics included having strippers at dances and hetero-patriarchy; violence against women concerning pornography, misogyny, and sexism; the relationship between lesbianism, feminism, women's issues, human rights issues, activism, and change; and oppression of trans and bisexual women within lesbian and 2SLGBTQ+ community spaces.[21] Despite impassioned calls for solidarity amid differences, some fractures occurred within the Womonspace community, and irreconcilable differences persisted.[22] For instance, Bobby Noble, an editor of *Womonspace News*, left the organization citing an inability to parse different aspects of their life, such as their identity and their activism in the world, and reconcile their lived experience with silences and secrecy expected within Womonspace.[23]

Womonspace tried to avoid politics and the ensuing visibility it brought and "adhered to the social mandate fearing that closeted members would [otherwise] turn away from the organization."[24] Womonspace organizer Agathe Gaulin asks, "How political could we be without jeopardizing this whole group of women who were counting on us to be their safe place?"[25] Safety for members meant Womonspace maintained a policy of discretion and secrecy through the years. Fears of being outed, especially in the 1980s and 1990s, came at a high cost for many women.

At one point, Womonspace took extreme measures to protect the safety and privacy of members. The Womonspace board controversially expelled members Liz Massiah and Jackie because their political activism had caused unwanted publicity and visibility to Womonspace members and the organization.[26] This expulsion occurred because Liz and Jackie had "challenged John Crosbie, Minister of Justice, to amend the Canadian Human Rights Code to include gays and lesbians."[27] "The organization was very closeted," Liz says, reflecting on her expulsion from the organization. "The people who initially started it did a great job and provided a safe place for women, but the overall message was 'Don't share, don't talk, don't let people know.'"[28]

Visibility for Womonspace might have jeopardized the organization—it might have lost membership, finances, and the ability to deliver resources and offer events—but members later questioned the necessity and prudence of Liz and Jackie's expulsion and the apolitical stance of the organization.[29] Several Womonspace members, including Liz Massiah, Maureen Irwin, and Bobby Noble, split off and joined Gay and Lesbian Awareness (GALA). In the 1990s, GALA also divided into two organizations, GALA Civil Rights Defense, which organized, supported, and funded the Vriend v. Alberta Supreme Court challenge; and the GALA Social Society, which later became the Edmonton Pride Festival Society and ceased operations in 2019.

Perhaps the division that occurred within GALA, which created separate spaces for political activism and social/recreational gatherings, highlights the challenges of many 2SLGBTQ+ organizations like Womonspace, which strove to develop and maintain safe spaces for its membership within the shifting and often fraught political landscape of Alberta in the 1980s and beyond.

Wallbridge and Imrie

In researching Edmonton's 2SLGBTQ+ history, there is only so far one can go back with any degree of ease. What records exist for people whose love was so secret and hidden? Oscar Wilde famously spoke of homosexuality as "the love that dare not speak its name." For so long same-sex couples dared not name their love; their relationships linger in history only as whispers, a hint of time past.

Some, however, found the strength to live their truth visibly and vocally. Long before there were gay bars, 2SLGBTQ+ organizations, or human rights protections, Jean Wallbridge and Mary Imrie found each other. Together, they built not only a business but a life in Edmonton. Their passion and commitment to each other and their architectural practice broke not only a closet door but also a glass ceiling. Wallbridge and Imrie were female architects at a time of male domination in the workplace and a lesbian couple when such a reality dared not speak its name.

Jean Wallbridge was born in Edmonton in 1912. She was privately educated, first in Edmonton, then in Victoria, Switzerland, and England; she later enrolled at the University of Alberta in an architecture program. She was one of four women to earn a Bachelor of Applied Sciences degree in the twenty-seven years of the program. She graduated in 1939 and received a Bachelor of Arts the following year. Fresh out of university, her first job was with the architectural firm of Rule Wynn and Rule. Wallbridge then went on to spend the World War II era working in New Brunswick with the St. John Town Planning Commission. Upon her return to Edmonton in 1946, Wallbridge began to work as a draughtsman in the department of the City Architect and Inspector of Buildings.

Mary Imrie was born in Toronto in 1918. She moved to Edmonton with her family in 1921. She enrolled at the University

▲ Mary Imrie canoeing / Jean Wallbridge at drafting table
▼ Wallbridge & Imrie Architects original location, present day (10344 Jasper Avenue)

of Alberta in 1938 but was able to complete only a year in the architecture program when the retirement of Professor Cecil Burgess abruptly ended the program; Burgess had earlier taught Wallbridge. Imrie was able to enroll as a second-year student in the architecture program at the University of Toronto. She returned home to Edmonton in the summers, where she found employment in the office of Rule Wynn and Rule. After completing her degree, she worked briefly in Toronto, then in Vancouver, before returning to Edmonton in 1944, where she was employed with the City Architect and Inspector of Buildings from 1946 to 1950. Whether through fate or circumstance, Imrie and Wallbridge found each other.

The impeccable work record of Wallbridge and Imrie spoke for itself; the City Architect recommended they be given a three-month study leave for a working tour of Europe. The tour was made up of architects from across North America and intended to study the devastation of the war and subsequent reconstruction. Wallbridge and Imrie were the only Canadians chosen to participate in the prestigious study group.[1] This accomplishment was celebrated with an article in the local press about their trip itinerary and study plans—and luggage. One wonders whether the *Edmonton Journal* would have devoted an entire paragraph to the difficulties of packing had the architects been male.

The European excursion proved to be invaluable for their careers. Not long after their return to the city, Max Dewar, City Architect and their boss, recommended their wages be increased—to three thousand dollars a year. Dewar told the City Commissioner, "Although these two persons are ladies, I see no reason why they should be treated differently than male employees."[2] The Commission declined on the grounds they couldn't justify "more than two registered architects." Dewar suggested a compromise in which the city would make Wallbridge a technical assistant in town planning and Imrie a junior architect. Not long after, Dewar quit working for the city and entered private practice. Subsequently, Wallbridge and Imrie resigned from their positions, intending to carry out a year of travel and personal research in South America.[3]

When the world travellers returned from their research trip, they opened a downtown office of their own at 8 Merrick Block. The practice, called Architects Folles, followed the larger trend of women in architecture, which involved taking on projects male architects wouldn't do.[4] Here, their time with the City Architect served them well. They knew some of the loopholes that builders needed to jump through, and their expertise in navigating city bureaucracy earned them their first commission: three medium-sized apartment buildings. These stand today as the Queen Mary apartments on 109 Avenue.

Wallbridge and Imrie remained in business for over 30 years, designing 224 projects, only 23 of which were commercial. The rest involved designing private residences and other domestic projects. Most other Edmonton (male) architects viewed domestic work as non-lucrative, especially given the extensive consultation time needed with clients. Imrie acknowledged this fact in a 1954 letter to her former professor, stating, "But that is probably one of the disadvantages of being female. People will get us to do their houses, be thrilled with them and go to larger male firms for their warehouses or office buildings."[5]

That clients were happy with the work of Wallbridge and Imrie wasn't in doubt. One client suggested that other architects could learn from them, particularly their "ability to combine business with pleasure. You didn't feel as if they were punching a time clock."[6] Another stated, "They listened and they advised" and was surprised that "they could produce a house that pleased us so well with so little instruction."[7] Even other architects noted their skills, one saying, "they were quick to understand what was wanted and able to interpret that architecturally."[8] He thought Wallbridge and Imrie "enjoyed doing houses, chiefly because they enjoyed people, and I think the two go hand in hand."[9]

Wallbridge and Imrie's firm received the Canadian Housing Design Council Award in 1957, the same year they closed their downtown office and built a new home and office in one.[10] This property, called Six Acres, would be home for the rest of their lives. Also in 1957, the two took another overseas trip, this time to Afghanistan, northern India, and the Middle East.[11] This trip was also extensively documented; all of their many travel diaries were later donated to the Provincial Archives of Alberta.

In September 1979, Jean Wallbridge passed away from cancer. Two days later, Imrie closed their firm. She finished her last project and retired from architectural practice. One more trip awaited Imrie: a 1980 return to South America and the Amazon.

After Imrie's death in 1989, Six Acres was bequeathed to the Alberta Recreation, Parks, and Wildlife Foundation.[12] A wetland reserve at the Devonian Botanical Garden bears Imrie's name.[13] *Canadian Architect* noted that "it is a bittersweet epitaph that she may be better remembered for this contribution to Alberta's natural heritage than for her contribution to Canadian architecture."[14]

Elna Nash, a friend of the couple, related that the women's personalities were as important to note as their architectural accomplishments. Nash spent many a Sunday afternoon with the two at their home in Six Acres and recalled them both as tomboys, "especially Mary." She observed, "She had to be pretty tough to survive in this world." Not only could Wallbridge and Imrie out-design most men, but also out-drink and out-golf them.

Their home at Six Acres reflected the simplicity with which they lived their lives. They had both grown up with wealth and privilege but had rejected it. The only signs of their status could be found in their many trips.[15] Mark Slater, a cousin of Imrie, recalled that "Mary Louise was always looking to help people who couldn't help themselves. That's why she and her partner focussed on schools and hospitals. I think they all felt a great sense of accomplishment while doing it, and on top of it, at the end, what a legacy she left."[16]

A tribute from the Province of Alberta noted, "the ingenuity, energy and exuberance of Mary Louise Imrie and her partner, Jean Wallbridge, coupled with the soundness of their architectural projects, attracted a large circle of business and professional people who soon became friends and admirers."[17] A love whose name may not have been publicly spoken at the time has left an imprint on our city, environment, and hearts.

TYSON MASTEL
Vice-Principal, Greenfield Elementary School

When I began my career in education, I did not come to work as my authentic self but chose instead to pass as straight, affording me the privilege of securing employment with ease and being free from mistreatment. Coming to work at Greenfield School and learning about the queer architects who designed it encouraged me to be my true self as an openly queer teacher and visible role model.

In June 2023, thanks to the Edmonton Queer History Project, we "introduced" Mary and Jean to our school community by highlighting many important aspects of their life, including their lifelong relationship, love of nature, and pioneering career, and the unique architectural projects they designed. Their story inspired me to write a children's picture book so others could learn about their incredible lives. I wrote the book as a way to honour Mary and Jean and to provide visible role models for our school community. As our school year wrapped up, some of our staff ventured to Mary and Jean's home at Six Acres and marvelled at the design similarities to our school.

At Greenfield, we work hard to create a safe space for our students, staff, and community. Knowing that two queer women designed our beautiful school has emboldened and encouraged us to support the next generation of brave queer leaders and allies. If Mary and Jean could walk into our school today, they would be greeted by a Pride flag, be welcomed by a gay administrator, and see a display highlighting their life's work. I know they would be as proud as I am.

Common Woman Books, Orlando Books, and Audreys

10702 JASPER AVE
(AUDREYS BOOKS)

In the northwest corner of Audreys Books shoppers can find the Orlando Corner. Here a selection of fiction and nonfiction books by and about 2SLGBTQ+ people has existed for almost twenty-five years. This corner is part of a legacy of queer bookstores in Edmonton dating back to the 1970s.

While North America had bookstores like Oscar Wilde Memorial Books, Giovanni's Room, Glad Day, and A Different Light focussed on 2SLGBTQ+ people even before the Stonewall Uprising, Edmonton's first such institution didn't come along until 1978. Common Woman Books, Alberta's first women's bookstore, began in Halyna Freeland's basement when she, along with Mair Smith and Julie Anne LeGras, identified the need to make feminist literature more available to local women.[1] This collective-run space moved locations a few times before opening on Whyte Avenue in 1981. Advertisements for that grand opening emphasized the space's dedication to feminist literature and non-sexist children's books. By 1987, that inventory was expanding. Staff member Andrea Ansbacher noted that "Although we branched out into selling socialist and gay men's books, it was still the feminist theory, lesbian and women's fiction which paid the rent."[2]

By that time, Common Woman Books had relocated to 109 Street in the Garneau Theatre building. With the inventory expanded, more volunteers were needed, a bigger board was formed, and the bookstore added "The Radical Bookseller" to its name. Volunteer Sheryl Ackerman remembers that Common Woman Books was the "first bookstore in Edmonton that used the word 'Lesbian' for its section on lesbian resources and fiction."[3]

Readings, book launches, and other drop-in programs were just some of the events in Common Woman's lineup of community activities. They eventually relocated back to

▲ Orlando Books entry in past Pride Parade
▼ Lesbian History tour stops at Audreys Books

JACQUI DUMAS
Owner, Orlando Books

My vision for Orlando Books was a feminist bookstore that would provide a safe, inclusive space for all—feminists, queer activists, anti-racist activists, members of the progressive left, small independent presses—who were working to enable the voices of the marginalized. We faced many challenges during those regressive Ralph Klein years, but what I remember most is the unwavering support from our community. The store was subject to hateful attacks, but each time a window was smashed in or smeared with homophobic graffiti, people showed up the next day with cash donations to fix the window. When a local high school refused to print an ad for the bookstore in their student newspaper, three educators responded by joining me in putting together a booklet to support queer youth. This booklet was published and distributed by the Alberta Teachers' Association. When I finally closed my doors, community members organized a fundraiser that helped pay off the bookstore debt. The store was a gathering place, and over its nine years, I felt as if I knew everyone and everything that was going on in the community, from fundraisers for court cases to hookups and breakups. I am left with only fond and grateful memories.

Whyte Avenue, but commercial bookstores had begun to carry more feminist literature. This competition, combined with "the usual problems" such as an economic recession and the introduction of the GST, contributed to Common Woman Books finally closing its doors, thirteen years after beginning as a single bookshelf. Freeland remarked that the store was always struggling against people's fear of "feminism and political activism," causing the store to "struggle to exist, right from the beginning."[4] Yet Common Woman Books' contributions to Edmonton's 2SLGBTQ+ history paved the way for other places to follow.[5]

203

One such place was Orlando Books, which opened on Whyte Avenue in 1993. Jacqueline Dumas opened her activist bookstore intending to carry "progressive political books; feminist books; poetry; a good selection of international literature; books from small, independent presses—and books by queer writers, of course."[6] At the time, Jacqueline was in the process of coming out and couldn't find either books about that or other Edmonton lesbians.[7] Named after Virginia Woolf's gender-bending bestseller, Orlando Books "became a gay bookstore by default."[8]

This default was both a positive and a negative for the bookstore. On the positive side, Jacqueline had created the space to be a community hub, and that it became, helping raise money for Vriend v. Alberta and Ms. T v. Alberta, participating in the Silly Summer and Pride Parades, and hosting meetings of the Edmonton Rainbow Business Association in the upstairs space called the Room for Change.[9] This area also hosted readings by writers from across the country, such as Daphne Marlatt, Dionne Brand, Gail Scott, Nicole Brossard, Shani Mootoo, Patricia Nell Warren, Paula Gunn Allen, Ivan Coyote, and Taste This.[10] The store also promoted events for lesbian entertainers like Cris Williamson and Suzanne Westenhoefer. With a group of educators Dumas authored *Safe and Caring Schools for Lesbian and Gay Youth: A Guide for Teachers*, published and

CREATING SPACE AND PLACE: LESBIAN HERSTORY

distributed by the Alberta Teachers' Association.[11] A University of Alberta undergraduate student entrance scholarship award was established and named after the bookstore, with its selection based on demonstrated leadership qualities and involvement in school and community activities, with preference given to students who have demonstrated commitment to the advancement of 2SLGBTQ+ communities.[12]

The drawbacks to being increasingly known as a gay bookstore were also, sadly, many. The queerer it became, the more marginalized it was. Media attention came to Orlando for queer issues only and seemingly never for the other literary events happening in the space. The store's bestseller lists stopped being included in the mainstream press, and the store was often subjected to homophobic graffiti and vandalism.[13]

One of the major financial challenges Orlando Books experienced was an ongoing battle with Canada Customs. As Dumas recalled, "Certain titles—primarily leather books from the US—were routinely stopped at the border, and when that happened our entire shipment of books would be stopped, which meant that dozens of titles (including customers' special orders) could be held up for months because of one title."[14] This problem was occurring while Vancouver-based Little Sister's Book and Art Emporium was engaged in a decades-long battle challenging Canada Customs over 2SLGBTQ+ censorship, which the Supreme Court of Canada eventually found to be discriminatory.[15] It was a fight against not only censorship, but also government-sponsored homophobia—and for the visibility and recognition of 2SLGBTQ+ communities.

In the end, Orlando Books experienced many of the same challenges other independent booksellers suffered, including the arrival of big-box outlets like Chapters and the rise of online book retailers such as Amazon. Independent bookstores around the world were dying. Following the closure of Orlando Books in 2002, Dumas began working at Audreys Books, an independent bookstore on Jasper Avenue. There she created the Orlando Corner. The February 2003 launch of the designated 2SLGBTQ+ corner featured music and refreshments as Audreys welcomed Orlando customers into their space.[16] In this corner, customers could find "the best in queer literature, erotica, sexuality, humour, books on coming out, relationships, and more."[17]

The Orlando Corner continues to this day, despite the continuing rise in online shopping and big bookstores. That Audreys continues to support and provide a home to the Orlando Corner is a sign of the importance of these spaces for Edmonton's 2SLGBTQ+ communities. The ongoing presence of the Orlando Corner is also a testament to the dedicated legacy of Edmonton's queer and feminist bookstores.

PART 4

Arts, Culture, and Nightlife

King Edward Hotel

10180 101 STREET

In a time long before gay bars, it was far more challenging for 2SLGBTQ+ Edmontonians to be able to openly socialize and find community. Club '70 (see page 216), Edmonton's first gay bar, did not open until 1969. Before that, folks often had to be more secretive and creative. Sometimes this meant hosting private house parties, searching for companionship along Edmonton's riverbanks, or seeking out other clandestine spaces.[1] There were only a few public spaces that 2SLGBTQ+ people could sometimes find and enjoy. They weren't gay in any official sense, but tolerant and safe, and sometimes they even catered to a gay and lesbian clientele. In Edmonton, these spaces were often found in hotel bars. Over the years, several downtown hotels were known at different times to be welcoming to the 2SLGBTQ+ community, so long as a person wasn't too loud or flamboyant. These hotels included the King Edward, the Royal George, the Corona, the Hotel Macdonald, and the Mayfair.

Maureen Irwin, a prominent local lesbian activist, described this subcultural world: "The queens frequented bars in the Mayfair Hotel. The gay and lesbian university crowd went to the Corona ... [and] the King Edward Hotel and Royal George Hotel were patronized by gay men and lesbians."[2] Paul Gessell noted that "the back five tables at the Mayfair Hotel were known as gay—even the doorman was aware that this was gay space."[3] A letter sent by the Gay Alliance Towards Equality (GATE) to the managing editor of *Butch* magazine in Sydney, Australia, in 1972 also indicated the popularity of bars in the Ambassador and the Grand; the letter noted that the Ambassador had "begun refusing service to gays," making the Grand the most popular space for gays and lesbians to socialize.[4]

Established in 1906, the King Edward (known affectionately as the King Eddy) was located in the heart of downtown

▲ Corona Hotel
▼ King Edward Hotel original location, present day (10180 101 Street)

DARRIN HAGEN

This prominent Art Deco hotel in the heart of the city was part of a pre-gay-bar, pre-1969 network of hotel taverns and bars that would "look the other way" as the queer people discreetly gathered in one corner. If you take the time to pore through old court transcripts from gross indecency cases, more than a few cases began with an encounter at one of these downtown watering holes. Staff, bellhops, and travellers could mix with the locals in the earliest days; later on in the 1960s and 1970s, Empress I Millie and her sidekicks Mother Jean and Trixie would start their party with afternoon draught beer (ten cents a glass) in the basement of the hotel before heading to the Mayfair for still more drinks.

It was easy to imagine that in the 1940s this would have been a great place to connect. It was close to the theatres, other hotels, The Hill, and many sundry men's rooms were mere footsteps away. Downtown Edmonton was small, and it wouldn't have taken long to stroll between spots to find where your people were congregating.

Edmonton, in the same spot where Holt Renfrew would later open.[5] The King Edward became a popular drinking spot during the pre-prohibition era. Designed by Edmonton architect Herbert Magoon, the hotel had a basement tavern accessible via the main lobby. Shortly after opening, many of the tables would be filled daily by gay men.[6]

The King Eddy was also a regular haunt of "Mother Jean" Lawson. The infamous Mother Jean would go on to be honoured as the first straight Empress of the Imperial Sovereign Court of the Wild Rose in Reign X. Mother Jean was a staunch ally and supporter of Edmonton's early 2SLGBTQ+ community. Long after her days at the King Eddy, Club '70's refusal to allow her in was a defining moment in the creation of the nightclub Flashback (see page 226).

Hotel owner and businessman John Calhoun had named the hotel after the reigning monarch of the day. Expansions during its early years gave the King Edward the most rooms of any hotel in Edmonton at the time. Even Prime Minister Wilfred Laurier stayed there during a 1909 visit to Edmonton. Further renovations occurred in 1945, 1951, and 1964, keeping the hotel a vibrant part of downtown.[7] In the late 1960s, the King Edward Hotel boasted Italian chef Angelo de Fanti.[8]

But in 1978, the King Eddy was destroyed by arson; two men died in the blaze.[9] Kitty-corner from the King Edward, in what is now City Centre East, stood the extravagant Royal George hotel. The founder of the Royal George was Abe Cristall, whose family were the first Jewish settlers in northern Alberta.[10] Cristall had visited Edmonton in 1893, immediately falling in love with the "dusty little town full of hookers, peasant immigrants, and rough-talking men."[11] Cristall soon won the respect of Edmonton's business community, including Frank Oliver, who had been quoted as saying, "Edmonton could well do without Mormons, Chinese, Slavs, Jews."[12] Cristall built the Royal George in 1910, boasting that each of its 117 rooms had a telephone and many had hot and cold running water.[13]

The Royal George became embroiled in a controversy when one of its staff members denied a room to Edmonton Eskimo player Rollie Miles because he was Black. Eskimos founder Henry Singer led a crusade against the hotel that didn't end until the employee was fired.[14] The Cristall family owned the Royal George until the 1970s when they sold it to Oxford Developments, who tore it down and built the present-day Edmonton City Centre shopping complex.

The Corona Hotel was also known as a safe and welcoming space for the 2SLGBTQ+ community. The Corona was located where First Edmonton Place currently stands, its name living on in the location of the Corona LRT station. The Corona Hotel was built by James Edward Wize in 1908, initially as an apartment building. During the First World War, it became "the city's leading hostel on the European plan."[15] The hotel was rebuilt in 1932 after being destroyed by an explosion and fire.[16] The lounge at the east end of the lobby became known as a friendly space for 2SLGBTQ+ Edmontonians.

In 1975, the Corona Hotel hosted a group called the Fantasy Follies. This troupe, which had previously existed in a slightly different iteration as the Fab Freaks, was a drag ensemble and had once performed at Club '70; the troupe was directed by Jamie Durette and Justin Ames. In an interesting and perhaps queer twist of fate, Ames went on to become the first male stripper at Chez Pierre.[17] In addition to their spring 1975 gig at the Corona, the Fantasy Follies put on a show at the Convention Inn South during the 1975 Klondike Days Festival.

The Corona also gained notoriety as the site of a well-publicized murder in 1977. Peter Paquette killed Ian McLaren, alleging self-defence. Paquette had recently been involved in the theft of amphetamines, resulting in a confrontation in the tavern. McLaren assaulted Paquette, and Paquette shot him dead.[18] In the fall of 1980, the Corona was demolished.

The Mayfair Hotel was located on Jasper Avenue and 108 Street, where a new apartment complex now stands. Featured as Canada's "first drive-in hotel," the Mayfair was the latest of the hotel hangouts to visit, having been built in 1944 at a cost of $1.6 million.[19] By 1955, the Mayfair was operating two lounges: a ladies' lounge, which seated seventy, and a larger men's lounge, which seated three hundred.[20] It wasn't until 1967 that Alberta liquor laws changed to permit men and women to drink together.[21]

The tavern at the Mayfair was accessible through a back door located down a back alley. This discretion was a vital part of the Mayfair's relationship with Edmonton's 2SLGBTQ+ community.[22] But that secrecy was needed only until gay and lesbian bars began to open. Then, instead of the hotels where 2SLGBTQ+ people found companionship and community for decades prior, Edmonton's 2SLGBTQ+ community could more openly explore the pubs and discotheques explicitly catering to them.

A proliferation of queer bars wasn't the end to the mutually supportive relationship between hotels and the 2SLGBTQ+ community. Community organizations like the Imperial Sovereign Court of the Wild Rose frequently hosted their annual Coronation Ball (see page 46), and a variety of other drag shows and events, in hotels across Edmonton for years. Likewise, groups such as the Fellowship of Alberta Bears also hosted hotel parties when gay bars weren't available. The Crash Hotel (which now has new life as inner city supportive housing) was located where the Grand Hotel once stood. For several years, Crash had hosted 2SLGBTQ+ pop-up events like the famous Fruit Loop parties. In 2019, the Fairmont Hotel Macdonald hosted a sold-out "drag brunch" sponsored as a fundraiser for the Edmonton Pride Festival Society. Drag brunches are now a staple in many hotels and restaurants across the city, helping to bring new visibility to Edmonton's 2SLGBTQ+ community.

Club '70

ORIGINAL LOCATION:
10593 101 STREET

FINAL LOCATION:
10242 106 STREET

After years of community interest, on December
21, 1969, a group of twelve people, including Edmontonians
Wayne Gordon, Judith Jerace, Stanley Hawkins, Roy Wilson,
Janet Wilkinson, and Paul Chisholm, came together to discuss
opening a dedicated gay club, intending to find funding for it
and navigate the legalities of successfully organizing a private
member's club dedicated to Edmonton's gay and lesbian community. On January 4, 1970, an expanded group of fifty-three
people met to continue these discussions, elect a board of
directors, adopt bylaws, and decide upon a club name. In an
amusing discussion, Club '70 was originally going to be called
Club 69, but that name was thought to be too risqué for the
times. Club '70 became Edmonton's first formally established
gay bar, officially registered on February 2, 1970.[1]

Before Club '70, members of Edmonton's 2SLGBTQ+ community often gathered together clandestinely in houses,
apartments, hotel car parks, tea rooms [public bathrooms],
and other fugitive spaces to find friends, relationships, and
spaces of safety. Some places like the King Edward Hotel (see
page 208) tolerated same-sex patrons so long as they were quiet
and did not drawn attention to themselves.

Club '70 was initially located in the basement of a Greek
restaurant on the southeast corner of 101 Street and 106 Avenue,
but the club's presence there was short-lived after the owner
discovered what "type of club" it was and demanded Club '70
vacate the premises.[2] Since membership information, including the names and addresses of club patrons, was stored in the
basement, a few dedicated club members broke in through a
window to retrieve the club records and ensure none of the
membership information would be misused or exposed.[3] The
publicizing of member names could have meant a person's
losing job, family, reputation, or worse.

219

▲ Club '70 membership card
▼ Second downtown location for Club '70, present day (10242 106 Street)

TWIGGY

Empress XV,
Imperial Sovereign Court of the Wild Rose

I still remember the very first time I went to a gay bar. It was called Boots 'N Saddle on 106 Street in Edmonton. I was with a friend who was nineteen and I was fifteen! I didn't know places like this existed. I hoped they did, so when he suggested we go, I was thrilled, excited, nervous, and petrified! I honestly didn't know what to expect, and the feelings and emotions were electric.

We arrived around two p.m., and the front door, which you usually needed to be "buzzed" into, was propped open, so there was no one checking IDs. We slowly went up to the bar. I asked for a Coke in a small rocks glass, and my friend got a bottle of beer. About fifteen or so guys were spread out around the room and by the pool table at the back. The bartender was very effeminate and balding, wearing a lavender silk outfit that looked like something from *I Dream of Jeannie*. Everyone called him Deidre, even though I later found out his actual given name was Ken.

The bar was long and thin, and the room had stucco walls and wagon wheels. A western saddle was placed on one of the railings separating the bar from the seating area, so we sat there. I was so nervous and worried that I would do or say something wrong and we would be kicked out.

When I returned from the bathroom, seven Black Russian drinks were on the table! My friend laughed and said, "You are young, blond, thin, and blue-eyed. What did you expect!?" I was so freaked out by all the attention (I was painfully shy) that I took the straw out of my Coke, had a sip out of all seven drinks, and then told my friend we had to go! And that was my introduction to the gay bars.

To this day, I still have all my drinks served in a small rocks glass.

Upon finding a new, more permanent home, Club '70 relocated to 10242 106 Street.[4] To maintain regular operations over the years, the club relied heavily on its members for support. For example, members with experience in renovations were asked to help paint the club, and those who knew something about music helped with the sound system.[5] It truly was a community venue that needed everyone to pitch for it to not only survive but thrive.

At the time, obtaining a liquor licence was a complicated process. Club '70 was required to apply for monthly permits, with police routinely entering the club on "dry nights" to ensure no liquor was being served.[6] In addition to their regular open nights on Wednesdays and the weekends, Club '70 hosted special community events open to members and non-members, such as a Hawaiian Night in September 1971 and annual Halloween and New Year's Eve celebrations.[7] Club '70 also organized and hosted many different shows and performances, with casting calls frequently advertised in their Club '70 newsletter.[8] The club permitted entry only to gays and lesbians; members who brought straight guests were subject to a thirty-day suspension of their membership and a fine.[9]

Barb Plaumann, assistant editor of *Carousel Capers* in Calgary, lamented that many gay clubs at the time were segregated by gender. In an article she wrote, later reprinted in *Club '70 News*, Plaumann argued that it was unwise for clubs to "split into even smaller groups" as they were already an "unwanted minority." Clubs that included both men and women were richer in their entertainment offerings and could provide a more diverse perspective on issues affecting the community.[10] Given Club '70's membership, which ranged between three hundred and four hundred people, the club's openness to entertain both gay and lesbian members and their guests speaks to its importance for Edmonton's growing gay and lesbian community and allies.[11]

In July 1971, the Montreal-based magazine *Long Time Coming* ran an article called "Two Dykes on a Bike," in which two lesbians travelled by motorcycle (and later train) across Canada, reporting on their experiences in gay bars. In Edmonton, they found the back of the Mayfair tavern to be "very swishy queen and hard-drinking butch," while Club '70 was "all gay and very private."[12] Historian Liz Millward has written that "judgmental statements reveal more about the authors than the people they encountered" and "one can only speculate that the 'two dykes on a bike' were young, anti-corporate, and distanced themselves from the 'hard-drinking butch' category."[13] While the two dykes' assessment of gay bars across Canada was far from unbiased, it did provide "information for other women who might travel to the same location, or even for those who lived locally but had not visited a particular venue."[14]

From the past to the present, 2SLGBTQ+ Edmontonians are used to being misjudged and overlooked by people and pundits from larger cities like Toronto, Montreal, and Vancouver. Queer life on the Prairies was often different from and harder than in big cities, and that difference is reflected in how social spaces were created and how the community organized amid active resistance. Club '70's focus was always to serve as a safe and social gathering space for Edmonton's gay and lesbian community. However, the club acknowledged that some members wanted to be more involved in the burgeoning gay and lesbian liberation movement. It was a time of change and demand in Canada, and the Prairies were no exception.

The arrest for gross indecency and the indefinite imprisonment of Everett Klippert as an "incurable homosexual" and "dangerous sexual offender" caused much shock and outrage (see page 131).[15] Klippert's case was a catalyst for then Justice Minister Pierre Elliott Trudeau to say famously, "There is no place for the state in the bedrooms of the nation" in support of efforts to partially decriminalize homosexuality by amending the Criminal Code of Canada.[16] These legal changes came about during the period of the infamous Stonewall Uprising in New York City and growing public calls for rights and recognition across North America. These events and legal changes would help to incite emerging gay consciousness and demands for equality as more communities began to organize and agitate for change.

In Edmonton, calls to become more politically active were often published in the *Club '70 News*, associated with the belief that political activity and proactive education of those outside of the gay and lesbian community were crucial in encouraging public understanding and fighting for gay and lesbian rights.[17] To this end, Club '70 often directed members who wanted to become more politically involved to join Gay Alliance Towards Equality (GATE; see page 18).[18] In the late 1970s, Club '70 permitted GATE to use the club as a drop-in centre, as GATE had recently lost the use of its premises on the south side of the city.[19] Club '70 also supported GATE by hosting special nights to raise funds for its new location. Once GATE found a new, more permanent home, Club '70 encouraged its members to seek and support political efforts outside of regular club activities.[20]

After eight years, Club '70 was forced to close its doors due to financial issues and competition from new queer bars and clubs like the legendary Flashback and the Roost. In 1978, Club '70 sold their premises, and the former club became the new location of the shortly lived Cha Cha Palace, which focussed on serving the lesbian community.[21] The Cha Cha Palace closed soon after, and Boots 'N Saddle, a members-only club owned by Conrad Dragu, opened in its place, becoming a well-known 2SLGBTQ+ community gathering space for some thirty years. After Boots closed in 2010, not long after the death of its co-owner Jim Schafer, Junction Bar and Eatery opened in its place. Junction was open for only two years before the location was sold and became an art gallery, ending the building's long-standing run as one of Edmonton's premier 2SLGBTQ+ entertainment venues.

ROB BROWATZKE

Junction was a truly special space because it only came about due to some fortunate timing. Prism was looking to relocate, Boots had just closed, and Play was closing. Deb and Tracey had a vision of bringing all of these groups and communities together, and it was truly a magical thing to watch happen. The bears from Boots, the cougars from Prism, the twinks from Play, and somehow everyone came together.

For me, the abruptness of Boots' closure in May 2010 was a real wound in my heart. The way Deb and Tracey immediately opened their bar and their hearts to all of us was unexpected. We'd had a rough go at Boots watching Jim Schafer slowly pass away, and we were left without a space to come together, but it was literally only twenty-four hours before Prism welcomed us all in, including me as a bartender. That was a saving grace for sure, and then being able to go back into that Boots space, to carry on, to build something new, all together, it was truly wonderful.

We talk a lot about chosen family in our community, and nowhere was that better understood by me than in the twenty-five months we had together at Junction. It was a space that truly tried to offer something for everyone, from all-day pool tournaments to Pride patio parties, karaoke nights, and dance parties. Boots had become well known for its Bear bashes in its last few years, and the way these events were welcomed by Junction was really amazing to see. Maybe they were less sexual, given the all-gender space they were suddenly in, but there was a new kind of liberation and unity that developed.

Losing Deb in 2023 brought our bar family back together, as loss often does. In the eleven years between the bar closing and her passing, life has taken us all on new journeys. We are all in new spaces in our life, but just like any family, being together was natural and comfortable and healing. That is the love that was at the heart of Junction.

Boots was a kind of home to me. I worked there maybe three or four different times. I would leave but always come back. There was a corner of the bar called the Princess Corner. It was where the guys sat at Happy Hour, heads turning in sync to see whoever came through the door. It was there where Jim Schafer served sambuca and laughter with equal gusto. It was also there where we watched him slowly die. We really were a family; we grieved together as much as we partied together. I'll always remember how Ross, Jim's partner in the bar, would dance, his hands together almost like in prayer; he loved music so much.

Sadly, Boots didn't last long after Jim died. It was incomprehensible really, having the bar without him. The night Boots closed, Ross and I drank into the wee hours of the night, sharing memories, laughing, and crying. I didn't see him again for over a decade, until one night he randomly showed up at Evolution. We picked up immediately where we had left off, sharing memories. Gay bars like Boots are places where memories are born and never forgotten.

Flashback

10330 104 STREET

John Reid began his coming-out process in Edmonton, but it was during travels to larger gay cities that he fell in love with the idea of gay nightclubs. As a result, it was only natural that, once he was ready to participate in Edmonton's 2SLGBTQ+ community, he headed to the only official gay bar in town, Club '70 (see page 216). Ironically, John was refused entry to the private member's club because no one knew him and therefore no one could vouch for his being gay.

229

Eventually, he was allowed entry into Club '70 and began his long tenure as a prominent member of Edmonton's early 2SLGBTQ+ community. As a patron of Club '70, John constantly lamented the lack of a real dance floor and sound booth. The only sound system was a jukebox, and so the music depended on the whim of the customers who arrived in the afternoon: if they had enough quarters, they could plug the machine and dictate what music would be played for hours, which drove John crazy!

When a long-time ally of the queer community, "Mother Jean" Lawson, a straight woman with deep roots in the emerging drag community, was refused entry into Club '70, Reid realized Edmonton needed a gay bar where allies and supporters of the community could be treated with fairness and respect. In 1974, John Reid, Paul Chisholm (Empress Millie), Pat Fortier, Harvey Jones, and others banded together to create Flashback, which became Edmonton's first gay disco. John said, "Gays deserved more than what Club '70 had to offer ... [which included] a more positive environment."[1]

This positive environment was reflected in John's founding vision: "Flashback is a place for human beings to accept one another. It is a place for those questioning their sexualities to feel comfortable in. An outlet that's easier to come out in ...

▲ Flashback's most iconic 104 Street location, present day (10330 104 Street)
▼ Flashback dance floor

NEON

I was originally from Calgary. I was fortunate enough to be taken under the wing of a group of crazy queens when I was fifteen. I had dabbled in doing backup for their shows for a while, but didn't have the nerve to step up to the spotlight. Then in 1983 we went to Edmonton for a Flashback crowning weekend. It changed me forever. I was asked to do a number. I was so nervous. My dearest friend (who was a superstar in Calgary) tried to talk me out of it, worrying I would be ridiculed… because I was fat and female. Fat was forgivable. Female? UNHEARD OF! (At least in Calgary.) But I really wanted it, so I did it. And never looked back. I may be female, but I was also one of the best drag queens of my time. I found my family, my people on the Flashback dance floor that night. It took about a year for me to move to Edmonton. The city has been all the more NEON for it.

I wanted to give every individual the right to party and bring in anyone they wanted to party with. When you want parity in a society, you can't expect total privacy."[2]

Flashback had three different incarnations during its sixteen years in operation. The first location was in the basement of a building on Jasper Avenue and 117 Street. After Flashback left this location, the Gymini, a gay bathhouse, relocated from downtown to the same spot, ultimately closing the day after the 1981 raid on the Pisces Spa (see page 84).

From the moment Flashback opened its doors, it was different. In an attempt to set itself apart from Club '70, Flashback welcomed and encouraged straight people to participate in the party. Flashback also featured a real dance floor and an actual sound booth. Naturally, the drag queens of Edmonton gravitated to the flashing lights of the Flashback stage. Even today, John speaks of the importance of drag to Flashback's success, having designed every incarnation of the club to nurture the performers who would bring so much life and vivacity to the club over the years. The dance floors doubled as a performance stage, along with a dressing room and costume storage for the countless numbers of drag shows and events Flashback hosted over the years.

In 1976, the formation of the Imperial Sovereign Court of the Wild Rose brought Edmonton's drag culture into the mainstream (see page 46). The election of Millie as Empress I of Edmonton cemented Flashback as the House of Drag. That same year, Flashback held its first drag pageant billed as the Mz. Flashback Competition. Millie ran for Mz. Flashback and won, becoming the only queen in Edmonton's history to hold both Imperial Sovereign Court of the Wild Rose and Flashback titles simultaneously. In the second year of the Court, John Reid ran for Emperor II alongside his friend Chatty Cathy Jackson. The duo became the second Empress and Emperor of the Imperial House of Millicent, further cementing Flashback as the centre stage for drag in Edmonton.

In the club's basement the Flashback Follies were formed. Under the expert direction of theatre professionals like choreographer John Kerr and director Allan McInnis, Edmonton queens began creating elaborate full-scale drag musical productions such as *Hello Dolly*, *A Chorus Line*, and *Cabaret*. As the Imperial Sovereign Court of the Wild Rose started to network with the International Court System in other cities, the Edmonton performances soon garnered wide acclaim.

The tiny disco, described by the *Edmonton Sun* as "the playground of the sexually confused," was packed from the moment it opened, and it soon became apparent that a larger location was needed.[3] In 1978, after losing some of its initial investors, Reid and Millie, with financial backing from Brent Earl and Dr. Henri Toupin, reopened Flashback on 104 Street. This would become Flashback's most iconic location—strategically located right across the street from Edmonton's newest gay bar, the Roost. This set off a legendary rivalry that would continue until there was only one club left standing.

Acclaimed playwright Brad Fraser recalls his first time at Flashback: "We were nervous and excited, taking in every detail of the place: the antique signs over the rustic wooden bar, the pinball and rudimentary video games flashing against one wall, in the next room a recessed lounge with a low-level backgammon table and matching stools, the main room with its bi-level dance floor and tacky Christmas lights on a patio-lattice ceiling." The whole place, he said, smelled of Aramis cologne, "as integral to a gay man's identity at the time as opening that extra button on your shirt."[4]

Former Mz. Flashback Cleo told *See* magazine that Flashback was all she could think about: "I just wanted to be gay, and I wanted to be gay in a place that was safe. That was my overriding memory, a sense of safety to be who I wanted to be."[5]

This magical location began to turn the party in Edmonton for the next decade, raising the bar for what a nightclub could be in a remote Prairie town. It was large, dark, loud, and on weekends, the party often lasted until the sun came up. It became a magnet for outcasts from every walk of life, and its legend spread far and wide. Part of the success was due to the best sound system in the city, an epic collection of dance music, and a superstar DJ in the form of DJ Mikee (Mikee Brennan). The club even had its own record store called Hot Trax, which supplied music not just for Flashback but also for more than a few other mainstream clubs and DJs in Edmonton. Flashback became the place people heard music they couldn't find anywhere else, often months before the radio stations would catch on. At its zenith, *Billboard* magazine named Flashback one of the ten best nightclubs in North America.[6]

It was also in this location that the annual Drag Races became part of the yearly pageant, crowning the new Mr. and Mz. Flashback. Every Victoria Day long weekend the outdoor event brought outrageous drag antics into the daylight by using the alley entrance and loading dock to present a bacchanalian barbecue and "sporting" event that featured hilarious antics and competitions in various states of drag or undress, in full view of passers-by.[7]

In 1981, Flashback made a short-lived entry into the after-hours scene, with the addition of Phase Four, a men-only club open until 5 a.m. (without liquor service). It didn't last.[8] Also in 1981, after the Pisces Health Spa raid, Flashback hosted at least one meeting of the found-ins as they planned their legal defence strategy. John Reid became one of the few gay Edmontonians of the time to speak publicly to the media on behalf of the community.

In 1982, Graham Hicks, an *Edmonton Sun* columnist, started mentioning Trash, the reigning Mz. Flashback, in his Page 6 gossip column. This public attention helped elevate drag gossip and machinations to local prominence. Some of the coverage included mention of a "cute as a button" columnist nominated for a Nellie Award and the popularity of the Josie Cotton classic "Johnny Are You Queer?" on the Flashback dance floor.[9]

DARRIN HAGEN

Someone once said that the first step to being a writer is to live a life worth writing about. By walking into Flashback, I was already partway there.

I have been writing about Flashback since the doors closed forever and I have yet to run out of stories of how a cavernous wooden warehouse space with a discrete alley entrance transformed my life—indeed, the way I view the world. Because once you have shared space with queer people who feel safe enough to finally reveal themselves, it's nearly impossible to retreat.

Within a year of being loudly buzzed through that squeaky wooden door, I had met the majority of the people who would be my new family for the rest of our lives. My destiny as an artist, as an activist, my history with Guys in Disguise, my lifelong partner ... they all began inside that club.

But it wasn't just the people, or the drag shows, or the crowds gyrating on a throbbing dance floor (although those were certainly draws); it was about seeing—for the first time—the future I hadn't been permitted to imagine. A freedom this unique couldn't have existed unless someone envisioned it, and being surrounded by so many courageous, defiant, fierce talents inspired the warrior in me. Diving in with both feet was the only option.

The joy of this discovery will always be shrouded by the darkness of that decade—plague, violence, discrimination, and murder ... but even after all the loss and heartbreak of my time within those walls—I would do it all again.

Flashback is the reason I stayed in Edmonton.

Still, this visibility had mixed results. One complaint sent to *Fineprint* magazine about the increased number of straight people coming to Flashback blamed the *Edmonton Sun* column.[10] Reid's response to complaints about straights was direct: "I am hurt that people would feel that way. Flashback provides a repertoire of clientele that can't be denounced ... Any hassles that I have encountered have been from the gays not the straight."[11] He went on to say, "It will take a lot of time to depend on the gay dollar in this city. We have a faithful [gay] clientele that I appreciate but it's not enough to pay the bills."[12]

Flashback hosted not just parties and pageants. For years, its dance floor was used to film a local weekly televised workout show, and in 1983 the club was chosen to host the International Designer of the Year Award, drawing fashion elite from across the country, as well as wealthy and influential patrons. Even the First Lady of Alberta, Jeannie Lougheed, was in attendance. That in itself made news the next day. The teaser airing on 630 CHED radio asked, "What was the wife of the Premier doing in a gay bar last night? Find out next." The story related that the Flashback coat check girl was fired after snarkily telling Mrs. Lougheed, "I don't care if you're the queen of fucking England, the coat check is full!"[13]

On September 15, 1983, a public community meeting was held at Flashback to discuss the growing spectre of AIDS. Fifty people attended, including Dr. Jerry Katz, a local physician well informed about AIDS. Community concern was starting to build and a 1984 meeting around Michael Phair's kitchen table led to the creation of the AIDS Network of Edmonton (see page 34).

In the mid-1980s, after years of harassment from the Alberta Liquor Control Board (ALCB), Flashback led a legal protest against provincial liquor laws in an attempt to have the cut-off hour for liquor service extended to two a.m., as in other provinces. The ALCB finally relented and extended service hours to two a.m. for all bars, except for private members' clubs.

This effectively meant all gay bars were excluded from the expanded hours. Flashback fought back again, this time with other gay bar owners joining the fight. Flashback finally won, and the liquor service hours were extended for all bars and clubs.[14]

Over the years, celebrities who might find themselves in Edmonton often asked, "Where does the wildest fun happen here?" They would all discover the answer was Flashback. Sarah McLachlan, Long John Baldry, Belinda Carlisle, Sylvester, Wayne Gretzky, The Nylons, The Great Imposters, Kurt Browning, Mark Messier, Steve Anthony, The Jazz Butchers, and The Kids in the Hall all spent time partying on the legendary dancefloor.[15] Flashback developed an international reputation. *Graffiti* magazine named it one of the top five clubs in North America, calling it "Edmonton's Alternative Underground."[16] This was perhaps a better description than the *Edmonton Sun*, which called it "the spiffy little club that serves as a second home to Edmonton's disco-n-Crisco set."[17]

In 1987, a group of Flashback drag queens led by a former Mz. Flashback, Darrin Hagen, and his partner, Kevin Hendricks, formed a performance troupe called Guys in Disguise and, in a very public debut, performed a sold-out run at the Edmonton International Fringe Festival, launching more than three decades of public performance and queer theatre creation, eventually touring and being produced internationally. In 1988, Craig Russell performed at Flashback as part of his cross-country comeback with the release of the sequel to his hit movie *Outrageous*. "Too Outrageous" eventually flopped, but his performance at Flashback gave a hint of the grandeur of the Russell magic that had captivated audiences around the world.

Flashback was one of the settings for the nightclub scenes depicted in Brad Fraser's play *Unidentified Human Remains and the True Nature of Love*, which became an international hit. When Denys Arcand's adaptation *Love and Human Remains* was filmed, it contained scenes set in Flashback. Likewise, Brad Fraser and Darrin Hagen's song "Give Me Tomorrow Back" was included as part of a 1991 AIDS Awareness benefit concert held at Flashback, part of a city-wide Day Without Art reflecting the loss of people who died from AIDS and all the art they might have created.[18]

In 1990, the 104 Street Millard Building owner passed away, leaving the building to his son. John Reid soon received word the club would be evicted: the building was to be sold and transformed into condominiums. Faced with the choice of relocating or shutting down for good, John shopped around for a new location, eventually finding the perfect spot directly across the back alley from the current Flashback. With investment from Michael Ritter, the third and final Flashback location was born. It immediately drew criticism from patrons because it was large, open, and sterile. The epic curved glass brick wall did strange things to the music by reflecting the sound in unpredictable ways. It wasn't open long before Reid and Ritter parted company, and John was left to carry on by himself. The damage to the club's reputation was fatal. The move, coupled with the changing times and Flashback's unfriendly entrance policies, eventually eroded support from the 2SLGBTQ+ community.

In 1992, Flashback closed its doors for good. The sound system, the lights, and the massive record collection were used to open Rebar on Whyte Avenue, which would become a mainstay in Edmonton's nightlife for the next decade. In 1996, the life and times of Flashback were immortalized in Darrin Hagen's play *The Edmonton Queen*, later published as a book. In 2024, a new documentary film about Flashback became a hit on the film festival circuit.[19] Today, Flashback may be gone, but the legend remains indelibly in our hearts and minds forever.

The Roost

10345 104 STREET

Today, the Excelsior Lofts sit across the street from a squat, square building housing the offices of the Canadian Border Patrol. It is an unremarkable stretch of road, one which, without the City's Neon Museum, you would drive down without a sideways glance. This wasn't always the case. Had you ventured down 104 Street in the 1980s, you would have found yourself in the heart of Edmonton's gay disco district, with the legendary Flashback to the west and the Roost to the east. These two juggernauts of 2SLGBTQ+ nightlife dominated Edmonton's gay culture for over a decade. Flashback was born in one location, came into its own in another, and finally died in a third. The Roost was born, grew, and died all in that red brick square; all that remains now is a fading and long-forgotten rainbow Pride flag painted across the front step.

For most of the 1970s, Club '70 (see page 216) was Edmonton's 2SLGBTQ+ watering hole, serving as a pub, dance club, and de facto community centre. Club '70 was a private members' space run by a volunteer board. The founding team of the Roost all served on that board at some point and as a result opened the Roost with some experience in Edmonton's nightlife. Seeing the business potential in a new venture, Dow Hicks, Eugene Keith, Robert (Bob) Dean (aka "Hannah"), and Paul Tilroe established the Roost in fall 1977, the same year that disco was dominating airwaves across the world.[1] Disco was of particular significance to gay male culture in the late 1970s and into the 1980s, when it lost commercial viability in the straight world with American campaigns like Disco Demolition Night and Disco Sucks.[2]

Originally known as the Cock's Roost,[3] the Roost initially opened as a gay men's club. Paul Tilroe recalls the pushback from Edmonton's lesbian community, resulting in the bar eventually becoming a mixed space for all genders, a focus that remained for the duration of the Roost's thirty-year run.[4]

▲ The Roost, 1982
▼ The Roost original location, present day (10345 104 Street)

CARL AUSTIN
Roost manager, 1995–2001

I started working at the Roost in 1988 when Pat hired me to work the door. It was an interesting turn of events in my life. I worked at sorting mail in the day and the Roost at night. Soon I worked full time at the Roost and it was here where I found my tribe/family. I started managing the Roost in the winter of 1995. Initially, the job was only temporary, but with Pat's departure I took on more and more responsibilities, which included programming all the music and community events. I tried to include as many groups as possible to have them feel that they had a home at the Roost. I created a Sunday show called *The Betty Ford Clinic's Recovery Show*, which featured Edmonton drag superstar Twiggy and newcomer Kitten. The Sunday show quickly became a staple with Kitten's amazing impersonation of Tina Turner. The Sunday show was the first time Edmonton queens were actually paid to perform.

We came up with new ways to use the upstairs as a venue for the Fringe and held private leather events and fundraisers. I left the Roost in 2001, not as a happy person as there is both a good and a dark side of the gay world. Overall, it was an amazing experience working at the Roost. I learned a lot on the business side from Dow [the owner] and met some truly amazing and talented people. When I finally left the Roost, I could see the tide turning and the crowd was getting smaller as the Internet was becoming more dominant. The landscape had changed, and the community changed with it. We started to see fewer and fewer LGBTQ bars and community spaces, and I'm not sure that was really such a great thing.

The first dedicated women's night at the Roost was on a Wednesday, less than ideal for Edmonton's lesbian community, but it was a start.[5] Carl Austin, who managed the Roost from 1995 to 2001, notes that once the strong lesbian faction took hold, they remained steadfastly loyal, even saving the Roost from closing in the early 1990s when competition arose in the form of the Option Room (see page 258).[6]

It wasn't long after the Roost opened that Flashback relocated directly across the street. The Flashback team had already been scoping out a new location, and it just so happened that Edmonton's two gay discos would soon be located right across the street from each other. Yes, this created competition, but it also created opportunities for collaboration, especially in a fight against the Alberta Liquor Control Board (ALCB), whose regulations prohibited basic actions like patrons walking around the bar with their own drinks.[7] Intense competition between the two clubs also resulted in the Roost expanding to include a second level in 1988.[8] The two levels enabled the Roost to play with different music formats and cater to trends, styles, and crowds over the years, often with country music playing downstairs and dance music upstairs.

The Roost opened up its popular outdoor patio in 1980, the first of its kind in Edmonton. This patio, located at the back of the building, was expanded in 1985 and then again in 1995.[9] Not only did the patio provide a place for patrons to cool down from the packed and sweat-soaked dance floors; it also provided space for the club and partner groups to host special events like barbeques and community gatherings. Originally designed to have an entirely outdoor bar station, the bar service was short lived due to intervention from ALCB. As government restrictions changed, the Roost always managed to adapt strategically.

Nightlife, particularly 2SLGBTQ+ nightlife, always comes with a dark side, and the Roost was no exception. Paul Tilroe recalls that "Many gay folks who were not as outgoing or good looking would hang out till the bitter end hoping to find a friend and other folks who clearly were unhappy and had drowned their sorrows."[10] Carl Austin also laments the amount of substance use and abuse that happened in the bar, noting that it could create an "unhealthy atmosphere for the staff" and customers. Carl relayed that "LGBT bars are lifesavers and on the flipside are unhealthy atmospheres for addictive personalities."[11]

Another dark aspect of the Roost was the risk of violence and harassment. Well into the 1990s, it was not uncommon for gay-bashers to drive around in trucks looking to cause trouble for patrons. And in September 1992, the *Edmonton Journal* ran a story in which then-manager Patrick Ryley bemoaned local taxi drivers pressuring the Roost's customers for sex in exchange for a free ride.[12]

Tilroe recalls the impact of the HIV/AIDS epidemic on venues such as the Roost, which rose to the challenge to help its community.[13] For more than twenty years, the November long weekend was home to the Roost's annual AIDS benefit.[14] This performance, which later evolved under beloved drag queen Sticky Vicky, started raising money for Kairos House, a hospice run by Catholic Social Services, before pivoting towards supporting HIV/AIDS research at the University of Alberta.[15] One of the staples of the fundraiser was a cut-a-thon where local stylists donated their time and talents to give patrons ten-dollar haircuts right in the Roost lobby. Austin isn't sure whether "the Roost was even given [enough] credit for the bigger picture of its charitable donations."[16]

With any long-running bar, the competition changed over time. The long-standing rivalry between the Roost and Flashback, which on occasion resulted in staff from one venue being barred from the other, began to wane when Flashback relocated for a second time, this time moving one block over to 105 Street. The third Flashback location was short lived, but equally fleeting was the Roost's dominance over Edmonton's 2SLGBTQ+ nightlife.

The Option Room rose to fill the void created by Flashback's departure from the scene, and while it had its own legal battles and issues, Austin recalls that it came close to putting the Roost out of business. In its later years, the Roost found competition in Buddys, which had opened as a pub in 1996 and rebuilt itself as a dance club in 2000. When the Roost finally closed, Buddys also enjoyed a short-lived dominance in Edmonton's 2SLGBTQ+ nightlife.

Dow Hicks attributed the Roost's success and longevity to its customer service. "We have been here so long that people really feel this is a home," Hicks told *Outlooks* magazine in the mid-1990s.[17] Austin admits that the competition sometimes got unfortunately ugly, with "bad blood between owners."[18]

One way the Roost was able to compete so well for so long was its second floor. Originally added to compete against Flashback and accommodate massive Saturday night crowds, the second floor was perfect for theatrical productions, Roost management realized in the late 1990s. Dow was eager to see the space used as much as possible during the rest of the week, and Joe Achtemichuk, manager from 2001 to 2007, convinced Dow that it was time to try something new.

Starting in 1996, the Roost became a Bring-Your-Own-Venue for the Edmonton International Fringe Festival, with plays such as Achtemichuk's own *Yes I Am* as well as drag productions like *Priscilla, Queen of the Tundra* and *Place Commercial Here*. The popularity of drag at the Fringe had been pioneered by Edmonton's Guys in Disguise, and the Roost was able to build upon that success. Achtemichuk had a deal with Dow: after every successful show, he could use the proceeds to improve the upstairs for future productions. In later years, the upstairs was used as a venue for drag shows produced by groups such as the Imperial Sovereign Court of the Wild Rose and Grant MacEwan College student groups.[19]

In September 2007, the Roost celebrated its thirtieth anniversary, making it the longest-running nightclub in Canada.[20]

ROB BROWATZKE

The Roost was my first gay bar. When I set foot in there that first time, I had no idea that queer nightlife would become my career and life. I wish I remembered more about that first night, my first feelings being inside a gay space, but sadly, so many memories blur and distort over time. I did end up working at the Roost later, in the early 2000s. I worked at the deli and soon discovered the Roost burgers were the best thing after a night out drinking. But what I didn't like about working in the deli was that it was on the wrong side of the wall. All of the fun, all the drama, and all the men were over there, and I was stuck in my little space flipping burgers and hoping they had to come buy some food or take out some money from the bank machine. I was a total Roost boy, though, basically there seven days a week. For so many of us, coming out is linked to coming of age, and I was lucky to have both happen in a place like the Roost. Miscellaneous Roost memories include Jazzy spinning "Groove Is in the Heart" every Saturday at midnight like clockwork, or all of us sitting on the floor around the stage chanting "Tina" to get Kitten Kaboodle to perform as Tina Turner on a Sunday night, or that liberation that we all felt when there's hundreds of us on a packed dance floor and we're all hot and sweaty and free.

What very few people knew at the time was that this would be the bar's last anniversary. Earlier that year, Dow had told a few key staff the bar would be closing at the end of the year.[21] Dow had owned the building for over a decade and had rejected many offers to purchase the space. One offer finally came along that was too good to pass up. As social acceptance of 2SLGBTQ+ people increased, there was less obvious need for dedicated gay bars, meaning business was declining. "You can't pay the bills with it full only one day a week," one of the staff's partners told the *Edmonton Journal*.[22]

The public announcement of the closure came late that fall, with the final party scheduled for New Year's Eve.[23] The reaction was immediate and felt far and wide. One "aging gay man" in Gloucester, England, lamented the loss, saying, "The Roost was the best watering hole that I have visited, not only in Canada but also in the world."[24] At first, there was talk of relocating to a smaller venue, but relocation plans never materialized. Paul Detta, one of the last staff to leave the Roost's employment, knew "it was time for the next generation to run their own party on their own terms."[25]

After a thirty-year run, the Roost is fondly remembered as a pillar of Edmonton's 2SLGBTQ+ community. A space where people found love, sex, intimacy, but perhaps above all else, an irreplaceable sense of safety, friendship, and community.

Secrets
and Prism

ORIGINAL LOCATION:
10249 107 STREET

FINAL LOCATION:
10524 105 STREET

SECRETS II:
10341 106 STREET

In the fall of 1998, Elizabeth (Liz) Gates relocated to Edmonton from Calgary with a mission: to open a bar for Edmonton's lesbian community. By the time Liz was ready to open, Edmonton's 2SLGBTQ+ nightlife scene had had a fraught and tumultuous relationship with lesbian customers.[1] At times, lesbians were outright excluded; at other times, lesbian events were relegated to mid-week or slower nights. While Club '70 was, for its duration, a space welcoming to both gay men and lesbians, other spaces in the 1970s, such as Boots 'N Saddle and the Roost (see page 238), originally opened as men-only spaces. The short-lived lesbian-owned Cha Cha Palace, located across the alley from where Secrets would eventually be established, was Edmonton's first venue focussed primarily on women.[2] Even though venues like the Roost and the Option Room hosted lesbian events, sometimes in partnership with Womonspace, it wasn't until Shakespear's opened in 1995 that Edmonton once again had a bar specifically dedicated to its lesbian community. When Shakespear's closed in 1998, Liz filled the void and opened Secrets Bar and Grill.[3] It opened in what had been the Hydrant Bar, so named because it was located next to a downtown fire hall.[4]

Prior to Secrets and its predecessor, Shakespear's, Edmonton's lesbian community had the option of existing gay clubs, which predominantly catered to gay men, or Womonspace, a social non-profit that had provided a safe space for lesbians, with activities like coffee nights, socials, and monthly dances since the early 1980s (see page 178).[5] In 1993, journalist Marilyn Moysa wrote a profile of lesbian nightlife for the *Edmonton Journal*. The piece is particularly instructive insofar as it serves as a window into the wants and needs of a community seeking spaces of kinship and conviviality while also trying to negotiate and maintain its diversity. Moysa's profile focussed

▲ Prism float in a past Pride Parade
▼ Cast of Save the Tatas, a breast cancer fundraiser at Junction

TWIGGY

Empress XV,
Imperial Sovereign Court of the Wild Rose

I worked at Secrets and then Prism from the first opening to the last closing. I got the job just by starting up a conversation with Liz when I ran into her at the bank; she was wearing a shirt with the Secrets logo. Secrets was a lot of fun, especially in the afternoons. On Wing Night, if you didn't get there by ten, you were out of luck because it was so popular and we always ran out. Dyna and Vera started a drag queen bingo to run alongside Wing Night as a fundraiser for the Imperial Sovereign Court of the Wild Rose. I knew a lot of lesbians from before in places like Shakespear's, Womonspace, Flashback, and "Dyke Alley" at Boots, but I sure met a lot more working at Secrets, some of whom went on to become very important in my life. Bartending at Secrets, I often became a lesbian counsellor, even talking a few people through their coming out. I also became an honorary member of the lesbian army.

I loved having the back and forth with Boots across the alley. That was a great time and helped break down the stigma that Boots was a men's bar and Secrets was a women's bar.

The transition from Secrets to Prism was very fast. I hadn't even met Cindy and Rae-Ann and suddenly I was working for them. They took over and started with a name-the-bar contest. It was Prism vs the Liquor Box for the top two names, but Prism ultimately won out. The bar got renamed and then we relocated. It was certainly different, not being close to Boots and being a bit further away from the other bars. Prism was very event driven with things like Dyke2Diva, and then when Deb and Tracey took over, the menu was elevated and people looked at us more for a good meal, rather than just as a place for drinks. Everyone loved the food, even if the neighbourhood and building weren't the best. At the time, I lived right next door, thirty-nine steps from the Macdonald Lofts to Prism—forty-two if you were in heels.

The promise of the Ice District was, even then, a light at the end of the tunnel. It was going to revitalize the neighbourhood, but that never happened. We eventually moved into the old Boots space, and my life had come full circle.

on Girl Crazy, a monthly dance event held in an unnamed warehouse in downtown Edmonton. Many of her interviewees aired indifference toward the Roost, with one declaring that she "hate[d] the place."[6] Above all, the women Moysa interviewed expressed the desire for multiple and diverse spaces for women. Sheila, who identified herself as a Womonspace member, stated, "Only a small number of women go to the gay clubs. There's so much diversity, there's got to be different venues for different interests. Straight women don't just go to Barry T's every night. We're not any different."[7]

Secrets Bar and Grill took its name from the secrecy Liz operated under while preparing to open. At the time, Edmonton had two dance clubs—the Roost and 109 Discotheque—and two pubs/bars—Buddys and Boots 'N Saddle. Liz built her space leaning closer to the pub side, with a kitchen to serve brunches and burgers. Secrets also had pool tables and a stage that could double as a dance floor. One of the most noticeable aspects, when one walked into Secrets, was Liz's motorcycle, which was suspended from the ceiling and provided many patrons with the opportunity for a great photo. When asked about the motorcycle, Liz remarked, "Every dyke likes a bike!"[8]

By Pride of the following year, Secrets had taken its spot in the 2SLGBTQ+ community scene, working with Boots and Buddys to host the Flamingo Pride Dance. Liz expressed her gratitude toward these other clubs and the way the community was collectively able to "let our fences down and work side by side."[9] Secrets had also secured working relationships with local 2SLGBTQ+ non-profit organizations such as the Imperial Sovereign Court of the Wild Rose (see page 46). Drag shows soon joined the lineup of entertainment, which included DJs, karaoke, open mike nights, and bingo.

In 2003, Rae-Anne Schatz Wood and her partner Cindy Goodwin assumed ownership of Secrets. With their current location slated for demolition, the new owners took the opportunity to relocate and rebrand. Now called Prism, the bar reopened at the end of that year on 101 Street, while continuing to offer the experiences Secrets was known for. In 2005, Liz returned briefly to the Edmonton 2SLGBTQ+ nightlife scene with a short-lived space she dubbed Secrets II. In all of Edmonton's years, this was the period with the most 2SLGBTQ+ clubs and bars (briefly maxing out at seven). It was truly the heyday of Edmonton's 2SLGBTQ+ entertainment scene.[10]

While Secrets II was short-lived, Prism continued. Bar manager Natasha knew what Prism offered wouldn't compete with the nightclubs of the time, so they didn't try. Instead, they came up with a rotation of events designed to entice people to visit them before heading to clubs like Buddys or the Roost.[11] One of these events was Straight 2 Diva, an evolution of the popular Dyke2Diva event Prism had been hosting. This new event saw straight men dressed in drag, typically as a fundraiser. This event was so popular that it was later adopted by the Calgary Eagle.[12]

Prism was eventually sold to Tracey Smith and Deborah Chymyshyn, who had been running the kitchen at Prism for about ten months before taking over the entire bar. With Prism's lease expiring, Tracey and Deborah were on the lookout for a new space, one that would allow them to host all-ages events. When Boots 'N Saddle closed abruptly, ending its tenure as Edmonton's longest-running gay bar, Tracey and Deborah took advantage of the timing to combine the spirits of both Boots and Prism by opening the Junction Bar and Eatery. This move brought the Secrets/Prism brand almost full circle address-wise: the Junction was located in the former Boots 'N Saddle space and right across the alley from the original Secrets.

Staff and patrons of both Prism and Boots came together to help with renovations, making the Junction something different from other incarnations of previous clubs and bars. Whereas bars like the Roost had opened as men-only and later welcomed in lesbians, and bars like Secrets opened with a lesbian focus but still embraced gay men, the Junction was from its inception a space for the entire community to come together. When it closed after just twenty-five months, it brought an end to those intertwined legacies.

Although lesbian-owned spaces like Mama's Gin Joint and Pink Noiz would later open, they did not last long. Other recent additions to Edmonton 2SLGBTQ+ nightlife, such as UpStares Ultralounge or Evolution Wonderlounge, geared some events towards Edmonton's lesbian community with mixed success. With Womonspace no longer active, Edmonton's queer women sought out pop-up or guerilla events through a variety of new and informal online groups such as Edmonton Lesbian Event Network and Sapphic Speakeasy. This phenomenon is not unique to Edmonton, as 2SLGBTQ+ bars across North America seek new ways to survive and thrive, and the communities in those cities find ways to do the same, often outside of bars entirely.[13]

ROB BROWATZKE

Secrets was a space we went for a change of scene, even though it was just across the alley. Wingo Bingo always pulled us in. I didn't know then, on those Wednesday nights at Secrets, that one day, Boots would close and Prism (the rechristened and relocated Secrets) would take us all in. Deb and Tracey always did an "orphans Christmas" where people who didn't have close relationships with family, or people who just wanted to spend holidays with found family, could gather together.

When Boots closed, we were literal orphans, and they took us all in. That's how Junction came to be, all these different people from different bars coming together. I didn't appreciate Junction enough when we had it. Given how big a part of my life it was, it's strange it was only around for two years. My sobriety was born there, thanks to some tough love from Deb and Tracey. There's something so poetic about how Boots and Secrets and Prism melded together and eventually ended together. But the relationships we made there in those walls? Those go on forever.

Sax and the
Option Room

10148 105 STREET

THE OptiON ROOM

423-HOMO
10148-105 STREET

Over the decades of Edmonton's diverse 2SLGBTQ+ nightlife, some venues have had a lasting presence and housed more than one gay club. Evolution Wonderlounge now stands where Play once existed. Woodys Pub closed and became Mama's Gin Joint. The building that currently houses Last Modern Event Venue previously hosted Club '70, the Cha Cha Palace, Boots 'N Saddle, and the Junction. The surprising record for most gay bars in one single location, however, goes to the building currently home to Shade Gentlemen's Club on 105 Street, which features exotic dancers and primarily caters to straight males.

Club Soda opened on March 20, 1985, billing itself as Edmonton's zaniest nightclub.[1] While surviving advertisements do not specifically brand Club Soda as a gay space, Ron Byers recalls the owners trying to cater to Edmonton's gay market after Ali Katz, their first attempt at a nightclub in this location, failed.[2] Club Soda featured an eclectic mix of Egyptian, Caribbean, and Hawaiian themes. The club was spread over two levels, with an upper balcony overlooking a sunken dance floor. It opened early for a nice lunch and then continued until last call, seven days a week. Over the next few years, the 105 Street location would be rebranded again and again, first as Lamborghinee's Playhouse Lounge (1987), then as Electric Banana (1987), and later as Reflexions (1988).

The nightclubs didn't all openly advertise themselves as exclusively gay spaces but were often frequented by the 2SLGBTQ+ community, some more than others. For example, Reflexions actively supported the Imperial Sovereign Court of the Wild Rose with an ad in the Coronation Ball program (see page 46).

The Electric Banana cast a spotlight on itself when management incorporated a fake confessional into the club, featuring a man in a monkey suit and priest's collar who would forgive the sins of nightclub goers. The most lurid confessions were

▲ The Option Room logo
▼ Sax Option Room 105 Street location, present day (10148 105 Street)

eligible for prizes. The publicity stunt caused outrage among some of Edmonton's religious communities.[3] Later, after another rebrand, Reflexions was shut down by the Alberta Liquor Control Board in December 1988 for failure to provide food service along with liquor sales.[4]

Things changed for the worse in 1989 when Carman Ahmed took over ownership of the building. He reopened the bar as Sax on Fifth and advertised that the new club was proudly NOT gay. "Before, it was owned by gays and run by gays. I'm giving notice this is going to be a straight restaurant," Ahmed proclaimed, prompting some of the remaining gay staff to give notice and quit.[5] Ahmed went further, stating that although gays were welcome, they must abide by his rules, which included no kissing or dancing together. When word reached local gay activists such as Wayne Hellard and GALA's Tom Edge, they called for an immediate community boycott.

Ahmed's problematic behaviour underscored a more significant issue in Alberta at the time. Gays and lesbians had no legal recourse against discrimination, as sexual orientation was not included in the province's Individual's Rights Protection Act. Tom Edge publicly compared Ahmed's actions to anti-Semitism, which would have been prohibited under the Act. Stan Scudder, then chairman of the Alberta Human Rights Commission, affirmed Ahmed's actions were indeed discriminatory but stated the Commission was helpless to act, saying, "The gay community [will] have to press your case with the government if you want an amendment to the legislation."[6]

Shortly after Sax opened, an incident inside the club turned violent. Ahmed claimed three men assaulted him after he told a group they couldn't dance in the establishment anymore. He expressed concerns the attack would lead him to contract AIDS.[7] Despite the building featuring a dance earlier in the year as part of Edmonton's AIDS Awareness Week, it was unclear whether the fundraiser was held there under Ahmed's ownership.[8] Wayne Hellard worried the incident would lead to further attacks against Edmonton's gay and lesbian community. The 2SLGBTQ+ community responded with a protest outside the business the day after the alleged assault. Michael Phair recalls the speed with which the protest was mobilized, and even though it was only around twenty people, the protest attracted the attention of local media. The issue of gay rights was already in the news, with Edmonton city council's recent rejection of yet another attempt by GALA to have Gay and Lesbian Awareness Day proclaimed.

Following the community protests, Sax on Fifth's days were numbered. Sax was repeatedly plagued by other troubles, including issues with the police in the weeks and months that followed.[9] When Sax closed, the building would eventually become queer again, but not without a different kind of legal issue.

In 1993, Tony C's opened on the ground floor of Capital Place (9707 110 Street), but the success of its grand opening was short-lived. Owner Tony Calara found himself locked out of his new business after just two days in operation. This wasn't the first time that a landlord had locked out an Edmonton gay bar, of course: the very first gay bar, Club '70 (see page 216), had gone through the exact situation a quarter of a century earlier. Capital Place owners Triple Five Corporation cited numerous so-called violations of the lease agreement, claiming their decision to lock out Tony had nothing to do with gay rights.[10] Other tenants in the building made anti-gay arguments, though. In the court's legal decision, Justice David McDonald stated, "Lesbians and gay men should not be considered lawbreakers just because of their sexual orientation."[11]

Although Tony eventually won his legal dispute against Triple Five, the business relationship was destroyed. Tony searched for a new location for his gay club and found it on 105 Street. In this new location, Tony C's was renamed the Option Room and (re)opened to great success. At the time, the Roost was the only nightclub specifically catering to Edmonton's 2SLGBTQ+ community. Bar manager Carl Austin recalls that the Option Room's opening severely affected the Roost's

263

MICHAEL PHAIR

This is the story of a 1989 "pop-up"! One morning, I received a phone call with the caller loudly announcing Sax nightclub had a sign posted reading "No Gays Allowed." We were both appalled at the audacity of Sax. Very quickly, we decided that a pop-up protest was to be held at four thirty p.m. We worked our phone lists, and the demonstration happened with about fifteen queer folks appearing with signs AND all the media—radio, TV, newspapers—covered the protest. The owners tried to say they didn't mean any harm, and the sign was removed!!

business, stating that gays were seemingly always attracted to new things. The Roost managed to survive only due to the loyalty of its lesbian customers. Yet the Option Room also tried to win over the lesbian crowd by inviting Womonspace to host events ranging from pool tournaments to live music nights. For a fleeting time, the Option Room was a smashing success.[12]

No matter the iteration, nothing seemed to last long in the 105 Street location. After the Option Room closed, Vicious Pink opened and began advertising itself as a gothic club with the best in rave, underground, and alternative music.[13] Vicious Pink was one of the few places in Edmonton that booked live electronic acts and played host to shows by 2SLGBTQ+ community groups like the Imperial Sovereign Court of the Wild Rose. Ultimately, Vicious Pink faced the same 105 Street curse and gave way to an even shorter-lived bar called Choices. Whether it was something about the building itself, the competition (Edmonton had four other gay bars at the time), or some other factor that led to so many venues opening and closing at this location is unknown.

Perhaps it was the storied queer history of the building that led JR White, the owner of Shade, to incorporate a drag element into the launch of ladies' night featuring the Men of Maximum Exposure. Male strip clubs with private lap dance rooms were unheard of in Western Canada at the time.[14] Local queens Miss Bianca and Krystall Ball often performed before the all-male revue took to the stage. Sadly, the drag performances had only a short but entertaining run. While none of the venues associated with the 105 Street building ever rose to the legendary status of long-running queer bars like Flashback or the Roost, their short-lived contributions to Edmonton 2SLGBTQ+ nightlife remain an important part of our community's history. Moreover, the media attention garnered by the events at Tony C's and Sax on Fifth demonstrated just how important it was for sexual orientation to be included as a protected ground against discrimination in Alberta's human rights legislation.

Evolution Wonderlounge

10220 103 STREET

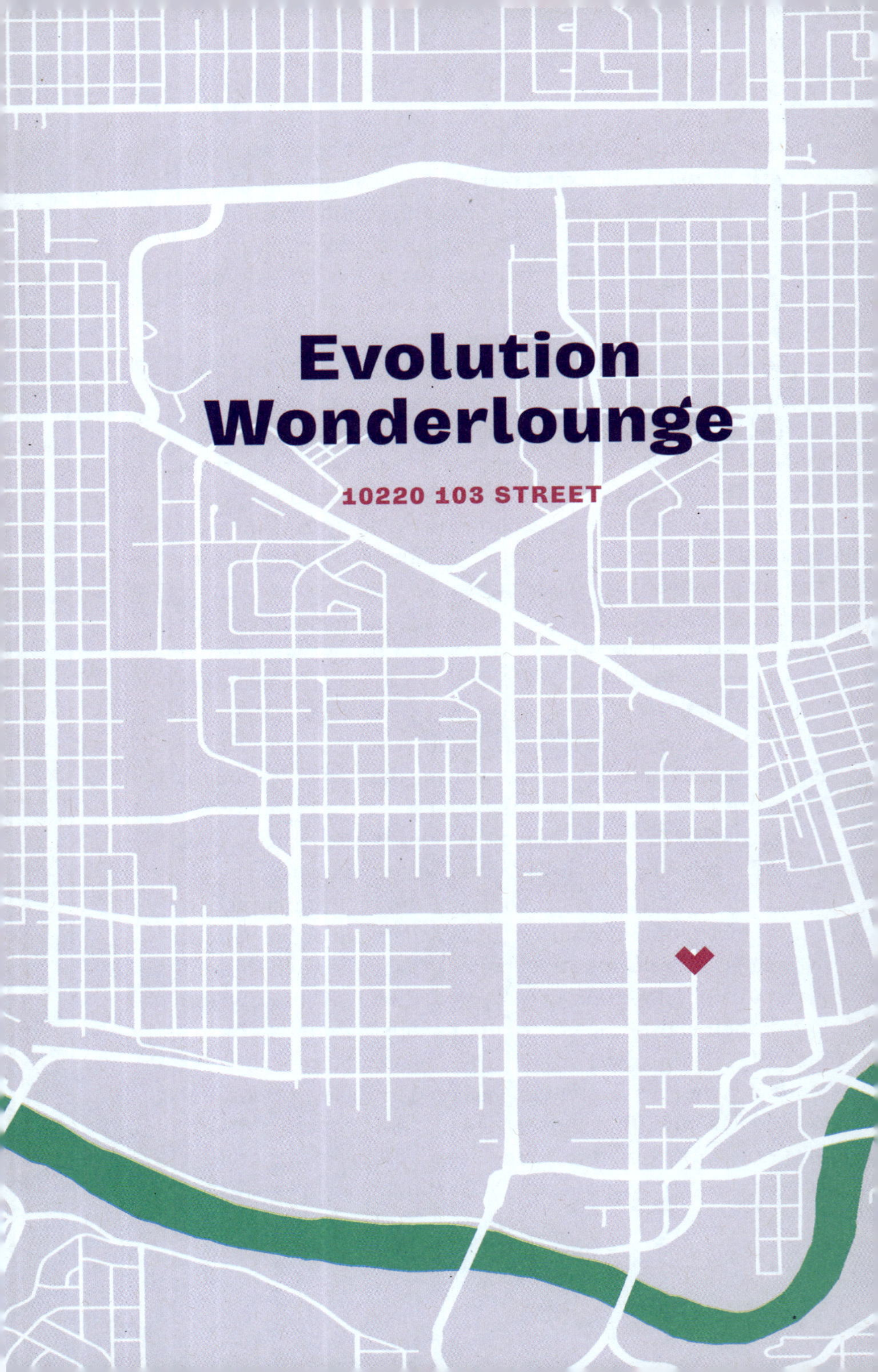

For thirty years, the Roost was a staple of Edmonton's 2SLGBTQ+ nightlife. It and Flashback dominated the 1980s. When Flashback closed, other clubs—such as the Option Room (see page 258), 109 Discotheque, and Buddys—rose to fill the void, but the Roost held its own with a loyal clientele. Late in 2007, the Roost announced it would be officially closing once and for all, leaving a significant gap in Edmonton's 2SLGBTQ+ nightlife.

The first to try to step into the space left by the Roost's closure was Uplift Entertainment. In summer 2008, Uplift owner Jamie Miller created a series of monthly parties called Pure. These parties, held initially at the Velvet Underground, focussed on twenty-five- to forty-year-olds as the target demographic. Miller said, "One gay dance bar isn't enough," but he didn't "feel comfortable in a room full of 18-year-olds." Miller also expressed concerns about opening an 2SLGBTQ+ nightclub on Whyte or Jasper Avenue, suggesting the "lack of discretion" wouldn't be popular with Edmonton's 2SLGBTQ+ community: "They don't want to stand in line, on a busy street, or have one of their friends from work drive by."[1] At the same time, several other groups were actively working on establishing a series of new 2SLGBTQ+ dance clubs.[2]

One of those new enterprises debuted on September 19, 2008, billed as a "high-end lounge and dance club under the Boardwalk Market."[3] Play Nightclub was co-owned by Mike Sainchuk, of the Bank Ultra Lounge and Oil City Roadhouse, and Bob Long, an Edmonton lawyer and board member of Team Edmonton, the city's 2SLGBTQ+ sports organization. Long referred to Play as "an evolution of the queer nightclub," saying he wanted a space where his friends could go after work, "gay and straight-but-queer friendly."[4] Play's general manager Corey Wyness described the venue as for "the queer and not so queer."

There was controversy right off the bat surrounding the use of the word *queer*. Some in the community found it triggering

▲ EVO Pride Block Party, 2019
▼ EVO original location, present day (10220 103 Street)

and hostile, but Wyness defended it, stating that Play bar was a safe space for everyone, not just 2SLGBTQ+ people. "Gay, trans, lesbian, bi or questioning," Wyness said, "queer is a word that encompasses everything."[5] Wyness also promised a strong working relationship with the Edmonton Police Service to help avoid some of the violence problems that had plagued other downtown venues owned by the same investment group.[6]

Another unique feature of Play Nightclub was its partnership with local community groups. HIV Edmonton and the Pride Centre were both on site during the opening weekend. With space dedicated for community groups to have board meetings, a notice board where groups could advertise freely, and multiple community fundraisers already planned, Wyness looked forward to Play's entry into Edmonton's bar scene.[7]

Play soon became a central part of Edmonton's 2SLGBTQ+ nightlife, continuing the trend that had long existed, where the weekend was unofficially divided between Edmonton's 2SLGBTQ+ dance clubs. The Roost had long captured Saturdays, while Friday was the night to go to Buddys. This stayed true with Play, which soon became the home of the Pure parties, now an annual Pride event rather than a monthly pop-up.

In spring 2010, a new dance club called Flash opened, located just south of the infamous Chez Pierre strip club on 105 Street. Not long after Flash's arrival, Play owners opted to rebrand their venue as Buffalo, and it was no longer an 2SLGBTQ+ club. Soon, Buffalo rebranded again as Warehouse, which also didn't last very long. After a short run, Flash closed in February 2013 and was quickly replaced by UpStares UltraLounge, which, for a time, was the Saturday night place to go for the 2SLGBTQ+ community.

At the time that UpStares opened, a new ownership group was looking for a venue in Edmonton to open an 2SLGBTQ+-focussed club. This group included Rob Browatzke, who had more than twenty years of experience working in Edmonton's 2SLGBTQ+ nightlife scene, and a partnership team that recently ran Helios, a pair of gay hotels in Palm Springs. This team included Murray Browatzke (uncle of Rob Browatzke), Scott Jarron, Drew Gromnicki, and Gord Cormie. The group originally began searching for a venue space for a new 2SLGBTQ+ club in Calgary without much success. When they came across the vacant space where Play used to be located, they jumped at the opportunity to make that space queer again.

Aware there would be immediate comparisons with the former Play Nightclub, the ownership group did their best to break the "dark and dingy gay bar stereotype."[8] Part of this refresh included white floors, white furniture, and a star-studded celebrity opening night lineup. The Helios team had extensive connections in the world of adult gay films, and infamous drag queen and porn director Chi Chi La Rue served as the DJ for the grand opening, which also featured a bevy of adult entertainment stars, including Matthew Rush, Christopher Daniels, and Tyler Saint.[9] Chi Chi and "her boys" remained a semi-regular fixture at Evolution from that night onward for years to come.

In the fall, Evolution partnered with UpStares Ultralounge on a pub crawl at two gay clubs for Halloween. UpStares announced it was rebranding that same night, leaving Evolution and Buddys as Edmonton's last remaining 2SLGBTQ+ dance clubs. Again, Edmonton's 2SLGBTQ+ community fell into the Friday/Saturday split that had dominated the scene for years.

Evolution began to build on Rob Browatzke's extensive contacts in the local 2SLGBTQ+ non-profit scene. Early Community Tuesdays included fundraisers for the Pride Centre, Womonspace, Curling with Pride, and the Imperial Sovereign Court of the Wild Rose. As with Play before, and many other gay spaces, fundraising was a central component of Evolution's programming and a way to support the local 2SLGBTQ+ community directly.

Evolution was initially open seven days a week, starting in the mid-afternoon. This attempt to capture the downtown after-work crowd was short lived. Located in a basement and without kitchen facilities, Evolution found it impossible to

MURRAY BROWATZKE
Evolution Wonderlounge co-owner

Evolution Wonderlounge has always been about family. Quite literally! Many people don't know we are a family-owned-and-operated gay bar. We opened in 2013 with myself, Scott Jarron, who is my partner of thirty-plus years, and our nephew Rob. Of course, since we opened, our family has grown. Spaces like ours create a found family, and we are blessed to have had so many people, groups, and events welcome us into theirs.

When we opened in 2013, it was with the intention of creating a little Vegas meets Circus. Our initial visions of the space had to adapt and evolve to fit the ever-changing scene. Then, we were one of four gay bars, and queer pop-ups were rare; now, we've been the only gay bar for several years, and queer pop-ups are everywhere. We are proud to be queer year-round in a city so progressive and inclusive that many venues now host queer dances, drag brunches, fundraisers, and more.

In the fall of 2023, Evolution celebrated one decade of queer joy. Over that time, dozens of community partners have helped to raise hundreds of thousands of dollars by hosting events in our space, including celebrity guests like Leslie Jordan, Bob the Drag Queen, and Chi Chi LaRue. We take great pride in being an inclusive place where queer people can find safety, joy, romance, and fun each and every week.

generate sustained interest in the Happy Hour market. Afternoons and early evenings were quickly scrapped.

Sunday nights had long been a drag show staple in many 2SLGBTQ+ bars, but since the closure of the Roost, this tradition had been sporadic in Edmonton. In early 2014, Evolution started its Sunday Revue night. The growing popularity of *RuPaul's Drag Race*, combined with Evolution's open stage policy, helped build the night and in turn Edmonton's drag community. Many shows had insisted queens "pay their dues" before getting show opportunities, but Evolution was open to new performers. This opportunity included the Haus of HOMOcidal, which helped launch the careers of Edmonton queens such as Gogo Fetch, Chelsea Horrendous, and Lilith Fair. The Sunday shows also debuted a 2015 event called the Stiletto Awards, which celebrated the best of Edmonton's drag community. The Stiletto Awards quickly became a celebrated annual event.

In spring 2014, Evolution partnered with Pure Pride to host the inaugural provincial drag show competition called the Search for Alberta's Next Drag Superstar, which featured the first of many "Ru Girls" to appear at Evolution. Courtney Act, a finalist from season six of *RuPaul's Drag Race*, was on hand to judge and crowned Tiara Manila the inaugural winner; Tiara went on to become the founding member of a troupe of Filipino drag queens known as Queens of the Orient. The following year, Evolution took over sole management of the competition, working with different Calgary venues.

Evolution sought to celebrate not only drag culture but all kinds of theatre and performance. This included participating in the Edmonton International Fringe Festival as a Bring-Your-Own-Venue (BYOV), a tradition previously established by the Roost. During the 2015 Fringe Festival, Evolution hosted the five-star debut of Man Up!, a troupe of four dancers who put on a male burlesque show described as "hilarious, heartbreaking, and damn funny."[10] Man Up! would go on to host multiple shows at a variety of venues over the years that followed.

Evolution continued to host fundraisers for several important community causes, ranging from a Red Cross fundraiser after the Fort McMurray wildfire to an event for the Edmonton Mennonite Centre for Newcomers following the election of Donald Trump in 2016 and an event for Making Waves to support their successful bid to host the 2016 International Gay and Lesbian Aquatics Championships.[11] Evolution and its patrons and business partners championed and supported many causes of significance to Edmonton's community. Other examples included ongoing fundraising for Amigos des Animales, a no-kill animal rescue in Mexico, and an annual May long weekend fundraiser to support mental health awareness.

On June 11, 2016, Evolution hosted a Pride party featuring queer rapper Cazwell. It was a busy Saturday night, and everyone was having fun. Shortly after midnight, social media reports circulated about a terrorist attack unfolding at an 2SLGBTQ+ nightclub in Orlando. In the early hours of the morning, forty-nine people were killed and dozens more were injured at Pulse Nightclub in what is considered one of the deadliest mass shootings in American history.[12] The effect on Evolution staff and partygoers in Edmonton was immediate and chilling. Indeed, the entire 2SLGBTQ+ community was deeply affected around the world. Rob Browatzke said, "This is a worst nightmare come true. That our safe places are being taken away from us."[13] Sadly, this was not the first, nor would it be the last attack on an 2SLGBTQ+ community venue.

By early 2017, Evolution Wonderlounge was Edmonton's only remaining 2SLGBTQ+ bar. With a shortage of 2SLGBTQ+ entertainment spaces, the Evolution team branched out to start a street festival during Edmonton's Pride celebrations. Evolution partnered with the City of Edmonton and closed down 103 Street for a Pride-themed dance party, drag show, and community festival as a downtown alternative to the main Pride Festival beer gardens and entertainment stage, which had been relocated near Whyte Avenue on 104 Street. Proceeds from the Evolution street party were split among participating 2SLGBTQ+ community groups.

In 2019, the unexpected cancellation of the Edmonton Pride Festival put pressure and new expectations on Evolution Wonderlounge and other community groups, such as Fruit Loop, to continue with the spirit of Pride. Rob Browatzke said Evolution was "trying to fill the void as best [we] can," by expanding the street festival to include more community partners as well as an all-ages area.[14]

In March 2020, Evolution, along with other nightclubs, was among the first local businesses to face restrictions as the Covid-19 pandemic began to explode across Canada. For the safety of the 2SLGBTQ+ community, Evolution opted to cancel upcoming events and close its doors just a few days before Alberta's provincial government instituted the first wave of lockdowns and community restrictions. Although Evolution was able to open briefly in the fall for a few small, socially distant shows, it soon closed again and did not officially reopen until late 2022.

Although pandemic restrictions were necessary to help limit the spread of the Covid-19 virus, they had a disproportionate impact on the 2SLGBTQ+ community. Without access to community venues and supports, many 2SLGBTQ+ youth and young adults were forced to isolate with non-supportive or hostile family members. Other 2SLGBTQ+ community members lost their jobs and experienced financial and housing insecurity.[15] Perhaps one of the most significant impacts was the loss of community, reminding us how essential spaces like bars and clubs have been throughout the history of the 2SLGBTQ+ community.

Evolution celebrated its tenth anniversary in fall 2023, making it one of a handful of Edmonton 2SLGBTQ+ bars to last more than a decade. In Edmonton, as in other cities, queer nightlife is rapidly evolving. What the future holds for Evolution, and Edmonton's 2SLGBTQ+ bar and club scene, is a story that is still developing.

The Citadel Theatre

ORIGINAL LOCATION:
10030 102 STREET
(SALVATION ARMY CITADEL)

CURRENT LOCATION
9828 101A AVENUE

When the Citadel Theatre opened its doors in 1965, Joseph Shoctor promised to bring world-class theatre to Edmonton.[1] Over its long and storied history, the Citadel has delivered on that commitment and in turn has had a significant impact on Edmonton's 2SLGBTQ+ community. In the more than five decades since, the Citadel Theatre has been home to three gay artistic directors, produced a myriad of plays by queer playwrights, and served as the creative workplace for hundreds of talented 2SLGBTQ+ artists and staff members.[2] The Citadel has also been a supportive community ally, hosting events such as Pride festivals, musical performances, exhibitions, and community dances.

The Citadel Theatre stage lit up for the first time on November 10, 1965, to great fanfare with Edward Albee's controversial play *Who's Afraid of Virginia Woolf?*, a mere three years after its acclaimed Broadway debut.[3] The play vaulted this gay playwright into the limelight, where many lauded him as "the new voice of his generation."[4] Albee was initially awarded his first Pulitzer Prize in Drama in 1963 for this groundbreaking play before the Pulitzer Prize Committee overturned its original decision, refusing to award the Pulitzer Prize in Drama to Albee or anyone else in 1963. Albee's professional experience was indicative of the many systemic barriers and experiences of discrimination faced by many 2SLGBTQ+ artists.

When the Citadel opened in its current iconic location in 1976 with a production of *Romeo and Juliet*, queer energy was all over the Shoctor stage. The production featured a young Brent Carver as Romeo and a young Tom Wood as Mercutio. Carver went on to become a Broadway sensation, winning the Tony for Best Actor in a Musical in 1993.

Over the decades, queer themes appeared as both playwrights and plays examined the closet from the inside looking

▲ Canadian AIDS memorial quilt
▼ The Citadel, present day (10030 102 Street)

LUC TELLIER
Director of Education and Outreach, Citadel Theatre

As a queer kid growing up in rural Alberta, theatrical institutions like the Citadel Theatre made my life not only possible but colourful. LGBTQ+ folks and allies come to Citadel productions and classes to exercise empathy like a muscle. This radical exchange of thoughts and ideas is one of the most integral parts of creating open-minded and forward-thinking community members.

I've worked in live theatre for nearly twenty years and currently serve as the Citadel's director of education and outreach. I did my first Citadel show when I was ten years old, and the experience taught me firsthand the importance of having queer role models in my life. Now, running the education department, I have the immense privilege of fostering safe and creative learning spaces with an outstanding team of diverse teaching artists.

Amongst the various land mines that I traverse as a queer Albertan on a daily basis, the Citadel has become my home. It has provided me with the opportunity to consume and create world-class theatre and to foster the next generation of artists. Through theatre, our students quickly come to understand that their differences are not setbacks; they are superpowers. With these young people as our future leaders, I know our province is in good hands.

out and the outside looking in. For instance, in 2010, when Tom Wood got the chance to direct gay playwright Tennessee William's *The Glass Menagerie*, he chose to highlight that Tom, the main character, was gay, suggesting that Tom's obsessive practice of going to the movies was a "1940's code word for what was really going on at those all-night sessions."[5] In *The Edmonton Queen* (2007), queer actor, playwright, and composer Darrin Hagen provides a beautiful and intimate portrait of how seeing the play *Hosanna* at the Citadel (written by queer playwright Michel Tremblay) affected him as an audience member through the different decades of his life: first as a fledgling drag queen and later as an actor.

> In 1983, a friend took me to see Tremblay's *Hosanna*. I had just started hanging out with Queens and had done my first few shows. In 1993, I saw *Hosanna* again. My career as a club queen was, for the most part, behind me. I was trying to launch a theatre career. In 2003, I starred as Hosanna alongside Jeff Page's Cuirette at Theatre Network. On closing night, I had trouble controlling the tears all the way through Act Two. Tremblay had written about my life before it happened. And I didn't want it to end. Even the painful stuff. It hurt too beautifully.[6]

From Hagen's and Wood's interpretations of scripts through live performance, one senses the dynamic interplay between art and life: queer theatre reaches out from the stage to affect audience members with both its power and promise.

The closet has always been a potent and complex metaphor for the 2SLGBTQ+ community. The exploration of its influence has been provocatively explored on The Citadel's stages, including in productions of Michel Tremblay's *Hosanna* (1975–76, 1983, and 1992–93); Manuel Puig's *Kiss of the Spider Woman* (1988–89); Tony Kushner's *Angels in America Part 2: Perestroika* (1996–97), Doug Wright's *I Am My Own Wife* (2005–06), and Brad Fraser's *True Love Lies* (2010–11).[7]

The groundbreaking *Hosanna*, written in 1973, was one of the first Canadian plays to feature a drag queen as the main character. Centred around a pivotal night in the relationship between Hosanna (a drag queen who dresses as Elizabeth Taylor in Cleopatra) and Cuirette, her ageing gay biker boyfriend, the play fearlessly exposes the cruelty of the marginalized community and asks the audience to consider and respect Hosanna's self-definition and a spectrum of shifting, porous, and intersecting gender identities and expressions.[8]

Argentinian playwright Manuel Puig's 1976 play *Kiss of the Spider Woman* draws strongly on the playwright's personal experiences.[9] Set in an Argentine prison, it focusses on a relationship between two cellmates—Molina, a middle-aged genderfluid person, and Valentin, a young, cisgender leftist revolutionary—and explores vital questions about the fluidity of gender, norms, assumptions, and expectations.

American Playwright Tony Kushner's *Angels in America Part 2: Perestroika* came to the Citadel just three years after its Broadway premiere. *Angels* is a complex and challenging play about the interplay of intersecting lives impacted by HIV/AIDS, politics, religion, homophobia, ignorance, fear, and hope. When *Angels* was produced in Edmonton, there was palpable enthusiasm for the Broadway sensation. There was also, predictably, strong opposition, as Conservative politicians and some journalists went out of their way to decry *Angels*, wringing their hands over so-called community standards. Theatre critic Liz Nicholls soundly called them out, stating, "Our box office is a happening place. Wielding the club of 'community standards' on a play that The People clearly want to see is a shabby, undemocratic proposition. *Angels* has attracted a big audience around the continent and seems poised to do so here. Who is this audience if not members of the community?"[10] Audiences may have been excited to see the play, but on the opening night of *Angels*, some patrons hid their eyes and expressed distaste when the two male characters kissed.

Doug Wright's Pulitzer Prize-winning one-person play *I Am My Own Wife* (2002) is based on Charlotte Von Mahlsdorf's autobiography and Wright's conversations with von Mahlsdorf (1929–2002), a German antique dealer and trans woman who lived through the horrors of Nazi Germany and the repressive Communist regime of East Berlin that followed.[11] Charlotte's story of grit and survival highlights the resilience of a trans woman and her determination to survive and thrive no matter the historical context.

In the 1990s and 2000s, some of Alberta's queer playwrights saw their plays and adaptations performed on the mainstage as part of the Citadel Theatre's regular season program.[12] In addition to plays appearing on the mainstage, the Citadel's Teen Festival for the Arts (1988–1994) gave many young local 2SLGBTQ+ playwrights, composers, set designers, and aspiring actors their start.[13] Teenfest featured notable queer playwrights such as Brad Fraser and Kent Staines, who were commissioned to write plays. Fraser's Teenfest works included *Blood Buddies* (with Jeffery Hirschfield), *Young Art*, and *Prom Night of the Living Dead* (with composer Darrin Hagen). Kent Staines contributed *Hero Bound*. With many queer artists at the helm of the artistic production, the Teen Festival provided a vital platform for young queer Edmonton artists to develop, hone, and begin showcasing their talents. The Festival also fostered relationships that proved foundational to emerging artists just beginning to establish professional networks.[14] Many of the 2SLGBTQ+ artists who took their initial steps at Teenfest remain active in the industry today.

In the broader community, the Citadel Theatre was also an important gathering place for education and remembrance. Early 2SLGBTQ+ community events at the Citadel included performances by Heather Bishop and Connie Caldor (1986), Day Without Art (1990), and The Names Project (1990–91). Day Without Art began in New York in 1989 and quickly spread to become an international day of mourning and remembrance

DR. MICHELLE LAVOIE

I remember it was mid-summer in 1990, either in June or July, when I visited the Citadel Theatre for the first time. Upon entering the Lee Pavilion, I recall the sound of water on rock, the smell of plants, the touch of humidity in the air, the sight of hundreds of people gathered, mostly in silence, and what felt like hundreds of quilts hanging floor to ceiling and filling the enormous space. For me, in my early twenties and just coming out, this was one of my first experiences of Edmonton's queer communities, coming together, just being together, to witness and to grieve.

I remember feeling an overwhelming sense of awe. The quilts were astonishingly beautiful, each handsewn with love and care. Each carefully crafted by lovers, partners, friends, parents, siblings, families, and chosen families to honour and uphold the memory of loved ones lost to AIDS. These were remembrances and notes of love, intimate and shared for all to see. There was a sense of words that had long been silent or silenced. They were being spoken here and now. There was an urgency even in loss, a sense of hope to be seen, to be heard, to be understood, to be loved. It was a taking back of space. We claimed space to be visible and stand together even amongst grief. It was palpable. It was powerful. The notes shared, bared, and held open space for all of us to witness and mourn and remember our common humanity and these people who loved and were loved just a short time before.

I'm writing this reflection on World AIDS Day, December 1, 2023. Although extraordinary medical strides have taken place over these past years, too many, especially vulnerable and marginalized communities, are still impacted by HIV and AIDS. Let's come together to work to end stigma and silence around HIV and AIDS and support quality health care here and abroad.

in honour of the millions of creative people whose lives were lost to HIV/AIDS. On December 1st, as part of World AIDS Day, galleries worldwide were closed and symbolically shuttered with window coverings, and theatres refrained from performances to commemorate lives lost.

Activist and producer Kevin Hendricks initiated Day Without Art in Edmonton. On December 1, 1990, Edmonton's arts community went dark. At the Citadel, all windows facing the street were covered with brown paper bearing a simple, stark logo as a visible sign of remembrance. In 1990 and 1991, in collaboration with the AIDS Network of Edmonton and the Works Art and Design Festival, Hendricks also brought the Citadel one of the most moving and significant works of activist art of the HIV/AIDS era: The Names Project. This Canadian instalment of the AIDS Quilt consisted of hundreds of individual quilts, which hung from the ceiling of the Lee Pavilion and formed a maze in the Shoctor Lobby. Each quilted panel was created by families, friends, and loved ones of people who had lost their lives to HIV/AIDS and honoured the courage, lives, and legacies of the people they loved.[15] The Names Project was both a moving homage to the strength and struggle of the many lives lost and a powerful educational platform to emphasize the scale and the far-reaching effects of HIV/AIDS.[16]

In June 1993, Edmonton's Pride Week film festival took place in the Citadel's Zeidler Hall. This event was preceded by two student-led 2SLGBTQ+ Pride Week film festivals in March 1992 and March 1993: Voice and Vision, which premiered *The Making of Monsters*, John Greyson's controversial film about gay bashing, and *Speaking in Tongues*.[17]

In 1997, award-winning playwright, composer, and actor Darrin Hagen launched his first book, *The Edmonton Queen*, in the Citadel's Rice Theatre lobby. It was a most fitting setting, as Darrin's New Year's Eve story in *The Edmonton Queen* ends with him losing a sequined high heel (as well as having a balloon breast deflate with exquisite timing) at the stroke of

KEVIN HENDRICKS

In 1990, the Works Art and Design Festival brought the Names Project to Edmonton. The quilt sections were displayed in the Citadel Theatre's Lee Pavilion as part of a national tour. During this tour, several new quilt panels created in Canada were submitted to the project; these remained in Canada and became the beginning of the Canadian version of the AIDS Quilt. I was extremely moved, not only by the display, but by the effect it had on everyone who experienced it.

By 1995, Canada had its own quilt. I was working at Living Positive/Edmonton Persons Living with HIV, and I worked to present the entire Canadian quilt for the first time. Co-presented again as part of the Works, *The Presence of Absence* was an awareness/fundraising campaign for Living Positive/Edmonton Persons Living with HIV Society benefitting the AIDS Network Edmonton, Feather of Hope Aboriginal AIDS Prevention Society, Alberta Society for Positive Women, and Interfaith Association on AIDS. This time I was lucky to meet many of the families who had shared their grief, and the memory of their lost loved one, through the act of creating a quilt panel to share with the world. It was during this display of the quilt that I was invited to become a board member of the Names Project-Canada/le projet des noms-Canada.

It was an honour to travel with the quilt to Saskatoon, Ottawa, and other locales. Each time the panels were unveiled, it was like reuniting with dear friends. The memories of their stories and their families would come flooding back. The Canadian quilt is now in the hands of the Canadian AIDS Society.

midnight in Shoctor Alley, metres from where the book was launched.

Also in 1997, the Loud and Proud Cabaret debuted at the Citadel after Catalyst Theatre decided to end its run of the highly successful Loud and Queer Cabaret. Citadel staff who had hands-on experience with Loud and Queer were inspired to create a brand-new event in its absence. Loud and Proud helped to launch that year's Pride Week festival. Sponsored by Edmonton Vocal Minority (EVM), Loud and Proud took over the Citadel stages with multiple events. Drag artist Christopher Peterson presented his "one-man/many women extravaganza" *Eyecons* on the Rice stage.[18] On the Maclab stage, Christopher Peterson and Darrin Hagen—both in drag—hosted Drag Fest '97, a cabaret, catwalk, and talent competition featuring four Edmonton queens vying for the title of DQ '97, dazzling in original creations designed by four queer Edmonton designers (winner: Paprika); the Maclab stage also saw a musical performance by EVM. Klodyne Rodney hosted Sister Sappho Stage in the Tucker Amphitheatre, a lesbian cabaret featuring Lin Elder with music, poetry, and comedy. Brad Fraser's film *Parade* was screened in Zeidler Hall. An après party followed all events at the Lee Pavilion. This may have been the most unapologetically queer week in the Citadel's history.

Other notable queer-positive events hosted at the Citadel over the years included Dave Jackson's infamous Hell Parties (all-night raves held in the Lee Pavilion); countless iterations of Late Night Madness and Women in Comedy on the Maclab stage, presented by the Edmonton International Street Performers' Festival (often featuring visiting queer artists from across the globe); the First Night Festival 2000 (Y2K), where Darrin Hagen performed *The Edmonton Queen* in the Rice Theatre; the Kaboom Festival (produced by Workshop West, also on the Rice stage), which featured Daniel MacIvor's play *In On It*; and dozens of other events like Pride dances and Fruit Loop parties.[19]

For many queer artists, directors, playwrights, and performers, the Citadel wasn't just a venue; it was a home. Edmonton has been fortunate to develop a world-class theatre community where queer lives are not just lived and performed but celebrated and elevated into art. The Citadel is proud to continue that tradition today.

PART 5

Sex and the City

Georgia Baths

9668 JASPER AVENUE

While the 1981 raid conducted by the Edmonton Police Service makes the Pisces Health Spa our city's most (in)famous bathhouse (see page 84), the Georgia Baths gained immortality when its famed neon sign was rescued and displayed as part of the City's Neon Museum on 104 Street. For almost a century, the Georgia was a licensed and operating bathhouse, although the nature of its business and clientele evolved and changed over time.

As a queer space, a bathhouse is "a medium for gay men to make social and sexual relations with other gay men."[1] Long before Georgia Baths filled this eventual role, however, it began as a Turkish bath. In 1913, the Edmonton Turkish Baths opened, providing a unique and luxurious space for men and women (separately) to enjoy steams and rubs, as well as providing access to bathing and barber facilities.[2] Around 1937, the business rebranded as the Georgia Turkish Baths, relocating in 1946 from the iconic Flat Iron Building to the fashionable Brighton Block.[3] By this time, the steam baths had already become one of "Edmonton's early gay destinations."[4]

Run first by Mike Bordian, and then by his son Ed after 1961, the Georgia was once a "Sunday social club" for older men to play cards, but those days didn't last.[5] Bordian knew many of his customers were gay, but stated, "As long as [they don't] raise any trouble down here, there are no problems."[6] Staff member Mike Robinson noted that the women's section lay unused due to low demand, but also highlighted that "three quarters of the 30 to 40 daily customers have been going for years."[7]

How the Georgia remained a gay space well into the 1970s is documented by a firsthand recounting of a visit by *Edmonton Journal* reporter James Adams, who ventured down with colleagues unsure if they would encounter a "fabled world of heavenly pleasure."[8] Expectation quickly led to disappointment

▲ Georgia Baths, 1988
▼ Georgia Baths sign (10330 104 Street)

ROB BROWATZKE

When I moved to Edmonton in 1999, I wanted a gay job to help me connect to my new community. I found a copy of the Edmonton Rainbow Business Association's *Pride Pages* and started applying everywhere. The Georgia Baths was the first business to hire me.

They were under new management and were proudly going after the gay market. Before that, Georgia had operated under the radar, even after the police raid on the Pisces Health Spa, and all through the AIDS crisis of the 1980s and 1990s. Down Under Baths, which opened in the Oliver neighbourhood in 1998, paved the way for Edmonton's baths to advertise more publicly. Georgia, and later Steamers, did just that boldly and unapologetically.

I'd always been comfortable with the world of bathhouses as spaces for both cruising and socializing. Although I worked at Georgia Baths only briefly before moving on to Down Under, I certainly appreciated that every space had its unique clientele and how the baths, in general, offered something wonderful for so many. There was always discretion available for those in the closet and those exploring their sexuality. The baths served as important alternatives to bars and were open 24/7. Most of all, I learned that everyone is attractive to someone. The lessons in body and sex positivity were sometimes surprising but always beneficial in understanding the beauty and diversity of our community.

when they were met with "moldy carpet," "towels with the texture of corrugated cardboard," and "pipes that began to blank and throb like the *Jaws* soundtrack"—a far cry from the Bette Midler experience he had been anticipating given the singer's recent start in New York City's famed bathhouse subculture.[9] Ads on the walls in the Georgia Baths indicated places where the gay community could be tested for "VD." The sight of two older men holding hands in the steam room was enough to prompt Adams's companion to press "his back to the wall."[10]

Only a few years after that visit, the Edmonton Police Service raided the Pisces Health Spa.[11] The Georgia Baths somehow escaped similar police action. While some sources indicate the Georgia Baths closed in 1991, it seems to have continued covertly into the late 1990s, when media attention returned to Edmonton's baths scene with the opening of Down Under Men's Bathhouse, located at the west end of Jasper Avenue.[12] The Georgia was still advertising as a gay men's bathhouse in the Edmonton Rainbow Business Association's 1998 guidebook.

In 2004, the Georgia Baths rebranded again, this time as Steamers. Down Under had since been joined by Steamworks, and Edmonton was now home to three gay bathhouses. Steamers, the final incarnation of the oldest of the three bathhouses, was short lived. Health inspectors closed it in 2005 for multiple public health violations.[13]

The neighbourhood around the Georgia Baths was also home to several adult peep shows, particularly Centrefold Adult Entertainment, which had a second location on Stony Plain Road. In 1994, when Centrefold first opened, the battle surrounding the shows' purpose and morality was already well underway. Video peeps, which are focussed on adult videos instead of live entertainment, arrived in Edmonton in 1990, generating immediate controversy. Those opposed to peep shows expressed concerns about their impact on children, as well as the potential health risks of ejaculation on the floor.[14]

Mayor Jan Reimer moved to block businesses such as live peep shows, with the support of many on city council. Alderman Michael Phair expressed concern over exploitation of women while alderwoman Sheila McKay used her position as a former nurse to bolster related health concerns.[15] Alderman Leroy Chahley proposed a bylaw that would limit where such adult entertainment businesses could operate.[16] Banner Amusements, owners of several peep shows, threatened to sue the City. The Alberta Court of Appeal eventually sided with the City, prohibiting Centrefold's expansion to live shows and limiting them to video offerings.[17]

The Centrefold issue wasn't the only time that public debate over sexual morality affected queer life in Edmonton. In 1998, when Down Under Men's Bathhouse was preparing to open, business owners and residents in Oliver expressed similar concerns to those surrounding Centrefold.[18] Owner Jim McBride told the local media that there would be "no prostitution or drugs" and expressed his "hopes the business will contribute to the gay community growing in that part of the city."[19] Fred Dicker of the Gay and Lesbian Community Centre of Edmonton said, "The bathhouse would help curtail the spread of sexually transmitted diseases. The alternative is Victoria Park, which is a lot less controlled environment. In a bathhouse, they hand you a condom on the way in."[20] Councillor Michael Phair expressed optimism the business would be licensed, and representatives from Alberta Health and the Edmonton Police Service also expressed no concerns, with EPS stating, "Opening a facility here, where consensual sex takes place primarily between men, is not a criminal offence."[21]

This change in stance from the Pisces Health Spa raid, or even the more recent peep show debates, is indicative of the growing mainstream acceptance of 2SLGBTQ+ people in Edmonton. Although many of these places have now since closed, it was not due to public morality, policing concerns, or homophobia, but because of the same changes that have affected many local 2SLGBTQ+ bars and clubs: the rise and growth of the Internet and dating apps. Currently, all the peep shows are now closed, and Steamworks is the only bathhouse remaining in Edmonton, now expanded to be "co-ed" and trans-inclusive on certain nights.

The Hill

**OLD LOCATION:
MACDONALD DRIVE
(100–102 STREET)**

**CURRENT LOCATION:
MACDONALD DRIVE
(100–102 STREET AND
BELLAMY HILL ROAD)**

MacDonald Drive overlooked the river valley from Edmonton's earliest incarnation, majestically marking the southern edge of downtown with a steep bank plunging to the valley below. The Hill, as it was known, actually represented a very short piece of city road (two blocks, at the most), which can be seen prominently in many of the early black and white cityscapes of downtown, with its namesake, the grand Hotel Macdonald, marking its eastern end. The water tower that rose on thick steel pillars behind the *Edmonton Journal* building marked the other boundary before the strip unceremoniously ended at 102 Street. At that time, there was no Bellamy Hill Road plunging down between hotels to the floodplain below. This was literally the end of downtown, with no way down to the river valley but steep paths. The Hill was one block away from the actual city centre, but for all intents and purposes, it was the end of the road.

The first short block of The Hill featured the elegant and original Edmonton Public Library and the burgeoning Alberta College campus, as well as the stately McDougall Church. It was a dignified strip of Edmonton real estate in the daylight, but at nighttime, it served a very different purpose. It would be nearly impossible to ascertain definitively when this strip of downtown became known as a place for gay men to meet, but by 1969, The Hill had a reputation as a place to cruise, as indicated by a unique gay guide making the rounds through underground networks across Canada.

This "guide to being gay" was created by Roedy Green, founder of the Gay Alliance Towards Equality chapter in Vancouver. Green's unofficial guide was called "The Naive Homosexual" and was written to instruct gay men about questions of identity, sex, intimacy, culture, and lifestyle—topics that were still largely taboo and censored from public eyes.[1]

▲ Bellamy Hill, 1919
▼ The Hill, present day (MacDonald Drive NW)

Green's witty and acerbic guide contained something that must have been a momentous discovery for the men who were lucky enough to get their hands on a copy: a very detailed listing of underground clubs, bars, and cruising spaces across Canada where men could meet others like themselves. Edmonton had an extensive entry, including a list of several bars, baths, and public cruising places. Throughout the 1970s, and even into the early 1980s, The Hill was not only a place to meet potential partners but also a place to buy and sell gay sex—although, depending on the year, sex workers of all genders could be found walking up and down the sidewalk stroll.[2]

Rarely acknowledged in public-facing queer history, public sex and sex work have been an important part of queer life in Edmonton and across Canada broadly.[3] Before 1969, gay sex in the private sphere was still illegal, as anal intercourse (or "buggery") laws prohibited sodomy even between consenting adults. Hotels and landlords did not have to serve or accommodate gay couples or people looking to hook up. Gay youths were regularly thrown out of their homes and disowned. As a result, gay street culture served as a vital site of kinship and conviviality. Public spaces such as washrooms, parks, and back alleys provided some degree of anonymity for those still in the closet or scared of entering gay clubs or bars, and were often the only sexual options in cities or towns with no such spaces.[4] Sex in public is also a sexual turn-on among some gay and straight men, as the thrill of anonymous encounters and the possibility of being caught builds sexual tension. Author Patrick Califia states, "While public sex is a mainstay for men who want sex with other men in rural or small-town [milieus], it is also a permanent fixture in many liberal areas, simply because it can be efficient, fun, and at least a little risky."[5]

MacDonald Drive had all the right attributes to make it perfect for cruising. All of the buildings that lined the scenic street were closed at night; there were only buildings on one side of the street, which meant far less chance of being surprised by someone appearing for nefarious or violent purposes. In 1971, MacDonald Drive became a one-way street, which meant the car cruising traffic moved in one direction with cars often circling repeatedly. With this change, sex workers and cruisers had to worry less about who was approaching behind them and customers looking for sex became more obvious. As queer historian Valerie J. Korinek observes, Edmonton's cruising spots were similar, spatially and geographically, to those in Saskatoon and Winnipeg. Thus, men who were "accustomed to cruising practices in their home communities could readily locate them in Edmonton."[6]

In the 1970s, the reputation of The Hill grew. It became not only a place for cruising and selling sex but also a gathering place after the only gay bar in town—Club '70—closed for the night. Club revellers would often head to The Hill and, even if cruising for sex wasn't the main objective, the socializing that occurred into the wee hours of the night was remarkable. On a weekend night, you could sometimes see several groups hanging out in different spots, socializing as the traffic circled. Sometimes cars would stop just to visit and smoke and gossip with the groups milling about on the sidewalk. It would not be uncommon to witness a drag queen or two strolling down the strip post-club performance, audaciously strutting their stuff. There was safety in numbers. It is no surprise that the closest apartment buildings—such as the Arlington, the Palisades, the towers on 104 Street, and the Avord Arms just a few blocks north—were filled with renters from the gay and lesbian community. The entire area took on a very queer flavour as downtown relaxed into its 1970s persona. The list of drag queens that lived in this section of the downtown core was impressive, and even Millie, the first Empress of Edmonton, lived with a gaggle of queens in a large rented house at the bottom of Bellamy Hill.

The late 1970s and early 1980s were undoubtedly the heydays of The Hill. By 1978, Edmonton had three gay bars and an emerging number of gay organizations. This was also the year the infamous Pisces Health Spa opened, adding another all-night option for socializing, sex, and community building. In 1980, the Dapple Grey Café opened on 102 Street, right at the spot where MacDonald Drive ended, adding a new all-night gay restaurant to the party and creating a bright moment on a dark stroll for those who were less inclined to cruise or needed a safe place to escape to if things got scary.

Eventually, higher visibility meant there were moments of violence and danger. In 1980, posters went up on lampposts lining the area warning gay men to "stay away from The Hill," as reports of anti-gay violence started to rise. The *Edmonton Journal* reported that roving gangs armed with knives and baseball bats were patrolling The Hill, and at least one gay male hustler had been beaten and castrated. Pat Fortier, the president of Boots 'N Saddle, stated, "I personally saw six men beat up one guy [on] April 24. He looked like a piece of hamburger when they were finished."[7] More infamously, reports came of gays fighting back and chasing the homophobes away. Fighting back would become a theme throughout the 1980s and 1990s as the 2SLGBTQ+ community fought not only for safety, but also for visibility and human rights.

The cruising action on The Hill morphed and shifted over the years. City construction changed the area and police "cleanups" routinely pushed cruising to different fugitive spaces across the city. For a while, The Hill would be nearly empty as the cruising action moved a block or two west, having taken root in the alleys between 102 and 104 Street and nearby dark parkades. Sometimes cruising centred around Veterans Park, a small pocket park located just across from the *Edmonton Journal* office building. In the late 1980s, 104 Street was where the girls worked, and The Hill was where the boys worked, with cruising occurring in all the alleyways in-between. The downtown streets were always alive with action if one knew where to look.

In August 1986, the community learned that a staff member at Flashback had been murdered by a trick he had met at the bar. A local blackjack dealer, Louis Verseghy, left Flashback nightclub with Richard Hall; Verseghy was found stabbed to death the next day. Soon after, John DiCarlo, known in the Edmonton drag scene as Lori St. John, was on his way to work at Cheddars restaurant, located at the spot where the Dapple Grey Café had closed. Cruising past The Hill, John spotted Hall, whom he had seen leaving Flashback. Hall was posing as a hustler on The Hill. Bravely, John pretended to be interested in a "date" and talked the man into joining him at Cheddars. Once the man was seated, John excused himself and used the restaurant's phone to call the police; Hall was arrested.[8] A few months later, he was tried and found guilty. That summer at the annual Imperial Sovereign Court of the Wild Rose's Coronation Ball, John was honoured with a special citation for his bravery in helping to keep the community safe.

In the 1990s, downtown street cruising began to wane, although the occasional hustler could still be found on The Hill. All was not lost, however, as the right bathrooms and bathhouses could still be found, along with the allure and legend of Victoria Park. Eventually, dating phone lines (literally called the "Cruise Line") and the growth of websites like Gay.com and apps such as Grindr transformed cruising. Today, The Hill is a quiet, picturesque street dotted with historic information signs, which tell some but not all of Edmonton's local history. And the view is still spectacular.

DARRIN HAGEN

Perched on the edge of the riverbank with one-way traffic circling, The Hill was practically designed for cruising. I missed out on the legendary years with tales of rumbles and parties and drag queens strutting their stuff, but even after 1982 there was almost always a car willing to let you get in, or strangers on a stroll hunting for adventure. There was even an exhaust grate from one of the high-rise office towers that blew warm air all night, so cold-weather lingering was an option as well, even in the bitterest winter, for those foolhardy or desperate enough.

It was a dark thrill to wander along that sidewalk to see who was out and about, then stop at Dapple Grey Café for a blueberry milkshake. It was not without its hint of danger too. When I was still a teen, before I knew what The Hill was, I recall seeing yellow flyers taped to the lampposts, warning of gay-bashers. Years later, the man who murdered a friend of mine was spotted on The Hill by the Queen who would never be Empress—and she took him to the Dapple Grey and sat him down and then called the police.

Dapple Grey Café

10024 102 STREET

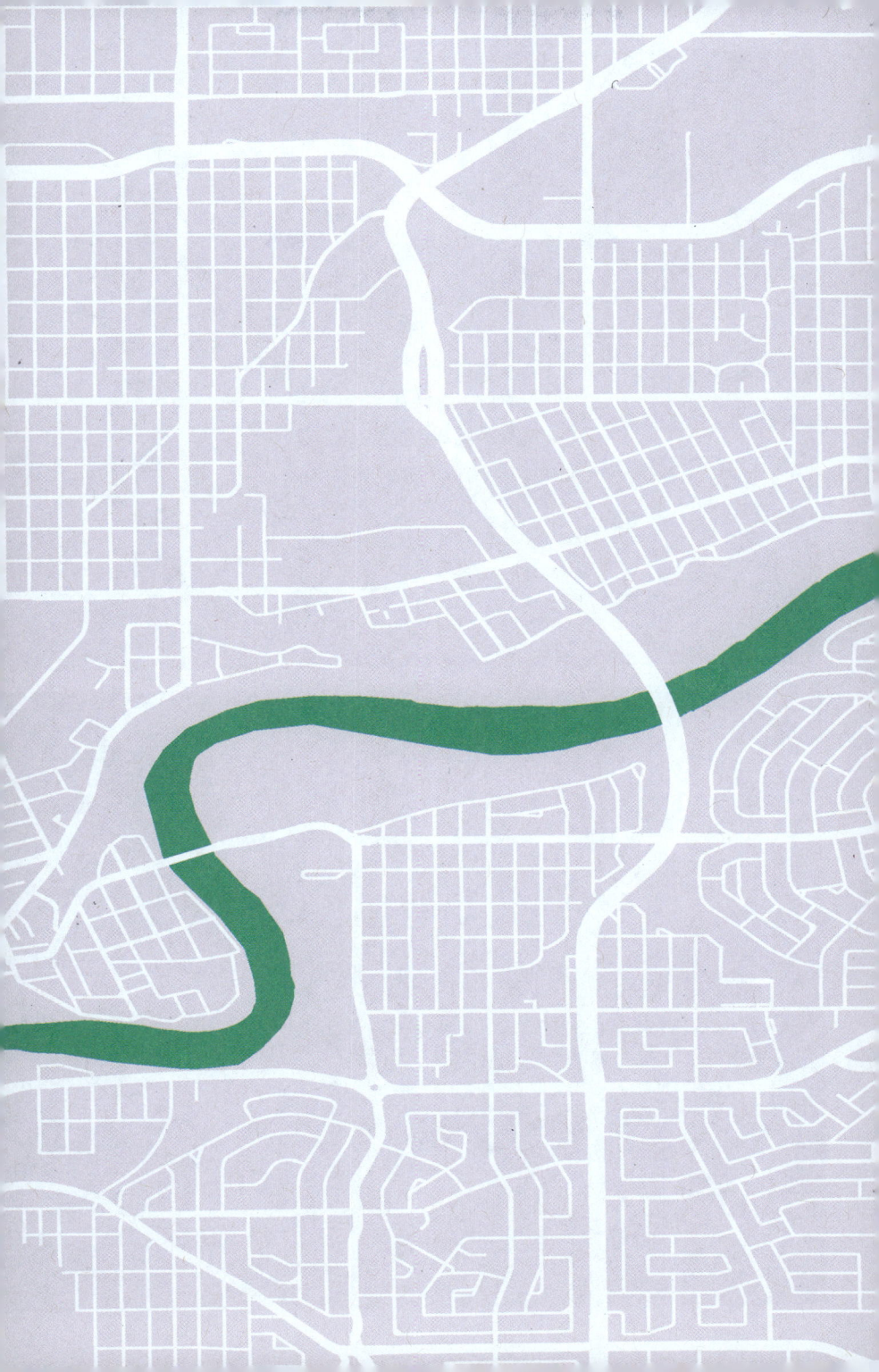

Cruising can be dangerous. Too often, the intention to have a fun sexual encounter has a violent end. Tragic examples of a date gone wrong include the 1998 murder of Edmontonian James Miles and the 2002 killing of Fort McMurray teen Richard Sneath.[1] Unfortunately, there are always more assaults than are reported to the police, often due to the shame or fear of victims coming forward.[2]

In the past, one way for gay and bisexual men to minimize the risks associated with hooking up was to meet first in a well-lit public place rather than heading directly to someone's home, car, or other space. In the 1990s, this meeting may have been at an openly gay coffee shop like Boystown Café and Gallery or the Second Cup (dubbed the "Gay Cup") on Jasper and 112 Street. Before the invention of smartphones, cyber cafés such as Naked or the Sugarbowl on 124 Street provided opportunities to chat on sites like #mIRC or Gay.com and then meet in the safety of the Internet café.

In the early 1980s, Dapple Grey Café was one of these safe spaces. Not only did the Dapple Grey deliver a legendary blueberry milkshake or an eggs benny that introduced Edmonton to the "farm-to-table" experience, but it was also open twenty-four hours a day.[3] When the gay clubs closed, the Dapple Grey was the place to go. It was located at the end of The Hill, an infamous downtown cruising strip (see page 298). The Dapple Grey provided a safe space for people cruising The Hill to take their prospective dates for a quick coffee before heading off to the main event. For many, the café was both a beacon and a refuge.

Although posters along The Hill often warned about the increased possibility of anti-gay violence, that didn't seem to affect its popularity as a cruising area. Beatings, robberies, and stabbings in the area were attributed not just to dates

▲ Dapple Grey Café, 1970
▼ Dapple Grey Café original location, present day (10024 102 Street)

DARRIN HAGEN

Dapple Grey was part of a new culture wave, consciously positioned against the corporate culture that was in the ascendance at the time. Nothing about it was a chain outlet. The berries were sourced locally; every beef patty was hand formed without filler. The ice cream was genuine quality. The eggs were from local Hutterite farms. The clientele was mohawked and counter-fashion of the New Wave sort. Bright and cheery, with club music playing, it was the perfect place for an eggs benny and an unforgettable huge blueberry milkshake—either before or after you checked out who was hanging out on The Hill.

that went wrong but to the pervasive anti-gay attitudes and violence of the time. Male sex workers on The Hill threatened to arm themselves if nothing was done to curb the violent swell.[4] Far too often, the 2SLGBTQ+ community had to take care of themselves.

A 1996 exhibit by Spencer Harrison explored the effects of gay bashing in Edmonton. Harrison interviewed thirty local men who were survivors of anti-gay attacks. The exhibit, displayed at Latitude 53 gallery, featured a massive central painting designed to duplicate the isolation a victim can experience before, during, and after an attack. The installation also included powerful quotes from victims. Harrison noted a common theme in the attacks, where the gay-bashers would stake out a local gay club to target victims. At a moment when the provincial government, under the leadership of Premier Ralph Klein, was actively fighting against equal rights for 2SLGBTQ+ people, the exhibit was a timely and powerful reminder of the consequences of hate and prejudice.[5]

Harrison also displayed an art installation at the Edmonton Police Service downtown headquarters, which included a black banner featuring three gay men with an ominous figure threatening them from the shadows. This provocative installation was created as a visible reminder to police of the ongoing violence against 2SLGBTQ+ people and its consequences.

The EPS Gay and Lesbian Liaison Committee, established in 1992, was a way to help connect the community with law enforcement. The committee's projects included a 1999 campaign bringing attention to gay bashing.[6] A special unit dedicated to investigating hate and bias crimes, which began tracking instances of gay bashing, was created in 2003.[7] In 2004, a new training activity was instituted to help police recruits understand what it was like to be an 2SLGBTQ+ person in Edmonton; this involved primarily male police recruits walking down Whyte Avenue holding each other's hands. Recruits were debriefed after the activity and often reported feeling uncomfortable and unsafe.[8] This activity was deemed so dangerous that an undercover unit had to be present in case the recruits were assaulted.

While working with the police to ensure the safety of 2SLGBTQ+ citizens is a constantly evolving and ongoing project, there is still much to celebrate in how far we have come as a community. As an example, the 2012 attack on Chevi Rabbit, a Two Spirit youth, was not only immediately investigated by the EPS Hate Crimes Unit; it was also met with a massive outpouring of community support. Chevi and supporters turned this incident into the Hate to Hope March and Rally, an ongoing community educational event.[9]

Today Edmonton is a very different world than it was in the days of The Hill and the Dapple Grey Café, but violence against 2SLGBTQ+ Canadians is still rampant. Another example occurred in 2014 when Demetrious Karahalios, a well-known cook at Woodys pub, was found murdered in his Oliver home. The police investigation soon linked the murder to Richard LaCarte, a drifter who frequented Woodys. Staff at the venue kept LaCarte's photograph prominently displayed as a reminder to always be vigilant. LaCarte was eventually arrested years later, finally bringing some closure to Karahalios's friends and family.[10] A recent Statistics Canada report highlighted that "gay, lesbian, bisexual and other sexual minority people in Canada were almost three times more likely than heterosexual Canadians to report that they had been physically or sexually assaulted in the previous 12 months" as well as being "more than twice as likely to report having been violently victimized since the age of 15."[11]

No one is born with hate in their heart. Homophobia, biphobia, and transphobia are learned behaviours. The hope is these prejudices can also be unlearned through education, empathy, and love.

PART 6

A History of Pride 1980–2024

In this section we provide a brief timeline highlighting the history of pride in Edmonton over the years, which demonstrates its origins, growth, successes, challenges, and setbacks. Pride is what we make it and is always in a state of continual contestation and evolution.

WARREN BECKER
Pride Festival volunteer and co-chair, 2008–2018

From my decade of volunteering with Edmonton's Pride Festival, there are so very many memories and moments of joy. I can still vividly recall one year when a young lady came up to me and expressed interest in volunteering. I could tell she was a bit apprehensive and very nervous. I asked her a few questions and signed her up to volunteer on Churchill Square. A few hours later, I stopped by to see how she was doing. When I spoke to her, she immediately burst into tears. I was thinking, Oh no! What happened? She said to me, between sobs, "I was unsure about coming to the Pride Festival, but being here and seeing all the people, I no longer feel alone. There are people just like me!" Both of us ended up with tears streaming down our faces. It was then, after all of those months of hard work putting this festival together, I knew it was worth it!

1980 Edmonton's first official Pride gathering is believed to have occurred at Camp Harris, with a campfire, softball game, and picnic that attracted about seventy-five people. Previously, Dignity Edmonton had held a smaller annual picnic in June.

1981 A small group of gay and lesbian Edmontonians launched the *S.S. Pisces*, billed as a gay 1890s bathhouse, as part of the Klondike Days Sourdough Raft Race. Michael Phair dressed as a rubber ducky as the crew of three gay men and three lesbian women sought to draw attention to the injustices of the Pisces Health Spa raid (see page 84).

1982 The first Gay Pride weekend (June 25–27) was launched with the theme Pride Through Unity, part of ongoing community organizing resulting from the Pisces Health Spa raid. Seven local lesbian and gay groups helped to organize Unity weekend, which kicked off with a drag show and buffet at Flashback sponsored by the Imperial Sovereign Court of the Wild Rose, and a Unity Dance held at the Phoenix Hall sponsored by GATE with about 250 people in attendance, followed by a picnic and barbeque at Camp Harris. Unity celebrations concluded with a softball tournament featuring gays versus lesbians and teams from Calgary and Red Deer. The games were held at Camp Harris and sponsored by the Roughnecks, Edmonton's gay and lesbian sports group. More than one hundred people came out to the ball games, barbeque, and sing-along.

Earlier this year, Dignity Edmonton hosted its sixth annual conference at the Hotel Macdonald (May 21–24), with the theme Free To Be. Conference workshops included freedom and authority in the church, gay freedom and gospel values, and freedom and women in the church.

1983 Edmonton's Gay Pride Week Committee organized ten days of activities (June 25 to July 3) to celebrate Pride throughout the city, including a fundraising food fair contest for the "culinary queens and ladle-swinging lesbians"—featuring a contest to find out if your buns win a prize![1]

Other Pride Week activities included a picnic in the park, sports games, film nights (with one night dedicated exclusively to women's films), lesbian book sale, gay and lesbian history discussion, musical performances, art show, community awards, pride dance, and an ecumenical church service sponsored by Metropolitan Community Church and Dignity. New this year was a special Gay Pride Week Pass, which allowed participants to take in all the events and celebrations!

Scott McConnell, one of the Pride committee organizers, stated that Gay Pride Week was an opportunity to "work with the straight community and become more unified."[2] Kathy Baker, a film night organizer, highlighted that Pride is "an acceptance of self and others within the community and facilitating good feelings about ourselves as lesbians and gay men and as individuals."[3]

1984 Gay Pride Week morphed into Gay and Lesbian Awareness Week (GALA '84), representing the coming together of several gay and lesbian community organizations to host a week full of planned activities. These initial organizing groups included Gay Alliance Toward Equality (GATE), Metropolitan Community Church, Edmonton Vocal Minority Chorus, and Womonspace. The new name was also deemed to be more reflective and inclusive of the involvement of the lesbian community.

The week of events (June 21–29) included a lesbian drop-in wine and cheese hosted by Womonspace. GATE held an open house, and there was an all-day picnic at Rundle Park with sporting events, games, an ecumenical church service, and a children's concert with Lynne Weeds. The week also featured two public forums: "Pornography: A Gay Perspective" and "Church, State, and Civil Rights." Other events included a film night at the Citadel Theatre, an art appreciation night at Flashback, and the annual GALA community Pride dance at Hazeldean

Community Hall. Common Woman Books also held its third annual lesbian book sale. Expenses for the week were about two thousand dollars, mostly covered by donations and fundraising.

For the first time, the newly formed GALA Society petitioned the City of Edmonton to declare June 27 Gay and Lesbian Awareness Day. Mayor Laurence Decore refused due to what he suggested was a lack of public appeal. Alderman Julian Kinisky stated he "would never in one minute endorse such a thing," adding that he had "no sympathy whatsoever" for gays and lesbians.[4] The *Edmonton Sun* published a virulently homophobic editorial comparing the request to supporting pederasty and chastised the gay and lesbian community for requesting an official proclamation. The *Sun* concluded its editorial by stating, "Have a nice week, people, but let the rest of us get on with our heterosexual lives in peace."[5]

1985   GALA '85 (June 20–27) continued to grow with events including a jazz concert, potluck picnic, poetry and film nights, a lesbian book fair, a GALA dance, an art show, and a public forum on Hepatitis B. The Camp Harris picnic day continued, with more than 150 people attending. Womonspace also continued to host its successful wine and cheese open house. GALA cited that Pride Week was necessary during "a time when AIDS stories dominated the news ... Positive exposure is vital in reminding Edmontonians that our city is home to a visible lesbian and gay community."

Alderman Ed Ewasiuk made a second attempt to officially proclaim Gay and Lesbian Awareness Day on June 27 in Edmonton. When the matter came before city council for discussion, "the mayor and aldermen smirked and chuckled like a pack of adolescents."[6] After the motion was defeated twelve to one, Bill Lee of GALA stated, "It's frustrating, but we're not giving up."[7] As justification for the rejection, the City noted the special day was denied because it represented "official recognition and endorsement of a particular lifestyle."[8]

1986   GALA '86 (June 18–26) hosted another impressive array of events, including an art show in the AIDS Network foyer, a lesbian wine and cheese reception hosted by Womonspace, film nights, an information seminar on safer sex, a public forum on homosexuality and the family held at the University of Alberta, the Common Woman lesbian book fair, a picnic, games and potluck at Rundle Park, and the annual GALA Pride dance. The week led up to International Lesbian and Gay Pride Day on June 27. For the first time, the entire schedule of Pride Week events was published in the *Edmonton Journal*, bringing even greater visibility to the 2SLGBTQ+ community.[9]

1987   GALA '87 (June 22–28) grew louder and prouder with the ever popular Womonspace wine and cheese drop-in, Common Woman book fair, annual Pride dance and a picnic, games, potluck, and ecumenical faith service at Rundle Park. New pride events included three plays—*Come Out, Come Out Wherever You Are, Retrospective: A Dramatization of Our Gay and Lesbian History*, and *Fit for Life: An Evening of Skits*—as well as a lesbian and gay Alcoholics Anonymous meeting at the Unitarian Church. Pride events continued to be published in the Neighborhood Calendar section of the *Edmonton Journal*.[10]

1988   GALA '88 (June 20–27) featured many favourite Pride events, including the Common Woman lesbian book fair, Womonspace wine and cheese drop-in, Pride dance, and a potluck picnic at Rundle Park featuring an All-Out Croquet Match between Guys in Disguise and Northern Chaps. This year, new Pride Week events included a coffeehouse performance at the Unitarian Church and the return of a public forum on homophobia and self-oppression at the University of Alberta.

1989   Edmonton, Calgary, Regina, and Winnipeg all hosted successful Pride weeks across the Prairies. In Edmonton, GALA

'89 featured the theme Celebrate Our Differences (June 16–27), and festivities grew to encompass twelve days of events. The Pride festival opened with a special concert by Lynn Lavner and David Sedera held at the Provincial Museum. The event was emceed by newly elected gay MP Svend Robinson from British Columbia.

Robinson was also on hand to help officially open the new Gay and Lesbian Community Centre of Edmonton (GLCCE) and participated in a community barbeque hosted by GALA's Civil Rights Committee, which had long been advocating for the inclusion of sexual orientation protections in Alberta's human rights legislation.

This year's Pride festivities included more than two dozen events, including a Womonspace dance; a workshop for people of colour, mixed ancestry and white allies hosted by Westwood Unitarian Church; a discussion on gays and lesbians and the law held at the University of Alberta's Faculty of Business; a panel discussion on Edmonton's lesbian and gay past at Common Woman Books; a film screening of *Torch Song Trilogy* at the Princess Theatre; a safer-sex workshop entitled "Hot, Healthy, and Horny" hosted by the AIDS Network of Edmonton; a lesbian photography exhibit; a GALA Pride dance with a 1960s dress-up theme; and a special twentieth-anniversary Stonewall Picnic at Victoria Park, which featured the second annual Northern Chaps Croquet Tournament.

Mayor Terry Cavanagh and city council continued to reject GALA's Pride proclamation request, leading GALA to self-proclaim Gay Day anyway, punctuated by a public rally and mock proclamation in the form of a special "silly city council meeting" held at Centennial Plaza (near City Hall; see page 114), with local actors playing the roles of city aldermen and the mayor.[11] A highlight was the portrayal of Alderman Julian Kinisky, who earlier had threatened to "run off to Australia where men are still men" if Gay and Lesbian Awareness Day was proclaimed in Edmonton.[12] The rally was attended by more than 150 community members, with two NDP MLAS addressing the assembled crowd.

Brian Mason, president of the Edmonton Voters Association, stated that Mayor Cavanagh's decision not to proclaim GALA day "displayed an unfortunate lack of political courage on his part and a lack of awareness." Only city councillors Lance White and Jan Reimer voted in favour of GALA's proclamation request.

As a lead-up to this year's GALA celebrations, Labour Minister Elaine McCoy publicly announced her support to amend Alberta's human rights statute to protect gays and lesbians from discrimination.[13] This political support was unprecedented as McCoy became the first provincial government minister on record to come out publicly in support of gay and lesbian civil rights. There was much to celebrate at Pride this year as Edmonton's community grew more visible and vocal and gained important new allies.

1990 Pride '90 (June 15–27) opened with a bang as newly elected Mayor Jan Reimer became the first mayor in Edmonton's history to participate in Pride festival activities. She joined a celebrity dunk tank held as part of the Something Wicked, Something Wild party at the Northern Light Theatre. Proceeds from the event were donated to the Ross Armstrong Memorial Fund/Names Project Quilt in support of AIDS awareness.

Other highlights of the twelve-day Pride festival included a special workshop for parents, a public forum entitled "Should I be tested for AIDS? What about AZT?," the annual Womonspace wine and cheese, a Stonewall picnic at Rundle Park, and an information fair at Centennial Plaza featuring gay Alderman Glen Murray from Winnipeg.

1991 Pride '91 (June 19–29) kicked off eleven days of events, including the first Pride march. Michael Phair and Maureen Irwin led a small informal group down Whyte Avenue. Several marchers were reported to have worn paper bags over their heads to protect their identities. The Pride march was organized, in part, to support Delwin Vriend (see page 105).

There was no formal request for a Pride proclamation this year as many felt there was no need. Earlier in the year, the City of Edmonton amended its Equal Opportunities Policy to include sexual orientation protections for all city employees. In recognition of Pride Week, Mayor Reimer issued a formal letter of support and sent cyclists to the bike-a-thon fundraiser, which raised over three thousand dollars to support the newly established Delwin Vriend Defense Fund.

Pride Week events this year included a well-attended outdoor concert featuring Mandy and Women in Comfortable Shoes, a film night, special bar/club nights, an evening with MP Svend Robinson, a poetry reading, a community picnic at Victoria Park, and a packed Pride dance with more than four hundred participants.

1992 The theme for this year's Pride festival was Pink, Pride, Power (June 18–27). This year Womonspace celebrated its tenth anniversary, and community leader Michael Phair was elected to city council, making him the first "out" politician in Alberta's history and one of only a few in Canada.

Despite the objections of Alderman Ken Kozak, who said proclaiming a Gay Pride Day would be akin to "having a day for flying elephants," city council approved the motion.[14] However, while Mayor Jan Riemer was away on vacation, acting Deputy Mayor Sheila McKay refused to sign the proclamation, stating, "I refuse to accept that burden. I am not a bigot. People in their private lives, if they're adults, can do what they want."[15]

Pride Week activities included a leather and safer-sex workshop. a Womonspace dance, a GLCCE garage sale, a three-night film festival, a safer-sex casino held by the AIDS Network of Edmonton, and a women's summer solstice dance. A Pride-a-Thon was held on Saturday, June 27, at the Kinsmen Field House, where Edmontonians walked, cycled, and jogged to raise money in support of the Delwin Vriend Defense Fund. A letter written and signed by Delwin Vriend was given to each participant, thanking them for their support. The letter stated, "This event is not only about raising funds for the legal battle I am now mounting, it is a visible demand for equality and justice."

With more time to organize this year, Edmonton's first "official" Pride parade marched down Whyte Avenue and concluded at McIntyre Park, where MP Svend Robinson addressed the rally with about two hundred people gathered, despite a few hecklers.[16] Pride Week events concluded with an evening concert at the Garneau Theatre and a Party in Pink night at the Roost.

1993   This year's Pride festival theme was A Family of Pride. The nine-day festival (June 18–27) involved more than twenty community groups and kicked off with a lesbian art exhibit at Latitude 53 gallery. Festivities throughout the week included a Mr. Drummer leather brunch and contest; a safer-sex workshop; Unitarian church service; multi-night film festival at The Citadel; live music and art show; and a LesBiGay, Motown, and Womyn only series of community dances.

Another notable event was the first-ever LesBiGay Business Fair, which featured forty vendors ranging from florists to lawyers. Alderman Michael Phair opened the fair and stated that it would be good for the city's economy: "People in the gay and lesbian community are not only involved in businesses but are consumers. It's easy for us to forget how important the business aspect is."[17]

On Saturday, June 26, the annual Gay and Lesbian Pride Day Parade and Rally were held at McIntyre Park, followed by a Pride picnic at Queen Elizabeth Park. The evening concluded with a Voices of Pride concert hosted by Edmonton Vocal Minority. The Pride-a-Thon returned on Sunday to close out the week of activities with funds being raised to support Team Edmonton, a new community gay and lesbian sports association.

The first-ever Pride awards were given to Michael Phair and Maureen Irwin for their many contributions in building Edmonton's gay and lesbian community. The Pride Awards, each year after that, would be named after them to honour their legacy contributions.

Mayor Jan Reimer officially proclaimed June 26, 1993, Gay and Lesbian Pride Day for the first time in Edmonton's history. Along with her proclamation, she wrote, "Dignity and respect for all people, without discrimination based on sexual orientation, is an important goal for a free and democratic society."[18] The proclamation was met with resistance from some city aldermen, including Rob Hayter, who stated, "I don't think this particular lifestyle should be promoted."[19] In response, newly elected alderman Michael Phair stated, "This has nothing to do with promoting a certain lifestyle ... the day is meant to represent that gays and lesbians exist in this city."[20]

1994 To commemorate the twenty-fifth anniversary of the Stonewall Uprising in New York City, the theme for Edmonton's Pride festival (June 17–25) was Stonewall 25. Mayor Reimer proclaimed June 25, 1994, Gay and Lesbian Awareness Day in Edmonton.

The successful LesBiGay Business Fair returned this year along with many other regular Pride events. Edmonton Vocal Minority held another sold-out concert. A draw was held for a special rainbow flag quilt by the Imperial Sovereign Court of the Wild Rose in support of Karios House. The Pride parade was held once again in Old Strathcona and attracted more than 450 participants, making it the largest in Edmonton's history thus far.[21] PFLAG also hosted a family picnic in the park following the parade.

The Delwin Vriend legal case was cited by many as the reason for the larger parade turnout, with more individuals joining the rally to protest the provincial government's refusal to grant legal protections against discrimination based on sexual orientation. David Sanders, one of the parade organizers, said, "We're here, and we're queer, and we'll be here if there's a Ralph Klein or not. In fact, the lesbian and gay community will be here long after the Klein government is ancient history."[22]

1995   The theme for this year's Pride celebrations was Past, Present, Pride: Celebrating Our History (June 16–24). Pride events included workshops on safer sex, a film festival, the Boystown Cabaret, and a rally and march down Whyte Avenue. Notably, during this year's Pride festival, Anne Erskine and George Davidson were honoured as recipients of the Maureen Irwin Award and Michael Phair Award, respectively. Erskine was recognized for her counselling efforts with women in the community, and Davidson for his supportive efforts in the Vriend case and other civil rights issues.[23]

The Pride parade marched down Whyte Avenue and attracted hundreds of participants. Still, it was also met with open disgust and disapproval from some businesses and protestors. Potter's House Christian Church members handed out pamphlets and preached to the crowd, stating that they do not hate, nor are they against gays and lesbians, but they want to inform them of a "better life."[24] And despite some community opposition, Mayor Reimer proclaimed Gay and Lesbian Pride Day for the third year in a row.

The Gay and Lesbian Archives of Edmonton were established this year as part of the City of Edmonton Archives to help preserve this important local history.

1996   In October 1995, Bill Smith was elected as the new mayor of Edmonton. Unlike his predecessor, Jan Reimer, Smith refused to proclaim Gay and Lesbian Pride Day in 1996. Smith told GALA their proclamation request was one of many he had denied. However, when pressed, the city's corporate communications office sent GALA a letter stating their proclamation request was the first and only one that the mayor had denied. GALA demanded an apology from the mayor. Alderman Michael

Phair said, "I was very disappointed. I'm surprised the mayor didn't have the courage to do this. I think that's sad. Personally, it hurt me as well."[25]

This year's Pride festival (June 15–28) continued with many familiar events, including a Womonspace picnic and dance, a public discussion on same-sex marriage sponsored by Metropolitan Community Church, a lesbian and gay history talk hosted by Maureen Irwin and Michael Phair, a PFLAG family picnic in Victoria Park, and an Edmonton Vocal Minority concert and Pride Awards ceremony at the University of Alberta's Convocation Hall.

In lieu of a city proclamation, a rally was held outside the Alberta Legislature protesting the provincial government's ongoing refusal to grant human rights protections based on sexual orientation. After the rally, the Pride parade marched from the Legislature grounds to Victoria Park.

1997   This year's Pride festival theme (June 20–29) was Celebrating our Diversity and Pride. For the second year, Mayor Bill Smith refused to proclaim Gay and Lesbian Awareness Day because "it isn't something he believes in."[26]

Pride festivities kicked off in a big way with a special Loud 'N Proud "fun-raiser" at the Citadel Theatre featuring Christopher Peterson in "EYECONS"; Darrin Hagen's "Drag Fest '97"; a screening of Brad Fraser's film *Parade*; Klodyne Rodney's "Sister Sappho Stage" cabaret; and an Après Party in the Lee Pavilion.

This year's Pride festival day started with a rally at Gazebo Park featuring Delwin Vriend, community lawyer Julie Lloyd, and Edmonton Vocal Minority, followed by a parade, which marched south down 104 street to Rollie Miles Park by Strathcona High School. Following the parade, PFLAG held a community picnic in the park featuring a "boys vs. girls" football game.

Other Pride Week events included a fundraiser for the Delwin Vriend Defense Fund and the Imperial Sovereign Court of the Wild Rose at the Roost; a Metropolitan Community

Church and Lambda ecumenical faith service; film festival at the Edmonton Art Gallery; Pride karaoke, talent shows, and drag performances; a literary salon event with costumes and impersonations at Orlando Books; a safer-sex workshop; the Womonspace Pride dance; and an Edmonton Vocal Minority concert and the annual Pride Awards.

1998 This was a milestone year as the Supreme Court of Canada ruled in favour of Delwin Vriend and read sexual orientation into Alberta's human rights statute, thereby making it illegal to discriminate on the basis of a person's sexual orientation. Premier Ralph Klein made national news when he threatened to use the Charter's notwithstanding clause to exempt Alberta from the ruling.

As this year's Pride festival approached, Mayor Bill Smith continued to refuse to proclaim Gay Pride Day, stating, "It's nothing I'm going to debate. My position has been that I'm not going to proclaim Gay Pride Days in Edmonton, and I'm pretty clear on that." Smith said he interpreted the issue differently than the Supreme Court of Canada, stating "There's only one judge in the Supreme Court here."[27]

This year's Pride festival (May 15–23) coincided with the Canadian GALA Choruses Festival (May 15–18), which brought together 2SLGBTQ+ choral groups from across Canada, the largest such gathering in Canadian history. This ground-breaking choral event was proudly organized and produced by Edmonton Vocal Minority.

Other Pride Festival activities for this year included the PFLAG-T family picnic, the Womonspace Pride dance, the Pride Awards, and a rally with several hundred people gathering at Churchill Square in front of City Hall. Notably, there was no Pride parade this year, likely due to the Festival's shift to May and a new City policy requiring the Pride festival to pay for road closure barriers, pylons, and security. The festival organizers couldn't afford to host a parade this year.

1999   Progress for lesbian and gay rights continued as same-sex couples were now legally allowed to privately adopt children in Alberta. The Pride Festival returned to June (12–19) with the theme Community, Celebration, Visibility. Festivities included the return of a vibrant, colourful, and growing Pride parade with five hundred-plus marchers and a very full week of activities, including an Equal Alberta town hall, a Flamingo Business Fair, an art show and craft sale, a drag fashion show at Vicious Pink, and the annual Edmonton Vocal Minority concert.

GALA decided not to ask Mayor Bill Smith for a proclamation and instead marched into City Hall and proclaimed the day themselves.[28] Mayor Smith stated that he would only proclaim a Pride Day if the courts forced him to, as had been the case in Ontario, where a few cities were taken to court and fined $10,000 for refusing to issue a proclamation.

This year's Pride rally started downtown at Grant Notley Park; followed by a Pride march to Oliver Park, where the parade attracted several thousand people and featured five floats; and concluded with a PFLAG-T picnic and beer gardens and the Pride Awards. The Pink Flamingo Pride Dance capped off the evening at the nearby Hellenic Hall.

The *Edmonton Journal* featured the Pride Festival as one of the "Ten Best Things to Do This Weekend," prompting some backlash in the letters to the editor.[29]

With the size and scope of the Pride festival growing rapidly, GALA members helped form the new Edmonton Pride Festival Society (EPFS), which took over all the planning and organizing of Pride Festival events and activities.

2000   This year's Pride Festival (June 10–17) theme was Proud in 2000. Festivities kicked off in Grant Notley Park, followed by a colourful parade winding down Victoria promenade, crossing Jasper Avenue on 121 Street, and ending in Oliver Park. Lasting about thirty minutes, this year's parade had doubled in size from the previous year. A new addition to the Pride Festival included a radio show showcasing Pride Week highlights and feature programs. Other Pride Week events included the Flamingo Business Fair, the Pride Awards, a large community dance, and an art exhibit by Steve Walker.

Still reluctant to proclaim a Gay and Lesbian Pride Day, Mayor Bill Smith instead issued a public letter of congratulations to the organizers of Pride. He wrote, "Thank you for lending your time to bridge understanding while strengthening unity within the Edmonton lesbian, gay, bisexual, and transgendered community."[30] Some saw this as a welcome message of support; others saw this as a cop-out and still demanded an official proclamation.

2001   Despite still not having any official support from Mayor Bill Smith and Premier Ralph Klein, Pride continued with the theme A Rainbow Odyssey. Pride Week began with a news conference outside City Hall and was followed by a parade down Jasper Avenue. Eighteen events made up this year's Pride Festival (June 16–23), including a street fair (with a youth carnival, a picnic, a business resource fair, and beer gardens). The week also included a musical cabaret, beach volleyball, dinner theatre, an Edmonton Vocal Minority concert, the annual Pride Awards, a literary night at Orlando Books, and a Flamingo Pride Dance at the Citadel. A highlight this year was the presence of federal Justice Minister Anne McLellan, Alberta NDP Leader Raj Pannu, and MLAs Laurie Blakeman and Brian Mason in the Pride parade.[31]

2002   Edmonton celebrated its annual Pride Festival (June 14–23) with the theme Many Faces—One Community. More than one thousand community members attended the increasingly large and colourful Pride parade down Jasper Avenue. Pride Festival events include a family picnic and barbecue, a drag pageant, a stand-up comedy show, a film festival, an inclusive church service, a public forum with members of the Edmonton Police Commission at City Hall, and the Pride Awards and dance at the Old Strathcona Art Barns. Importantly, this year Pride also celebrated the twentieth anniversary of Womonspace and the thirtieth anniversary of the Gay and Lesbian Community Centre of Edmonton.

Mayor Bill Smith continued his steadfast refusal to proclaim a Gay and Lesbian Pride Day. In response, EPFS announced that they were formally initiating a human rights complaint against Mayor Smith. Roz Ostendorf, Pride Festival Co-Chair, said, "For some people, it is very important that Mr. Smith be dragged kicking and screaming into a liberal society."[32]

2003   This year's Pride theme was The Flame Within. The Pride Festival (June 13–22) began with the largest Pride parade to date, with nearly six thousand people in attendance. Notable festival events included two public forums on community health and a discussion on hate crimes, police, and the LGBT community at City Hall. Other events included karaoke, dances and dinners, live music, sporting events, and the annual Pride Awards.

Earlier in 2003, a formal human rights complaint was filed against Mayor Bill Smith (Pride vs. City of Edmonton vs. Bill Smith) for his failure to proclaim a Gay and Lesbian Pride Day. Despite the mayor's refusal, seven city councillors issued a joint letter, published in the official Pride Festival Guide, welcoming the event to Edmonton. Councillor Michael Phair stated that Mayor Smith's refusal to issue a Pride proclamation felt like a personal slap in the face.[33]

Finally, upon the advice of City lawyers, Mayor Bill Smith reluctantly proclaimed Gay Pride Week and issued an official proclamation. *Edmonton Journal* columnist Paula Simons described Smith's proclamation as "delivered not with gracious generosity, but churlishly through clenched teeth."[34]

2004 This year Stephen Mandel was elected mayor and without hesitation proclaimed June 18–27 as Gay Pride Week. In response the Better Canada Coalition, a local anti-gay group, gathered a petition with more than one thousand signatures requesting the City cancel the annual Pride Parade.[35] The petition was ignored

This year's Pride Festival theme was Pioneering Pride Pride Week officially kicked off at City Hall with the reading of the official proclamation and the raising of the rainbow flag, which flew proudly for the week. Pride Festival events include the annual parade, the Pride Awards; a queer history display showcasing Edmonton's LGBTQ pioneers at City Hall, a Two Spirit awareness workshop, a pancake breakfast, a youth art display, and Edmonton Vocal Minority concert, a silent auction; community dances; and a public forum on same-sex marriage that closed out the week's festivities.

2005 A historic year for lesbian and gay rights in Canada as Bill C-38 was passed into law, changing the legal definition of marriage to "a union between two persons." Canada became the fourth country in the world to legalize same-sex marriage Dissatisfied with the decision, Premier Klein threatened to use the Charter's notwithstanding clause. Klein was advised not to fight against the law, however; his legal advisors suggested "our chances of winning are virtually none."[36]

Grow Pride was selected as the theme for this year's Pride Festival celebrations (June 17–26). Mayor Stephen Mandel officially proclaimed Pride Week and became the first mayor in Edmonton's history to participate in the Pride Parade. When asked about his participation, he stated, "I'm supporting my friend Michael Phair ... People who are gay are people. I don't know what the big deal is."[37] The mayor also hosted the inaugural Mayor's Pride Brunch in Support of Camp fYrefly, which would become an annual event.

This year's Pride Festival began with the Pride Awards and rainbow flag raising at City Hall with a performance by

Edmonton Vocal Minority. The ever-growing Pride parade featured Deputy Prime Minister Anne McLellan as the Grand Marshal who led the parade down Jasper Avenue alongside Mayor Stephen Mandel and Councillor Michael Phair. The parade concluded with a large festival at Churchill Square. About six protestors from Potter's House Christian Church walked along the sidewalks during the parade holding anti-gay signs.[38]

Pride events this year also included a Womonspace Pride Dance; a public forum called "Pride, Community, the Police Commission, and the Police Service" at City Hall; a Bonfire of the Rainbows punk entertainment extravaganza at the University of Alberta; an Edmonton Vocal Minority concert at the Provincial Museum of Alberta; Acts of Pride featuring an evening of music, comedy and theatre at La Cité francophone; and a family brunch and penny carnival.

2006   This year's Pride theme was Pride Power (June 16–25) and was officially recognized with a proclamation by Mayor Mandel. The Pride Festival kicked off at City Hall by once again raising the rainbow flag and hosting the annual Pride Awards. Other activities included the annual Pride parade and Festival at Churchill Square, a joint concert and dance organized by Edmonton Vocal Minority and Womonspace, the Mayor's Pride Brunch, a new Pride Challenge softball game with the Edmonton Police Service, the first EPS Pride Week Reception hosted by Chief Mike Boyd, Acts of Pride Cabaret and Silent Auction at La Cité francophone, and other regular Pride events.

2007   This year's Pride Festival theme was Pride 007–License to Thrill (June 15–24) and was officially recognized by Mayor Stephen Mandel and the City with a proclamation. The Pride Awards and rainbow flag-raising were the first events to open up the Pride Festival, and a parade was held the day after, travelling down Jasper Avenue and ending with a celebration on Churchill Square. Other Pride events included a Pride run, sporting games, a PFLAG picnic, Pride and Womonspace dances, a Pride in Transit barbeque hosted by Councillor Michael Phair, a Pride Centre Family Brunch, a concert by Edmonton Vocal Minority, and the annual Mayor's Pride Brunch.

2008 This year marked the tenth anniversary of the landmark Delwin Vriend decision. Unmasked and Outrageous was the theme for the Pride Festival (June 13–22). Pride celebrations kicked off with the Pride Awards at City Hall and a large parade with fifty entries marching down Jasper Avenue, followed by a community celebration at Churchill Square. Throughout the week, numerous Pride events took place, including a Womonspace Unity Dance, a two-day film festival at Metro Cinema, an Edmonton Vocal Minority concert, and a masquerade ball.

2009 Edmonton celebrated this year's Pride Festival with the theme Age of A-Queer-ius (June 12–21). Mayor Stephen Mandel issued a proclamation officially declaring Gay Pride Week in the city.

This year's Pride Parade was the largest to date, with sixty entries and more than ten thousand spectators. Heather Klimchuk, Fred Horne, and Doug Elinski became the first Progressive Conservative MLAs to participate in Edmonton's Pride Parade. Klimchuk, the first government minister to participate formally, was greeted with jeers over the recent passage of Bill 44, which placed parental restrictions on openly discussing sexual orientation in Alberta's K-12 schools.[39]

Other Pride Festival events included an open house at the Edmonton Public Library, the Edmonton Police Chief's Pride Reception, a queer history bus tour hosted by Michael Phair and Darrin Hagen, a Devonian Gardens Rainbow Tour, the Queer Images film festival, the Edmonton Vocal Minority Rainbow Madness concert, and the annual Mayor's Pride Brunch.

2010   Edmonton celebrated this year's Pride Festival with the theme
A Pride Odyssey (June 11–20), which included more than forty
events. Mayor Stephen Mandel continued to be a key supporter
and once again issued an official city proclamation. Like
previous years, a large parade down Jasper Avenue kicked
off the Pride Festival with a massive celebration at Churchill
Square. Ten-year-old parade participant Kia Rand stated,
"I think it's really fun ... especially because they don't have to
hide anymore."[40]

Pride Festival events included a queer history bus tour, film
nights, a self-defence workshop, community dances, art shows,
the annual Gay Cup softball game, an Edmonton Police Service
Pride Reception, an Eskimos Pride Party Bus, the Pride Awards
at the Art Gallery of Alberta, and the Fifth Annual Mayor's
Pride Brunch, among many other activities.

As the Pride Festival continued to grow, concerns began to
be raised about the expansion of corporate sponsorship and
the shifting meaning of Pride from its activist roots.

2011   Edmonton's Pride Festival continued to grow by leaps and
bounds and now had an estimated cost of $250,000 per year.
This year's celebrations were part of a new multi-year theme,
Stand Up! Stand Out! Stand Proud! (June 10–19), and the Pride
Parade featured students from Edmonton's Gay-Straight Student Alliances as the Grand Marshals. More than twenty thousand people packed the streets, making this one of Edmonton's
largest and most colourful festivals in the city's history.

Pride Festival events this year included the annual Pride
Awards at City Hall; a Pride Festival pancake breakfast at
the Legislature grounds; a forum called "Gay–Straight Alliances Making It Better in Schools," hosted at the Art Gallery
of Alberta; a Rainbow Gallery Art Show at the Arts Barns;
queer history bus tours; a Laugh Out Proud night at Yuk Yuk's
Comedy Club; Edmonton Vocal Minority Our Proud Voices
concert nights at Catalyst Theatre; a business professionals'

Pride mixer; a Womonspace picnic and music festival a Seniors' Strawberry Tea at the Pride Centre of Edmonton a variety of inclusive church services and discussions; a Come Out and Play Day at Kinsmen Park; the annual Mayor's Pride Brunch; and a luncheon with Michael Phair on "Community Challenges: The End of Gay-NOT!"

An *Edmonton Journal* editorial observed, "It's a time to celebrate the important steps forward society has taken, and a reminder we must all continue fighting for full, unqualified gender and sexual equality in the years to come."[41]

2012   Edmonton's Pride Festival had grown into one of the largest in Canada, with more than twenty-four thousand people attending this year's parade and celebration in the square This year's Festival theme was Stand Out! (June 8–18), and it was historic. The Edmonton Public School Board trustees, who recently passed the first standalone Sexual Orientation and Gender Identity Policy in western Canada, were selected as the Pride parade's Grand Marshals for their work in support of 2SLGBTQ+ inclusive education.[42]

Not only did Mayor Stephen Mandel once again proudly proclaim Pride Week in the city; Premier Alison Redford also joined the celebrations. Redford became the first premier in Alberta's history to participate in Pride and gave an im passioned speech in front of thousands after the parade in Churchill Square: "We are in a province where people are inclusive, they respect diversity. And it's important for our political leaders to understand that ... I think we're a very different province than we were many years ago and I'm very proud of that."[43]

Support for this year's Pride Festival represented a seismic shift in attitudes and Alberta's changing political culture Support for the 2SLGBTQ+ community galvanized after Wild rose party candidate Allan Hunsperger famously condemned gays and lesbians to burn in the eternal "Lake of Fire."[44]

This year's Pride Festival included more than thirty events and began with the Pride Awards at City Hall. The week also included a special panel discussion entitled "Standing OUT: Educational Leadership for Social Justice in the 21st Century," featuring Deputy Premier Thomas Lukaszuk at the Art Gallery of Alberta. Other Pride Festival events included the Edmonton Vocal Minority concert A Touch of Goth, Pride church services, barbeques and dances, movie nights, a downtown and Whyte Avenue queer history bus tour, a business professionals' Pride mixer, a Rainbow Art Gallery, the Edmonton Police Service Chief's Pride reception, Laugh Out Proud comedy night at Yuk Yuk's, Come Out and Play Day at Kinsmen Sports Centre (including the Gay Cup volleyball tournament and a dance party at Queen Elizabeth Pool), and the annual Mayor's Pride Brunch.

2013   This year's Pride festival theme was Stand Proud! (June 7–16) and marked Stephen Mandel's last year as mayor of Edmonton. During his time in office, the Pride Festival grew and was officially recognized each and every year by the mayor and city council. At the annual Mayor's Pride Brunch, Mandel was celebrated for his unwavering support of Edmonton's 2SLGBTQ+ community. Michael Phair described Mandel's inclusive leadership as "the start of a new era .... The mayor's Pride proclamation was an enormous step toward making Edmonton a very inclusive city." In recognition of the mayor's allyship, a new leadership award was created in his name to support 2SLGBTQ+ students at the University of Alberta. As well, the University of Alberta held its first campus Pride parade, with Michael Phair in attendance, stating that Pride on-campus shows that 2SLGBTQ+ individuals are "respected like every other citizen ... it's a chance to say we're here, and we make a difference."[45]

A crowd of more than thirty thousand people attended this year's Pride parade, the largest in the city's history with

more than seventy-five entries. The Pride Centre of Edmonton
led the parade as the featured Grand Marshal. Pride Festival
events included movie nights, dances, and pageants; Pancakes
for Pride at Oliver Hall; queer history bus tours; Come Out
and Play Day; a Beef Bear Bust barbeque; and a family picnic
Of particular note, the Canadian Forces Base in Edmonton
became the first military base in Canada to raise the Pride flag
during a ceremony attended by senior officers and members
of the local 2SLGBTQ+ community.

2014   Both Mayor Don Iveson and Premier Dave Hancock partici
pated in the Pride Parade as more than 35,000 people lined
the streets of downtown Edmonton to watch some 80 floats
and 2,300 parade marchers, which ended with a celebration in
Churchill Square organized by Fruit Loop. Edmonton Oilers
captain Andrew Ference made history as the first NHL hockey
player to march in Edmonton's Pride Parade; in fact, Ference
was the first team captain of any professional sport in North
America to march in a Pride parade.[46]

This year's Pride Festival theme was Together in Pride
Worldwide (June 6–15), and events included the Rainbow Art
Gallery and Pride Awards Night, Womonspace Colour Yourself
Proud Dance, a Come Out and Play pool party; queer history
bus tours; Paintball for Pride, a Pride sock hop, and the annual
Mayor's Pride Brunch, among dozens of other events.

New this year, the colourful Pride parade was broadcast
live on Shaw TV, and the Edmonton Police Service Pipe and
Drum Band joined the parade for the first time. Also notable
was Provincial Justice Minister Jonathan Denis's funding
announcement for an LGBTQ youth mentorship program
organized by the Pride Centre of Edmonton.[47]

2015   This year's Pride Festival (June 5–14) returned home to its roots
in Old Strathcona, where it began thirty-five years earlier. The
theme was Together in Pride: 35 (1980–2015). The Pride parade

marched down Whyte Avenue to End of Steel Park, featured some ninety entries and more than two thousand parade participants, and lasted about ninety minutes. Soon to be elected Prime Minister Justin Trudeau, NDP Premier Rachel Notley, Mayor Don Iveson, RCMP Assistant Commissioner Marianne Ryan, and Edmonton Oilers goaltender Ben Scrivens joined the record-breaking parade. Former city councillor Michael Phair was this year's Parade Grand Marshal. In total, the Pride parade was estimated to have attracted a crowd of more than fifty-five thousand people, making it the fourth-largest Pride parade in Canada and one of the longest running.[48]

New and notable this year was the installation of the first inclusive Pride crosswalk in Old Strathcona. A special kids' area was created for Pride in the Park, along with a Pride interfaith service and the first Women and Trans mini-fest. Also new this year was the inaugural Edmonton Pride Run and Walk and the first Trans March, which included about eighty participants who walked to the Alberta Legislature. Other Pride Festival events included a week-long queer film festival at Metro Cinema, the Rainbow Art Gallery and Pride Awards, an Over the Rainbow Strawberry Seniors' Tea, an Edmonton Vocal Minority concert, Pride dodgeball, the first St. Albert Pride Picnic and Barbeque, and a Strathcona County Pride social. This year also marked the tenth anniversary of the Mayor's Pride Brunch.

To commemorate the thirty-fifth anniversary of Edmonton's Pride Festival, the Edmonton Queer History Project hosted a specially curated multimedia exhibition entitled *We Are Here* at the Art Gallery of Alberta.[49]

2016 This year's Pride Festival theme was Dive into Pride (June 3–19) and featured a large and colourful parade down Whyte Avenue followed by Pride in the Park in Old Strathcona. The Pride parade Grand Marshals were Edmonton's Making Waves Aquatics Club, which tied into the swimming theme as a lead-up to the

International Gay and Lesbian Aquatic Championships held August 8–14 in Edmonton. The Pride Festival also featured the inaugural Sherry McKibben Mojito Golf Tournament and Pride Dinner. McKibben was the first openly lesbian city councillor elected in a 1994 by-election; McKibben later went on to become the Executive Director of HIV Edmonton.

Other Pride Festival events included the second Queer Women and Trans Festival and March at Oliver Park, a Bears in the Park Pride barbeque, a government-sponsored information session on fostering and adoption, the long-running Laugh Out Proud night at Yuk Yuk's Comedy Club, Edmonton Pride Walk and Run, Pride church services, a family picnic, and the annual Mayor's Pride Brunch. St. Albert also hosted another successful Pride barbeque.

In May of this year, just before Pride month, a small pocket park on 104 Street was named after Edmonton's first openly gay city councillor, Michael Phair, who would later also have an Edmonton public school named after him.[50] The Rainbow Visions film festival also continued into its second year in November.

2017   This year's Pride theme was One Pride, Many Voices (June 9–18), with a concerted effort to make the Pride Festival into a community-building event. For the first time in the Festival's history, Edmonton's Two Spirit community members were the Pride parade Grand Marshals, with approximately one hundred Two Spirit individuals leading the parade down Whyte Avenue.[51]

This year, a new event was the addition of a "human library" at Strathcona Park. Pride attendees were able to engage in conversation with volunteers who acted as books to answer questions, listen to stories, and learn from their lived experiences. Volunteers included Boyd Whiskeyjack, the Two Spirit coordinator with the Pride Centre, and other active members of the 2SLGBTQ+ community.[52]

Other notable events for this year's festival included the annual Pride Awards; a Movie in the Park night at the End of Steel Park; Pride church services; Edmonton Pride Run and Walk; an Edmonton Queer History Project exhibit; art shows, barbeques, mixers, dances, and book readings; the annual Mayor's Pride Brunch; an Edmonton Vocal Minority concert; and the debut of Over the Rainbow storytime sessions where local drag queens read picture books to children at the Edmonton Public Library. St. Albert Pride continued to grow with a barbeque and local entertainment. Pride Day @ KDays was also a new and very successful event held on July 26 as part of the long-standing KDays festival.

With increasing visibility also came more vocal resistance. Raising a Canadian Pride flag at a local high school resulted in vandals cutting it down a few hours later. A high school principal ordered students to wash away their Pride chalk art and take down Pride banners at their school. A slew of hate-filled comments targeted the Edmonton Public Library's Strathcona branch for their involvement in hosting Over the Rainbow storytime sessions.[53]

2018 This year's Pride Festival theme was One Pride (June 8–17), which highlighted the full spectrum of 2SLGBTQ+ identities, representing that no one is alone in the fight to change the world. Reflective of this theme, more than twenty diverse individuals served as the Grand Marshals for the parade, which included NDP MLA Ricardo Miranda, Alberta's first openly gay cabinet minister.

The United Conservative Party applied to the Edmonton Pride Festival Society to march in this year's Pride parade, but was rejected due to the party's long-standing opposition to the 2SLGBTQ+ community and for voting against many pro-2SLGBTQ+ inclusive bills, such as Bill 24, which protected and supported GSAs in schools.[54] In light of this rejection, the UCP held its own sparsely attended pancake breakfast, described as being "open to anyone who wants to celebrate Pride."[55]

This year's Pride parade once again marched down Whyte Avenue, where it was met with protests over police and military participation, both of whom were asked to participate out of official uniform. Dozens of protestors halted the parade in protest with a list of demands and signs stating, "No Justice No Pride" and "Racism is a Queer Issue".[56]

Pride Festival events this year included the official Pride flag raising at City Hall; a youth social; a pancake breakfast; a Battle of the Queens talent show; a Pride on 103 downtown street festival organized and hosted by Evolution Wonder lounge; the annual Pride Awards; Pride and interfaith church services; drag queen bingo; book readings; community barbe ques; film screenings; and a Fruit Loop wrap-up party. A new event this year featured Pride Night @ the Ballpark hosted by the Edmonton Prospects downtown at Re/Max Field, which included many fun-filled family Pride activities.

This year's Pride Festival also marked the twenty-fifth anniversary of Edmonton Vocal Minority, with a concert at the Westbury Theatre featuring the choir and guest conductor Darrin Hagen. This year also celebrated the fortieth anniver sary of the Pride Centre of Edmonton.

2019   For the first time in nearly forty years, the annual Pride Festival was cancelled due to rising community tensions and the social and political climate. This decision resulted from the struggle to meet growing concerns over increasing corporate, military and police involvement and issues raised by trans people, queer people, and people of colour about Festival operations, funding, and programming.[57]

Despite having no official Pride events organized by EPFS, local businesses and groups celebrated Pride in their own unique ways.[58] Evolution Wonderlounge spearheaded a com munity street festival to support local queer and trans non profit groups; Edmonton's 2 Spirit Society held its first barbeque; Spotlight Cabaret hosted a drag brunch; and RaricaNow and Shades of Colour organized a rally to commemorate the fiftieth anniversary of the Stonewall Uprising at the Alberta Legislature. The Pride Run and Walk returned to a new venue in Rossdale. Also new this year was the debut of the Edmonton Transit Service's Pride Bus.

2020   Due to increasing community pressure, EPFS ceased operations. Pride was cancelled due to the Covid-19 pandemic and no public Pride events were held in an effort to help stop the spread of the virus.

To respond to community needs, some Stonewall and Pride events went virtual.[59] New virtual events included the Indigi-Queer Gayla 2020 created by the Edmonton 2 Spirit Society with the Calgary Pride Festival and RaricaNow's Edmonton Stonewall Black Trans Lives Matter march and rally. Fruit Loop also broadcast performances from the Starlite Room for a special Pride at Home event. Edmonton's High Level Bridge was also lit up in rainbow colours.

2021   Once again, there were no in-person Pride festivities due to the ongoing Covid-19 restrictions. To help keep the spirit of Pride alive, Fruit Loop developed a virtual, augmented-reality Pride tour, which was "designed to educate and entertain." Using a mobile device with a virtual map, individuals could travel to ten locations in the city's downtown core that "showcase [Edmonton's] diverse community's past, present, and future."[60] Each stop on the tour included videos of over fifty drag performances and speakers discussing the significance and importance of the location to Edmonton's queer history. The tour opened at Beaver Hills Park ᐊᒥᐢᑲᐧᒌᐧᐋᐢᑲᐦᐃᑲᐣ (amiskwacîy-wâskahikan) with a land acknowledgement and cultural performance by Edmonton 2 Spirit Society. Other virtual tour locations included Evolution Wonderlounge, Michael

Phair Park, the old Flashback and Roost locations, and the Neon Sign Museum.

The Pride Centre of Edmonton also hosted virtual Pride events, including a virtual queer prom and printmaking workshop with The Society of Northern Alberta Print-Artists (SNAP). RaricaNow hosted an online Stonewall event: The International Stonewall Symposium, featuring local and international speakers, a healing circle, and performances by BIPOC 2SLGBTQ+ artists.

2022 After two years with few in-person events, this year several small and diverse Pride activities were organized. Billed as the Ruby Red Celebration to mark the fortieth anniversary of the first community Pride weekend in Edmonton held in 1982, this year's festival took place over June, July, and August.[61]

In the wake of the dissolution of the Edmonton Pride Festival Society in 2020, two new organizations formed: Capital Pride and Edmonton Pride Fest. Capital Pride kicked off the month of June with ceremonies and speakers at City Hall, with a special focus on QTBIPOC community members. Pride Fest focussed its energies on organizing a two-day event at the end of June, returning to Churchill Square for an entertainment garden that included acts like Virginia 2 Vegas and Fefe Dobson. Local 2SLGBTQ+ non-profits and vendors were also on-site at the square, with an afternoon of local entertainment following a pancake breakfast hosted by Capital Pride.

Other community and non-profit groups provided programming throughout June, including a three-day family-friendly event at the Grindstone organized by Fruit Loop, a beer garden and dance party on 104 Street, and a drag queen ballgame at Re/Max Field, featuring Party Queens and the Imperial Sovereign Court of the Wild Rose. The Edmonton Oil Kings, Edmonton Stingers, Edmonton Riverhawks, and Edmonton Oilers all hosted pride events over the summer months. The Oilers hosted the inaugural Pride Cup, held in August featuring a Battle of Alberta for inclusive hockey with the Calgary Pioneers squaring off against the Edmonton Rage in the Edmonton Ice District Plaza.

St. Albert, Fort Saskatchewan, and Strathcona County all hosted their own colourful Pride events as well. Inclusive faith services, a queer choral event hosted by Edmonton Vocal Minority, Edmonton Queer History Project summer walking and bus tours, and multiple drag brunches all over the city helped make this first post-Covid Pride a special summer to remember. An expanded Pride Day at KDAYS in late July helped keep the celebrations going well into the summer.

2023 By June 2023, the pandemic was feeling pretty far behind. Capital Pride, one of the groups that rose up during the pandemic, had already stopped planning events, but Edmonton Pride Fest was still going. Pride Fest opted to move to August; other community groups and businesses, however, hosted their pride events in June. This created a new Summer of Pride with three months of fabulous programming.[62]

More than one hundred events were held during the Summer of Pride, including some new and notable ones. Edmonton's first Drag Festival, a full day of drag performances, was held at Louise McKinney Park; the weather didn't cooperate but that didn't stop dozens of local and celebrity drag performers from entertaining their wet audience. MacEwan University's Centre for Sexual and Gender Diversity held their first Pride patio party, which included a barbeque and drag queen bingo. Evolution Wonderlounge hosted a riverboat party in late August to end the summer. Some favourite parties also returned for a second year, including Drag Me Out to the Ballgame, a collaboration between the Imperial Sovereign Court of the Wild Rose and Party Queens that raised over thirty thousand dollars for charity, and the Pride Cup in partnership with the Oilers Entertainment Group and Pride Tape.

Mid-summer, Pride Day at KDAYS expanded with ten full days of 2SLGBTQ+ programming, including drag acts, DJs, and live musicians. KDAYS hosted its first drag brunch entitled the Empress 1 Millicent's Brunch Royale, in support of the Imperial Sovereign Court of the Wild Rose, celebrating our city's queer history by acknowledging Edmonton's first drag empress. Even Taste of Edmonton incorporated a drag production on the main stage.

Pride Fest anchored the celebrations in August with three nights of programming at Churchill Square, including Alberta's first Two Spirit powwow and a Nineties Night featuring music acts like Snap!, Love Inc., and Prozzak. Pride was back downtown and in the heart of the city!

2024 The Summer of Pride returned to Alberta's Capital City with another three months of spectacular community programming. In its second year, the Edmonton Drag Festival relocated to Churchill Square and grew to three days, which included hosting a Two Spirit powwow and drag brunch, expanding the celebration of the art of drag. Fruit Loop also helped to kick off celebrations in June by continuing its popular Pride Street Fair at Grindstone.

Queer history was featured and celebrated all summer long with free walking and bus tours hosted by the Edmonton Queer History Project, as well as the powerful Len & Cub Photo Exhibit presented by the MacEwan Centre for Sexual and Gender Diversity, plus a new exhibition at Fort Edmonton Park entitled "Regulating Morality," which highlighted 100 years of Edmonton's 2SLGBTQ+ history. The Summer of Pride also featured the debut of two local documentary films, *Pride vs Prejudice: The Delwin Vriend Story* and *Flashback*.

This year, a lot of Edmonton's favourite Pride events returned. June included the third annual Drag Me To The Ballgame, which raised over $30,000 in support of the ISCWR's John M Kerr Memorial Bursary and Bent Arrow Traditional

Healing Society. The Riverhawks held their annual "Strike Out Hate" Pride Night with record attendance of over 5,000 fans. August included the third Annual Pride Cup, where Calgary beat Edmonton for the second year in a row at the Battle of Alberta. Pride Night at KDAYS was bigger than ever, with some epic special guests, including Naomi Smalls and Bosco from *RuPaul's Drag Race*. Drag returned to Taste of Edmonton with Legends of Drag, who also brought their iconic drag excellence to the YEG Xmas Market for the second time, proving that pride in Edmonton truly happens all year long. And to end the summer, Pride Fest returned to Churchill Square in late August for three days of festivities.

Now in its sixth year without a parade, Edmonton held a community engagement meeting to discuss whether the time was right for the return of the Pride parade. Although the meeting highlighted the shared importance of a parade, especially for queer and trans kids and at a time when discriminatory anti-2SLGBTQ+ legislation was introduced by Alberta's UCP government, consensus on how the parade should look or be run could not be achieved. In a year when parades in other cities like Winnipeg, Toronto, Ottawa, and Vancouver were also disrupted by conversations around corporate sponsorship, police participation, and the war in Gaza, we were all reminded that pride has its roots in protest and that it remains a protest in 2024.

BEING GAY IS NOT A CRIME

GAY BASHING IS

EDMONTON
POLICE
SERVICE

In cooperation with the Edmonton Gay and Lesbian Community
to contact the Liason Committee, call 421-2277

GLCCE
(Gay & Lesbian
Community Centre)
Telephone 488-3234

PFLAG/T
(Parents, Friends of
Lesbians & Gays/Transgender)
Telephone 462-5958

While we have been working on this book,
hate crimes targeting 2SLGBTQ+ individuals and communities have been increasing across Canada as the global tide of right-wing populism rises. Almost daily, rainbow crosswalks are vandalized, pride flags are torn down, drag queen story time events are protested, and so-called parental rights protestors and far-right provincial governments seek to erase 2SLGBTQ+ identities from all facets of public life. The UCP government introduced some of the most discriminatory anti-2SLGBTQ+ legislation in Canadian history. After decades of hard-won social progress, Canadian society seems to be moving backwards.

A lot is clearly at stake for 2SLGBTQ+ communities and our allies. This is why our history matters more now than ever. We have always been here. Even when it wasn't safe to be visible. We have always existed and persisted thanks to our community's incredible strength, creativity, and resiliency—to which many of the stories in this book attest.

Our communities and identities are part of what makes our province and country such an incredibly rich, diverse, and beautiful cultural mosaic. We must never lose sight of the fact that our strength as a society lies within our diversity. And this diversity includes our 2SLGBTQ+ communities, which have existed in every faith, religion, culture, and community in the world—both in the past and in the present.

Without a past it is hard to imagine a healthy and hopeful future. Our 2SLGBTQ+ young people need to be able to grow up knowing that they are not alone, that they are part of a rich history of queer, trans and Two Spirit people. When you have access to history and role models, it not only fundamentally changes who you are, but gives you a sense of possibility for the future.

We hope the stories in this book serve not only as an archive but also as a powerful reminder about the incredible strength, resilience, and determination of our 2SLGBTQ+ communities, and as a testament to and celebration of the people, places, moments, and memories that have come to define our city and province. While this book looks to the past, we trust it will also serve as an incitement to build a more inclusive future with the belief that our history is worth preserving and unapologetically celebrating. The fight for equality must continue.

MICHAEL PHAIR PARK

1. Destiny Swiderski, who designed the park's original artwork, is a Métis Canadian artist who explores how public art can be a vehicle for place-making; see http://www.arttouryeg.ca/15-destiny-swiderski.
2. That early meeting around Michael's kitchen table was instrumental in the formation of the AIDS Network of Edmonton. This legacy was captured in the title of Leslie Goldstone's book *Around the Kitchen Table: 25 Years of AIDS in Edmonton* (HIV Network of Edmonton Society, 2010).
3. For more on the history of the Canadian AIDS Society, see https://www.cdnaids.ca/about-us/history.
4. Fil Fraser, "It's Up to Premier Klein to Protect Gays Against Discrimination," *Edmonton Journal*, 15 April 1994, A14.
5. Don Retson, "Bloody Scuffle with Gays Worries Club Owner," *Edmonton Journal*, 11 May 1989, B1.
6. Fraser, "It's up to Premier Klein."
7. Paula Simons, "How the Vriend case established LGBTQ rights 20 years ago in Alberta—and Across Canada," *Edmonton Journal*, 22 March 2018. https://edmontonjournal.com/news/insight/paula-simons-how-the-vriend-case-established-lgbtq-rights-20-years-ago-in-alberta-and-across-canada
8. See Matthew Hays, "The Legacy of Edmonton's Michael Phair," *XTRA*, 28 October 2007, https://xtramagazine.com/power/the-legacy-of-edmontons-michael-phair-17423.
9. While the Vriend decision officially read sexual orientation into Alberta's Individuals Rights Protection Act, it took the Alberta government eleven years to agree to write the actual words into the Act with the passage of Bill 44 in 2009. Bill 44 represented a backwards step for equality, however, when it added the legal right for parents to remove their children from any classroom where human sexuality, sexual orientation, or religion was to be discussed. This legislation was described as homophobic in its attempt to prevent students from learning about 2SLGBTQ+ identities, histories, and cultures.
10. "Michael Phair to Have Edmonton School Named for Him," *CBC News*, 21 June 2015, https://www.cbc.ca/news/canada/edmonton/michael-phair-to-have-edmonton-school-named-for-him-1.3122281.
11. McKibben was narrowly elected in a city by-election in 1994. She became the first openly lesbian city councillor; she was defeated in the 1995 municipal election, however, coming in third place.

GAY ALLIANCE TOWARD EQUALITY

1. Erin Gallagher-Cohoon, "'Ultra Activists' in a 'Very Closeted Place': The Early Years of Edmonton's Gay Alliance Toward Equality, 1972–77," in *Bucking Conservatism: Alternative Stories of Alberta from the 1960s and 1970s* (Edmonton: Athabasca University Press, 2021).
2. Early organizers, often referred to as the founding five, included Michael Roberts, Bob Emery, Bill Booth, Tom Hutchinson, and M.A. Mumert. GATE eventually became a registered society with S.V. Landberg, Constance

Beaulieu, Bob Emery, Bill Booth, and Bob Radke serving as signatories on the official application.

3   Michael Roberts, "Homosexuals," *Edmonton Journal*, December 6, 1971, 4.
4   More information on Manus Sasonkin and his work can be found at https://www.thecanadianencyclopedia.ca/en/article/manus-sasonkin-emc.
5   1972 Press Release from Michael Roberts.
6   "Homosexual Albertans Seek Rights," *Edmonton Journal*, November 4, 1972, 33; Tom Warner, *Never Going Back: A History of Queer Activism in Canada* (Toronto: University of Toronto Press, 2002), 74.
7   "Homosexual Albertans," 33.
8   Valerie J. Korinek, *Prairie Fairies: A History of Queer Communities and People in Western Canada, 1930–1985* (Toronto: University of Toronto Press, 2018), 236.
9   GATE moved and opened its first commercial office space on 109 Street in spring 1974.
10 Some of the women involved in the early days of GATE included Jeannette Perreault and Maureen Malloy, who were part of the Edmonton Lesbian Feminists (ELF).
11 Korinek, *Prairie Fairies*, 239.
12 Gallagher-Cohoon, "'Ultra Activists'."
13 Korinek, *Prairie Fairies*, 359.
14 "Irate Gays Bitter over CBC decision," *Edmonton Journal*, February 22, 1977, 25.
15 Norman Provencher, "In Comes Anita Heavily Guarded," *Edmonton Sun*, 30 April 1978, 4.
16 *GATE Newsletter*, October 1984, 4.
17 "After the Raid," *The Newsletter*, June 1981, 12.
18 "Gate Retains Legal Counsel," *The Newsletter*, June 1981, 1.
19 Korinek, *Prairie Fairies*, 244.
20 Gallagher-Cohoon, "'Ultra Activists'," 133.
21 Sheelagh Caygill, "AIDS Threat Defined by Health Service," *Edmonton Journal*, 31 July 1984, F14.
22 "Gay Group Urges AIDS Awareness," *Edmonton Journal*, 8 May 1985, G2.
23 Chris Zdeb Montgomery, "Gay Groups Want City to Help AIDS Agency," *Edmonton Journal*, 20 August 1985, B8.
24 "Gay Youth of Edmonton," *Fine Print*, May 1983, 19. https://archive.org/details/fine-print-1983-05
25 *GATE Newsletter*, August 1984.
26 *GATE Newsletter*, February-March 1985, 3.
27 Korinek, *Prairie Fairies*, 235–246.

AIDS NETWORK OF EDMONTON

1   David Quigley, "Doctor Suspected of Having AIDS," *Edmonton Sun*, May 9, 1985, 2.
2   "Doctor Sues Newspaper for $2 Million," *Edmonton Journal*, 28 June 1985, B3.
3   Valerie Korinek, *Prairie Fairies: A History of Queer Communities and Peoples in Western Canada, 1930–1985* (Toronto: University of Toronto Press, 2018), 389.
4   Korinek, *Prairie Fairies*, 26.
5   Edmonton Public Library, *Queer History in Edmonton: The Founding of the AIDS Network*, 16 July 2020, https://www.youtube.com/watch?v=t-kVH-4QBCAA.
6   "HIV/AIDS Support," Catholic Social Services, https://www.cssalberta.ca/Our-Services/HIV-AIDS-Support.
7   Edmonton Public Library, *Queer History in Edmonton*.
8   Greg Barker, "Ross, a big splash!" *Roughnecks Newsletter*, October 1982, 1; see archive.org/details/roughnecksvol3no35unse.

9   Jamie Sarkonak, "Edmonton's Forgotten Epidemic," *The Gateway*, 16 March 2016, https://thegatewayonline.ca/2016/03/feature-edmontons-forgotten-epidemic/.

10 "Faces of Edmonton."

11 Lasha Morningstar, "City AIDS Victim Facing the Future," *Edmonton Journal*, 18 April 1986. E13.

12 HIV Network of Edmonton Society, https://www.hivedmonton.com/get-help/ross-armstrong-centre.

13 The stories of Barry, David, Allison, and Dennis are drawn from Valerie Gervais, "AIDS Grief and Multiple Loss: The Experiences of Individuals Within an AIDS Service Organization" (Master's Thesis, University of Regina, 1985).

14 Jason Clevett, "23rd Annual AIDS Benefit: Roost Fundraises for AIDS Research," *GayCalgary.com Magazine*, November 2006, http://www.gaycalgary.com/Magazine.aspx?id=37&article=140

15 Heritage Savings Trust Fund Act, 1988, https://docs.assembly.ab.ca/LADDAR_files/docs/committees/hs/legislature_21/session_2/19880107_1400_01_hs.pdf (page 145).

16 "Awards," HIV Edmonton, https://hivedmonton.com/about/awards.

17 Sarkonak, "Edmonton's Forgotten Epidemic."

IMPERIAL SOVEREIGN COURT OF THE WILD ROSE

1   The Executive Hotel is now known as the Coast Plaza Executive Hotel and has been the host for many ISCWR coronation balls.

2   Founded in 1965, the International Court System is one of the longest-running 2SLGBTQ+ charitable networks in the world. For more information on Edmonton's chapter, see: Ron Byers, "The Imperial Sovereign Court of the Wild Rose, Part 1: The First Twenty-Five Years," Edmonton City as Museum Project, November 18, 2020, https://citymuseumedmonton.ca/2020/11/18/the-imperial-sovereign-court-of-the-wild-rose-part-1-the-first-twenty-five-years.

3   While perhaps not as well known as drag performance or the vogue ball scene popularized in the movie *Paris Is Burning* (1991) and in the television series *Pose* (2018–21), the International Court System has been a mainstay of North American drag culture and one of the community's most successful fundraising initiatives.

4   Bob Remington, "Homosexual Ball Attracts Little Attention," *Edmonton Journal*, 8 August 1977, 19.

5   Remington, "Homosexual Ball."

6   Remington, "Homosexual Ball."

7   Michael Phair, "Giving: The Ross Armstrong Fund," *Times.10*, December 1994–January 1995, 6, 21.

8   "Red Carpet Diaries." *Edmonton Journal*, 14 March 2009, F7.

9   John Kerr was a well-liked and respected member of the court and community, who once worked the door at Club '70, welcoming members to the club for many years. See this feature story about John "Grandma" Kerr: Darrin Hagen "After the Pisces Bathhouse Raid: John Kerr—Dance for Grandma," Edmonton City as Museum Project, 18 May 2021. https://citymuseumedmonton.ca/2021/05/18/after-the-pisces-bathhouse-raid-john-kerr-dance-for-gramma

10 Byers, "The Imperial Sovereign Court."

11 Rob Browatzke, "The Imperial Sovereign Court of the Wild Rose, Part 2: The Next Twenty Years," Edmonton City as Museum Project, 25 November 2020, https://citymuseumedmonton.ca/2020/11/25/the-imperial-sovereign-court-of-the-wild-rose-part-2-the-next-twenty-years.

12 Valerie J. Korinek, *Prairie Fairies: A History of Queer Communities and People in Canada, 1930–1985* (Toronto: University of Toronto Press, 2018), 385.

13 Learn more about the CHEW Project at https://www.ualberta.ca/fyrefly-institute/programs-and-services/chew-project.html.

14 History: Imperial Sovereign Court of the Wild Rose," https://iscwryeg.ca/history.

EDMONTON 2 SPIRIT SOCIETY

1 amiskwacîy-wâskahikan ᐊᒥᐢᑿᒌ·ᐄᐧᐄᐧᐢᑲᐦᐃᑲᐣ, Edmonton is Treaty 6 Territory; this is the traditional meeting ground, gathering place, and travelling route of the nehiyawak (Cree), Anishinaabe (Saulteaux), Niitsitapi (Blackfoot), Métis, Dene, and Nakota Sioux.

2 "History: 2 Spirit History in Edmonton," Edmonton 2 Spirit Society, https://e2s.ca/about.

3 Edward Lavallee, "Indigenous Pride: Plains Cree Believe Two Spirit People Inhabit Both Male and Female Spirits," *The Rainbow Effect: Commemorative Issue 2015—Together in Pride* 35, 21. Cheyenne Mihko Kihêw, community liaison for E2S, describes the term Two Spirit as a placeholder. They state, "it's not a term that is meant to be concrete for every person. It is meant to act as a placeholder for us as we explore our own traditional languages and teachings. For those who are on that journey, who are figuring out their different genders and teachings—there's a name for that and that's Two Spirit" (personal communication, 19 August 2021) The term Two Spirit is also described by Geo Neptune, a Two Spirit Passamaquoddy educator, as an umbrella term meant to bridge understandings between Indigenous people and non-Indigenous people, to help educate non-Indigenous people about the cultural teachings regarding gender and sexual diversity of First Nations people. In 1990, the term Two Spirit was proposed and approved by consensus at the Third Annual Native American Gay and Lesbian Gathering (now the International Two Spirit Gathering) to address the challenges of naming the vast diversity of gender and sexual identities and expressions of Indigenous people across First Nations. Although Two Spirit may be a contemporary term, it was chosen by Indigenous people because it was thought to reflect long-held beliefs and cultural teachings of many First Nations. See Geo Neptune, "inQueery: What Does Two Spirit Mean," https://guides.library.utoronto.ca/2spirit. Cheyenne Mihko Kihêw traces the contemporary use of the term Two Spirit to 1989, when Elder Myra Laramee "saw this term in a pipe ceremony and with great clarity and strength in her mind said, 'You are as we are and you have been here as long as we have. You are as time immemorial as we are.' And she knew that it was the ancestors coming to talk to her." Elder Myra Laramee later shared her vision and Two Spirit teachings with Elders and Knowledge Carriers at the Third Annual Native American Gay and Lesbian Gathering and the term was adopted (personal communication, January 10, 2022).

4 In an educational video created by E2S, kêhtêyayah (Elder) Jo-Ann Saddleback describes ihkwew—all genders/Two Spirit within Cree society. Expanding on these on teachings, Elder Saddleback highlights eight neheyaw (Cree) genders; these are man, woman, Two Spirit, intersex, asexual or agender, contrary, androgynous, and transgender. The language around the eight neheyaw genders continues to evolve (Cheyenne Mihko Kihêw, personal communication, January 10, 2022). See Edmonton 2 Spirit Society, "Two Spirit Identity," https://youtu.be/8N7JcYbdlmo?si=2bd0roIARAcPVXp1.

5 Lavallee, "Indigenous Pride," 21.

6 Lavallee recalls that many Two Spirit people and wihtikokanak (contraries) perform as Spirit Dancers. See Lavallee, "Indigenous Pride," 21.

7 Lavallee, "Indigenous Pride," 21.

8 Niya Frida Sakebow, a nehiyaw (Cree) Knowledge Carrier, states, "I believe

some of the reasons why Two Spirit awareness and Two Spirit knowledge went underground is the impact of colonization and especially residential schools." See Edmonton 2 Spirit Society, "Two Spirit Identity," https://youtu.be/8N7JcYbdlmo?si=2bdorolARAcPVXp1.

9 Lavallee, "Indigenous Pride," 21. Rob Gurney, an E2S community member, describes a gentle teaching he practises using the acronym 2SLGBTQ, instead of LGBTQ2S, to remind people inside and outside of the queer community that Two Spirit people were here first. Cheyenne Mihko Kihêw notes they often write 2S-LGBTQ, instead of the more common 2SLGBTQ+ acronym, to remind people that some who identify as Two Spirit may not identify or feel comfortable defining themselves with LGBTQ acronyms and identities.

10 Lavallee, "Indigenous Pride," 21

11 Lavallee, "Indigenous Pride," 21.

12 Edmonton 2 Spirit Society, "Who We Are," https://e2s.ca/about-us.

13 Rob was the Kokum of Indigi-Hauz, an all-Indigenous drag performance house co-founded by Rob Gurney and Boyd Whiskeyjack. Indigi-Hauz (now 1+1=2S) performed a show at the Legislature Grounds as a fundraiser to support the office space for E2S, originally located across from Beaver Hills Park. The fundraiser also included a silent auction supported in part by the Imperial Sovereign Court of the Wild Rose.

14 Rob Gurney, personal communication, 19 August 2021.

15 The Sixties Scoop is a shameful part of Canada's history that began in the late 1950s and persisted into the mid-1980s in some provinces. See Christopher Dart, "The Sixties Scoop Explained," http://www.cbc.ca/cbc docspov/features/the sixties-scoop-explained. The Sixties Scoop was a Government of Canada policy that enabled child welfare agencies to take Indigenous children away from their families and communities and place them in foster homes for adoption to Caucasian families. The term was coined in 1983 by researcher Patrick Johnson in a report on Indigenous child welfare. In 1985 Justice Edwin Kimelman released a review of Indigenous child apprehension by child welfare agencies called *No Safe Place: Review Committee on Indian and Metis Adoptions and Placements*. Justice Kimelman stated: "cultural genocide has been taking place in a systematic, routine manner" and this treatment represented "an abysmal lack of sensitivity to children and families." The Kimelman Report ended the Sixties Scoop. Importantly, while Canada's Truth and Reconciliation Commission (TRC) cites the Sixties Scoop alongside residential schools as a source of intergenerational trauma reverberating still in lives of Indigenous peoples and their communities, Cheyenne Mihko Kihêw notes that the TRC and the United Nations Declaration of the Rights of Indigenous Peoples make no mention of Two Spirit peoples, effectively erasing the significance of Two Spirit identity in any mention of reconciliation or reparations (Cheyenne Mihko Kihêw, personal communication, 19 August 2021).

16 Gurney, personal communication.

17 Gurney, personal communication.

18 Gurney, personal communication.

19 Kihêw, personal communication.

20 The Two Spirit teaching on eight genders is specifically a Cree concept; within this teaching, each of the genders has its own teachings (Kihêw, personal communication).

21 Kihêw, personal communication.

22 Edmonton 2 Spirit Society, "Who We Are."

23 Edmonton 2 Spirit Society, "Who We Are."

24 Edmonton 2 Spirit Society, "Who We Are."

25 Edmonton 2 Spirit Society, "Who We Are."

26 Edmonton 2 Spirit Society, "Who We Are."

27 Edmonton 2 Spirit Society, "Who We Are."

28 Edmonton 2 Spirit Society, "Who We Are."

29 In 2017, for the first time in the history of Edmonton's Pride Festival, a member of Edmonton's Two Spirit community, Boyd Whiskeyjack, was asked to be the Grand Marshal and lead Edmonton's Pride Parade.

30 Elise Stolte, "Forum Focuses on 'Two-Spirit' Life," *Edmonton Journal*, November 3, 2021, A5. Cheyenne Mihko Kihêw explains, "Within our own communities, there is a lateral violence that comes from not understanding what Two Spirit is. We have extremely gendered spaces that come out of the residential school system, because that isn't really something that existed before colonization. We had teaching around men's roles and women's roles and we had different Two Spirit teachings depending on what Nation you were in, but when residential schools happened, it was boy/girls, short hair/bob; there was no room for the in-between people. Where did we go?" (personal communication).

31 "E2S Facebook," https://www.facebook.com/E2S.ca.

32 Kihêw, personal communication.

33 Gurney, personal communication.

34 Gurney, personal communication.

METROPOLITAN COMMUNITY CHURCH & DIGNITY EDMONTON

1 MCC began when Pentecostal pastor Troy Perry was defrocked because of his sexuality. Pastor Perry had a spiritual awakening following a suicide attempt, inspiring him to host a spiritual service in his Los Angeles home for twelve people who had left or been rejected by their church communities. Perry's first sermon focussed on being true to yourself, and interest and attendance grew quickly, with more than two hundred people soon attending; requests began to come from individuals in other cities to open new chapters. MCC services are ecumenical, open to everyone, and focussed on helping people from all denominations, sexual orientations, and gender identities to feel at home in their faith. MCC reports that at least twenty percent of its congregants identify as heterosexual. See Metropolitan Community Churches, "History of MCC," https://insidemcc.org/about-mcc/mcc-history.

2 Charles Bidwell, "A Brief History of Metropolitan Community Church of Edmonton," April 2015.

3 Canadian stops on the tour included Toronto/Peterborough (January), Edmonton and Winnipeg (April), and Moose Jaw (July) to "celebrate" the city's hundredth birthday. See Valerie Korinek, *Prairie Fairies: A History of Queer Communities and People in Western Canada, 1930–1985* (Toronto: University of Toronto Press, 2018), 283–287, 327.

4 Korinek, *Prairie Fairies*, 326–27.

5 Korinek, *Prairie Fairies*, 326–27.

6 "Police Guard Anita Bryant in Edmonton," *Globe and Mail*, 1 May 1978.

7 Julia Pyryeskina, "'A Remarkable Dense Historical and Political Juncture': Anita Bryant, The Body Politic, and the Canadian Lesbian and Gay Community in January 1978," *Canadian Journal of History* 53, no. 1 (2018): 58–85.

8 "Alberta Passes Law Allowing Parents to Pull Kids Out of Class," *CBC News*, 2 June 2009, https://www.cbc.ca/news/canada/alberta-passes-law-allowing-parents-to-pull-kids-out-of-class-1.777604.

9 Protests occurred at each stop of the Canadian tour. In Toronto, more than one thousand people came out to protest Bryant's visit, representing the city's largest gay rights demonstration to date. See Pyryeskina, "A Remarkable Dense Historical and Political Juncture."

10 *The Body Politic*, May 1978, Internet Archives, https://archive.org/details/bodypolitic43toro. Footage of these protests is available through the Provincial Archives of Alberta.

11 Pyryeskina, "Remarkable Dense Historical."
12 "Chapter Activities and Highlights," May 1979 to June 1980; *Conference Program: Sixth Annual Dignity Canada Dignité Conference*, Edmonton, Alberta, 1982. Both from MS-595, GALA, Series 12, Box 37, File 81, Edmonton City Archives, Prince of Wales Armouries Heritage Centre, Edmonton, Alberta, Canada.
13 Bidwell, "A Brief History."
14 Bidwell, "A Brief History."
15 "Mission Statement," Diversity Conferences of Alberta Society http://web.archive.org/web/20220525143215/https://sites.ualberta.ca/~cbidwell/DCAS.
16 David Staples, "Gay-Rights Supporters Fuelled by Simple Love," *Edmonton Journal*, 8 March 1998, A6.
17 Bidwell, "A Brief History"; Mission Statement," Diversity Conferences of Alberta Society, http://web.archive.org/web/20220525143215/https://sites.ualberta.ca/~cbidwell/DCAS/.
18 Emil Tiedemann, "A few minutes with Mickey Wilson," I Heart Edmonton, http://iheartedmonton.ca/2015/07/a-few-minutes-with-mickey-wilson.html.
19 Bidwell, "A Brief History."
20 Dignity Canada Dignité was founded in April 1981 with chapters in Edmonton, Calgary, Vancouver, Regina, Winnipeg, Ottawa, Toronto, London, and Montreal (with two French and English chapters). Dignity Edmonton Dignité was also a chapter of Region 11 of Dignity USA. For more information on Dignity Edmonton, see "Application for Incorporation as a Society under the Societies Act Being Chapter 347 of the Revised Statutes of Alberta, 1970, and Amendments Thereof," 6 May, 1980, MS-595, GALA, Series 12, Box 37, File 81, Edmonton City Archives, Prince of Wales Armouries Heritage Centre, Edmonton, Alberta, Canada.
21 "Statement of Position and Purpose," n.d., MS-595, GALA, Series 12, Box 37, File 81, Edmonton City Archives, Prince of Wales Armouries Heritage Centre, Edmonton, Alberta, Canada.
22 "Statement of Position and Purpose."
23 "Dignity Edmonton Calendar of Events," October/November 1984; "Dignity Schedule—Edmonton," January 1988. Both from MS-595, GALA, Series 12, Box 37, File 81, Edmonton City Archives, Prince of Wales Armouries Heritage Centre, Edmonton, Alberta, Canada.
24 Bernard Dousse, "Letter to Members and Friends, Dignity—Edmonton—Dignité," 10 September 1987, MS-595, GALA, Series 12, Box 37, File 81, Edmonton City Archives, Prince of Wales Armouries Heritage Centre, Edmonton, Alberta, Canada.
25 Dignity was invited to host meetings at Catholic Social Services with support from the CEO, Father Bill Irwin, who also helped to establish Kairos House, which supports persons living with HIV/AIDS. Father Irwin also endorsed Michael Phair's 1992 inaugural election campaign.
26 Joseph Cardinal Ratzinger, "Congregation for the Doctrine of the Faith: Letter to the Bishops of the Catholic Church on Pastoral Care to Homosexual Persons," 1 October 1986, https://www.vatican.va/roman_curia/congregations/cfaith/documents/rc_con_cfaith_doc_19861001_homosexual-persons_en.html.
27 "Dignity Edmonton Calendar of Events," November/December 1985, MS-595, GALA, Series 12, Box 37, File 81, Edmonton City Archives, Prince of Wales Armouries Heritage Centre, Edmonton, Alberta, Canada.
28 "Dignity Edmonton Calendar of Events."
29 Conference Program: Sixth Annual Dignity Canada Dignité Conference. Edmonton, AB, 1982, MS-595, GALA, Series 12, Box 37, File 81, Edmonton City Archives, Prince of Wales Armouries Heritage Centre, Edmonton, Alberta, Canada.

30 Stephen Weatherbe, "The Error of their Ways," *Alberta Report*, 7 June 1982, MS-595, GALA, Series 12, Box 37, File 81, Edmonton City Archives, Prince of Wales Armouries Heritage Centre, Edmonton, Alberta, Canada.

31 Joe Sornberger, "Gay Catholics struggle for Dignity," *Edmonton Journal*, 9 January 1982, F11.

32 Roma de Robertis, "Local Gay Says Church Persecutes," *Western Catholic Reporter*, 31 May 1982, MS-595, GALA, Series 12, Box 37, File 81, Edmonton City Archives, Prince of Wales Armouries Heritage Centre, Edmonton, Alberta, Canada.

33 Leslie Goldstone, *Around the Kitchen Table: 25 Years of AIDS in Edmonton* (Edmonton: HIV Network of Edmonton Society, 2010).

34 "Synopsis of the November 9, 1982 Meeting," 1982, MS-595, GALA, Series 12, Box 37, File 81, Edmonton City Archives, Prince of Wales Armouries Heritage Centre, Edmonton, Alberta, Canada. By 1984, this library was held at member Dennis' house ("Dignity Edmonton Calendar of Events," October/November 1984, MS-595, GALA, Series 12, Box 37, File 81, Edmonton City Archives, Prince of Wales Armouries Heritage Centre, Edmonton, Alberta, Canada). It is unclear how often or how many times the location of the library moved.

35 "The Church and the Gay Catholics of 'Dignity,'" n.d., MS-595, GALA, Series 12, Box 37, File 81, Edmonton City Archives, Prince of Wales Armouries Heritage Centre, Edmonton, Alberta, Canada.

PISCES HEALTH SPA

1 This article is adapted with permission from: Darrin Hagen, "The Pisces Bathhouse Raid: Igniting Four Decades of Activism," *Edmonton City as Museum Project*, 2021, https://citymuseumedmonton.ca/2021/05/18/the-pisces-bathhouse-raid-igniting-four-decades-of-activism.

2 Michael Rocke, *Forbidden Friendships: Homosexuality and Male Culture in Renaissance Florence* (Oxford: Oxford University Press, 1998), 203.

3 David Higgs, *Queer Sites: Gay Urban Histories Since 1600* (London: Routledge, 2009), 30.

4 George Chauncey, *Gay New York: Gender Urban Culture and the Making of the Gay Male World 1890–1940* (New York: Basic Books, 1994), 214.

5 Gymini Health and Sauna was originally located in the basement of 10166 100 Street and operated from the mid-1970s until 1981. See Hagen, "The Pisces Bathhouse Raid."

6 Pisces Health Spa was owned by Dr. Henri Toupin and his partner Eric Stein. Dr. Toupin is reported to have invested $130,000 to renovate and open the spa (roughly $400,000 in 2025 dollars). Dr. Toupin was a prominent neurologist whose medical practice was located in the front of the same building. As a private member's club, Pisces was reported to have a membership list of more than 2000 patrons and revenue of $20,000 a month.

7 Tom Hooper, "Bathhouse Raids in Canada, 1968–2004," https://anti-69.ca/wp-content/uploads/2019/01/Chart_Bathhouse_raids_in_Canada_1968-200-3.pdf.

8 Hooper, "Bathhouse Raids."

9 Griffis's identity was revealed via subpoena from a defence lawyer during a trial for one of the found-ins. There are different theories concerning Griffis's motivations. One report alleges Griffis's boyfriend was a regular member of Pisces; Griffis was jealous and wanted revenge. Other reports suggest Griffis went to Pisces several times at the request of the police to collect information, thereby making him an agent of the state. Griffis stated that places like Pisces gave the gay community a bad name and suggested he was just being a "good citizen" by making the complaint to the police. See G. Hannon, "More guilty in Pisces Trials but Court Lowers Owners' Fines," *The Body Politic*, October 1981, 14.

10 Rae Hull, Darcy Henton, and Robin Barstow, "Gay Spy Led Police to Raid Spa," *Edmonton Journal*, 4 June 1981, B1.

11 Gerald Hannon, "Edmonton: Bath Raids Move West," *The Body Politic*, No. 75, July 1981, 7.

12 Hagen, "Pisces Bathhouse Raid." EPS members were assigned to work in pairs, reportedly for their safety. They would often pose as couples when attending the spa and made detailed notes and maps of the facility. At least ten officers are documented to have gone undercover, each with his own elaborate cover story. During one evening at the Spa, an undercover officer reported seeing a local corrections officer he recognized. They are reported to have had a conversation to ensure the officer's cover was not revealed.

13 No charges of prostitution were ever laid in the Pisces raid, which some commentators argue is an example of how common bawdy house laws were used to unfairly target non-normative forms of sexuality, and in particular gay and bisexual men. In 2013, the Supreme Court of Canada struck down the common bawdy house provisions in the Criminal Code, and in 2014 Bill C-36, The Protection of Communities and Exploited Persons Act, was passed in the House of Commons and received Royal Assent into law.

14 Hagen, "Pisces Bathhouse Raid."

15 Hagen, "Pisces Bathhouse Raid."

16 Initial members of the Privacy Defence Committee included George Davison, Andy Hopykins, and Michael Phair.

17 Lois Sweet, "Gay Spa Raid a Step Toward Erosion of Individual Privacy," *Edmonton Journal*, 8 June 1981, A6.

18 Rae Hull, "Gays Say Raid Strengthens Cause," *Edmonton Journal*, 27 June 1981, A11.

19 Gilbert Bouchard, "Effects of '81 Spa Raid Still Concern Local Gays," *Edmonton Journal*, 30 May 1986, G12.

20 Michael Phair, "Pisces Revisited: The Conclusion," *Fine Print*, April 1983, 8, https://archive.org/details/fine-print-1983-04.

21 Rae Hull, "Guilty Pleas Betray Gays." *Edmonton Journal*, 9 June 1981, B2.

22 "Crown Calls Pisces Place for 'Depraved,'" *Edmonton Journal*, 31 July 1981, B6.

23 Hagen, "Pisces Bathhouse Raid."

24 Phair, "Pisces Revisited," 8.

25 Upon appeal, fines were reduced by more than half: Pisces Health Spa Ltd. ($6,000), Toupin ($4,000), Stein ($1,500), and Kerr ($4,000).

26 The last legal appeal of a found-in is documented to have concluded in 1985, four years after the initial police raid and arrests occurred.

27 Robin Barstow, "Raid Drove Gays Back into Closet," *Edmonton Journal*, 30 May 1982, B1.

28 Bouchard, "Effects," G12. The average cost of a court trial in 1981 was reported to be $12,000. With inflation, that amounts to roughly $35,000 in 2025. If we multiply that figure by sixty (not including appeal trials), the total cost would have been approximately $720,000 in 1981 or more than $2.5 million dollars in 2025. See "Court Costs Soar," *Edmonton Sun*, 10 September 1981, 4.

29 "Police Chief Apologizes to City's LGBTQ2S+ Community," *CTV News*, 3 May 2019, https://edmonton.ctvnews.ca/police-chief-apologizes-to-city-s-2SLGBTQ+s-community-1.4407102.

30 Dylan Short, "'Our Actions Caused Pain': Edmonton Police Chief Apologizes to LGBTQ Community," *Edmonton Journal*, May 3, 2019, https://edmontonjournal.com/news/local-news/edmontons-new-police-chief-to-apologize-to-lgbtq-community-today.

31 Michael Phair, "Pisces Revisited: Part II," *Fine Print*, March 1983, 5.

1   In 1996, the IRPA was changed to become the Alberta Human Rights Act.
2   "Gain for Gays Loss to Others," *Edmonton Journal*, November 24, 1979, B3.
3   "Gain for Gays," B3
4   "Gain for Gays," B3
5   Wendy Koenig, "Gays Surrounded by Fear Without Human Rights Law," *Edmonton Journal*, 7 February 1980, B5.
6   Agnes Buttner, "Gays Seek Legal Job Protection," *Edmonton Journal*, 24 January 1985, B1.
7   Bob Boehm, "Fear Blocks Rights: Gay Spokesman," *Edmonton Journal*, 18 July 1987, B2.
8   Boehm, "Fear Blocks Rights," B2.
9   Karen Sherlock, "Legal Status Won in 1969, But Rights Still Unprotected; Gays Say Homophobia, AIDS May Prove Deadly Combination; Quest for Rights Still Explosive"[Special Report], *Edmonton Journal*, 20 August 1989, A1.
10 Sherlock, "Legal Status," A1.
11 Sherlock, "Legal Status," A1.
12 Sherlock, "Legal Status," A1.
13 Lynda Shorten, "MLA Ejected for 1st Time in 38 Years in Dispute Over Rights Law for Gays," *Edmonton Journal*, 11 April 1990, A7.
14 Brian Laghi, "Gays Could Face 10-year Wait on Rights, MLA Says," *Edmonton Journal*, 24 May 1990, A8.
15 Bruce MacDougall, *Queer Judgements: Homosexuality Expression and the Courts in Canada* (Toronto: University of Toronto Press, 2000), 107.
16 This was an impressive legal team. Stollery would go on to become the first 2SLGBTQ+ Chancellor in the history of the University of Alberta and would receive the Order of Canada for his human rights work. Julie Lloyd represented the Canadian Bar Association at the Supreme Court of Canada. Sheila Greckol and Julie Lloyd were both appointed as judges to the Alberta Provincial Court, with Justice Greckol rising to the Provincial Court of Appeal, the same court that had previously overturned the Vriend decision and ruled against him.
17 Bruce MacDougall, *Queer Judgements: Homosexuality Expression and the Courts in Canada* (Toronto: University of Toronto Press, 2000), 107.
18 "Labor Minister Says Discrimination Against Gays Not a Problem in Alberta," *Canadian Press NewsWire*, May 1, 1996.
19 Paula Simons, "From the Archives: The Vriend Case is About Bigotry," *Edmonton Journal*, March 15, 2018, https://edmontonjournal.com/news/insight/from-the-archives-the-vriend-case-is-about-bigotry
20 It would take the provincial government eleven more years to write the words "sexual orientation" into the Alberta Human Rights Act, and they did so by passing Bill 44, which introduced parental notification requirements any time sexual orientation, human sexuality, or religion was taught in schools. These parental opt-out provisions were an attempt to limit a student's exposure to 2SLGBTQ+ issues and were modelled after similar "don't say gay" laws in the United States.
21 Steve Chase, "Klein Won't Fight Ruling on Gays: 'Ha-Ha, I win!' Says Delwin Vriend as High Court Rules Alberta Must Explicitly Include Homosexuals in Human Rights Law," *Calgary Herald*, 3 April 1998, A1.
22 Paula Simons, "How the Vriend Case Established LGBTQ Rights 20 Years Ago in Alberta—and Across Canada " *Edmonton Journal*, 15 March 2018. https://edmontonjournal.com/news/insight/paula-simons-how-the-vriend-case-established-lgbtq-rights-20-years-ago-in-alberta-and-across-canada
23 Lisa Gregoire, "Klein Will Use Charter to Ban Gay Marriages: Premier to Use Notwithstanding Clause to Protect 'Sanctity of Marriage'," *Ottawa Citizen*, 19 July 2002, A5.

24 Jason Fekete, "Federal and Provincial Tories at Odds Over Same-Sex Marriage," *Calgary Herald*, 15 December 2004, A6.

25 Jason Markusoff, "Gov't Positions Itself to Override Same-Sex Marriage," *Edmonton Journal*, 27 July 2005, A6.

26 Charles Russnell, "Are Gay Parents as Good? The Experts Say Yes," *Edmonton Journal*, 22 September 1997, A12.

27 Charlie Gillis, "Lesbian Mom Appeals Provincial Ruling," *Edmonton Journal*, 21 March 1997, A6.

28 This announcement did not apply to public (that is, government) adoptions involving same-sex couples, which had never been approved by the province. That policy changed in 2007.

29 Shawn Ohler, "Alberta Shift on Same-Sex Adoption a Ploy to Head off Judges: Minister: Key Term is 'Step-Parents': Gay Rights Activists Applaud Surprise Announcement," *National Post*, 23 April 1999, A11.

30 Mike Sadava, "Gay Couple Leaps 'Walls' to Adopt Son: Breakthrough Case Faced Gov't Obstacles," *Edmonton Journal*, 19 February 2007, A1.

31 Kathy Mueller, "Smith Douses 'Lake of Fire'," *Edmonton Sun*, 16 April 2012.

32 Kelly Cryderman, "Alberta NDP, UCP Square Off Over Gay-Straight Alliances Bill," *Globe and Mail*, 2 November 2017. https://www.theglobe andmail.com/news/alberta/alberta-ndp-tables-bill-to-protect-privacy-of-students-joining-gay-straight-alliances/article36823213

33 Janet French, "UCP would roll back school protections for LGBTQ students, add new provincial exams," *Edmonton Journal*, 25 March 2019, https://edmontonjournal.com/news/local-news/ucp-would-roll-back-school-protections-for-lgbtq-students-add-new-provincial-exams. The Kenney government's Bill 8 (nicknamed "Bill Hate") undid much of the Notley government's work to support GSAs, including removing the time limit for school principals to grant a student's request to start one, and even removing the guarantee that words like *gay* or *queer* could be used in the club's name. The passage of Bill 8 led to the UCP being banned from participating in Pride festivities across the province. As a further attack on the 2SLGBTQ+ community, the UCP quickly put an end to a provincial working group, established under the Notley government, to provide recommendations to prohibit so-called conversion therapy practices, which are designed to change, supress, or deny same-sex attraction or gender affirmation.

33 Sammy Hudes, "UCP Raises Pride Flag Outside McDougall Centre, But Political Parties Still Banned from Marching in Parade," *Calgary Herald*, 26 August 2019. https://calgaryherald.com/news/local-news/ucp-raises-pride-flag-outside-mcdougall-centre-but-political-parties-still-banned-from-marching-in-parade

34 Janet French, "Alberta premier says legislation on gender policies for children, youth coming this fall," *CBC News*, 1 February 2024. https://www.cbc.ca/news/canada/edmonton/danielle-smith-1.7101595.

35 Kristopher Wells, "Statements About Premier Danielle Smith's Trans & 2SLGBTQ+ Policy Proposals," MacEwan University. https://www.macewan.ca/c/documents/dr-kristopher-wells-statements.pdf

36 "Alberta premier, UCP banned from 2024 Pride events," *CBC News*, 19 May 2024. https://www.cbc.ca/news/canada/calgary/alberta-pride-event-ban-danielle-smith-ucp-1.7208832#

CITY HALL

1 John Zazula, "June 26, 1993: Pride Day Marches with Edmonton's First Mayoral Proclamation," CBC News Archive. https://www.cbc.ca/news/canada/edmonton/throwback-thursday-edmonton-pride-parade-proclamation-1.4182694

2   Marta Gold, "Newest Alderman Plunges Right in: Ward 3 Winner Takes Her Oath Just in Time for First Meeting Monday," *Edmonton Journal*, January 23, 1994, B1.

3   Ralph Armstrong (Ed.), "Mayor's Gay Day Proclamation Has Edmontonians in a Tizzy," *Edmonton Journal*, 8 June 1993, A11.

4   Zazula, "June 26, 1993."

5   City employees made these anti-discrimination measures part of their CUPE Local collective bargaining negotiations. Public service unions have long been on the front lines of pushing for 2SLGBTQ+ equality in Canada. Toronto City Council passed a similar motion in 1973, Vancouver in 1989, and Calgary in 1990.

6   Helen Metella, "Gay Groups Applaud City Hiring Policy," *Edmonton Journal*, 29 May 1991, B3.

7   Ashley Geddes, "City Hall to Provide Same-Sex Benefits," *Edmonton Journal*, 7 July 1998, B1.

8   "Anti-Gay Pride Protesters Bring Petition to Edmonton City Hall," Canadian Press NewsWire, 9 June 2004.

9   Liz Nicholls, "Hagen's the Man When it Comes to Drag: Edmonton Queen Gets an Overhaul for the Stage," *Edmonton Journal*, 11 July 2000, C3.

10 "About EVM." Edmonton Vocal Minority, http://evmchoir.com/About.htm

11 Two scholarships were created at the University of Alberta in the name of Michael Phair and Stephen Mandel, in recognition of their long-standing support for the 2SLGBTQ+ community. https://www.ualberta.ca/en/fyrefly-institute/scholarships-and-awards/index.html

12 Jeff Labine, "Edmonton officially bans conversion therapy," *Calgary Herald*, 10 December 2019, https://calgaryherald.com/news/local-news/banning-conversion-therapy/wcm/a7948338-7887-4ab4-9245-92b9e86d1a6b.

EDMONTON COURTHOUSE

1   The original Edmonton Courthouse was established in 1913 and eventually replaced by Edmonton City Centre Mall.

2   See, for example, Brenda Cossman, Shannon Bell, Lise Gotell, and Becki L. Ross, *Bad Attitude/s on Trial: Pornography, Feminism, and the Butler Decision* 2nd ed. (Toronto: University of Toronto Press, 2017); Bruce MacDougall, *Queer Judgements: Homosexuality, Expression, and the Courts in Canada* (Toronto: University of Toronto Press, 2000). See also work by Ummni Khan, Kyle Kirkup, Robert Leckey, Viviane Namaste, and Bruce Ryder.

3   Gary Kinsman and Patrizia Gentile, *The Canadian War on Queers: National Security as Sexual Regulation* (Vancouver: University of British Columbia Press, 2010).

4   Vriend v. Alberta [1998] 1 SCR 493, https://scc-csc.lexum.com/scc-csc/scc-csc/en/item/1607/index.do.

5   See, for example, Valerie Korinek's *Prairie Fairies: A History of Queer Communities and People in Western Canada, 1930–1985* (Toronto: University of Toronto Press, 2018), 377–83.

6   R. v. Graham [1977] ALTASCAD 90, https://canlii.ca/t/fp3b7.

7   In 1954, gross indecency was changed in the Criminal Code to include "anyone," meaning women, including lesbians and bisexuals, could now be charged. Divorce laws were also changed in 1968, adding "engaging in a homosexual act" as new grounds for a divorce, which was designed to protect heterosexual men who were married to a "practicing lesbian."

8   Lyle Dick, "The 1942 Same-Sex Trials in Edmonton: On the State's Repression of Sexual Minorities, Archives, and Human Rights in Canada," *Archivaria* 68 (2009): 186.

9   Paula Simons, "Witch hunt at the strand lifts curtain on an ugly chapter of Edmonton history," *Edmonton Journal*, 15 August 2015. https://

edmontonjournal.com/news/edmonton/alberta/simons-witch-hunt-at-the-strand-lifts-curtain-on-an-ugly-chapter-of-edmonton-history

10 See, for example, R. v. Dick [1942] CanLII 447 (AB QB), https://canlii.ca/t/gcgkb.

11 As historian Valerie Korinek remarks, much of this media hysteria had national and geopolitical overtones: "During this time period, Cold War anxieties about social, sexual, and political abnormality, and worries about how best to reconvert from the total war effort to civilian life, preoccupied educators, doctors, governments, and the criminal courts" (Korinek, *Prairie Fairies*, 48).

12 R. v. McDonald [1948] CanLII 223 (AB CA), https://canlii.ca/t/gbd6n

13 Brenda Cossman and Shannon Bell, Introduction to *Bad Attitude/s on Trial*, 14–21.

14 "Clerics 'Accused' of Inspiring Teen-Agers to Live in Sin," *Edmonton Journal*, 26 April 1966, 25.

15 Kyle Kirkup, "The Gross Indecency of Criminalizing HIV Non-Disclosure," *University of Toronto Law Journal* 70, no. 3 (2020): 266.

16 Kirkup, "Gross Indecency," 266. For more on the history of the "criminal sexual psychopath" in queer Canadian history, see Elise Chenier, "The Criminal Sexual Psychopath in Canada: Sex, Psychiatry and the Law at Mid-Century," *Canadian Bulletin of Medical History* 20, no. 1 (2003): 75–101.

17 Gary Kinsman, "Not a Gift from Above: The Mythology of Homosexual Law Reform and the Making of Neoliberal Queer Histories," in *No Place for the State: The Origins and Legacies of the 1969 Omnibus Bill*, eds. Christabelle Sethna, Christopher Dummitt (Vancouver: University of British Columbia Press, 2020), 75–100.

18 Tom Hooper, "Queering '69: The Recriminalization of Homosexuality in Canada," *Canadian Historical Review* 100, no. 2 (2019): 257–273. See also Tom Hooper, Gary Kinsman, and Karen Pearlston, "Against the Mythologies of the 1969 Criminal Code Reform," https://anti-69.ca/faq/

19 The "gay blood ban" finally ended in 2022 when Canadian Blood Services changed its criteria specific to men who have sex with men and instituted new sexual behaviour-based screening criteria for all donors, regardless of sexual orientation or gender identity.

20 R. v. Graham [1977] ALTASCAD 90, https://canlii.ca/t/fp3b7

21 Towne Cinema Theatres, Ltd. v. the Queen [1985] 1 SCR 494, https://scc-csc.lexum.com/scc-csc/scc-csc/en/49/1/document.do

22 Towne Cinema Theatres, Ltd. v. the Queen [1985] 1 SCR 494

23 Korinek, *Prairie Fairies*, 377.

24 Rosemary Ray, "Men arrested for kissing," *The Body Politic*, March 1977, 5–6. https://archive.org/details/bodypolitic31toro/

25 "Local Gays Upset Over Park Incidents," *Edmonton Journal*, 30 July 1988, B2.

26 David Howell, "Homosexuals Meet in Three City Parks," *Edmonton Journal*, 23 October 1989, C2.

27 Helen Plischke, "Police Tried a New Tactic in Park-Sex Investigation," *Edmonton Journal*, 8 October 1993, B1.

28 Ian Hamilton, "Province Drops Park Sex Cases," *Edmonton Journal*, 27 November 1993, B1.

EDMONTON POLICE SERVICE

1 It is a common misconception that homosexuality was decriminalized in Canada in 1969, when in fact the reforms led by then Justice Minister Pierre Elliott Trudeau only resulted in the partial decriminalization of "gross indecency" and "buggery," and then only in private and between two persons age twenty-one or older. Policing and differential age of consent laws have long been a concern for 2SLGBTQ+ community activists.

2 Lyle Dick, "The 1942 Same-Sex Trials in Edmonton: On the State's Repression of Sexual Minorities, Archives, and Human Rights in Canada," *Archivaria* 68 (2009): 193.

3 Lyle Dick and Ron Frohwerk. "State Repression of Sexual Minorities" *Canadian Dimension*, July 2009, https://canadiandimension.com/articles/view/state-repression-of-sexual-minorities

4 Dick and Frohwerk, "State Repression."

5 Dick and Frohwerk, "State Repression."

6 "Indecency Count Brings Jail Term," *Edmonton Journal*, January 21, 1955, 24. Ron Levy, "The 1969 Amendment and the (De)criminalization of Homosexuality," The Canadian Encyclopedia. November 26, 2019, https://www.thecanadianencyclopedia.ca/en/article/the-1969-amendment-and-the-de-criminalization-of-homosexuality.

7 Rosemary Ray, "Men Arrested for Kissing," *The Body Politic*, March 1977, 8–9, https://archive.org/details/bodypolitic31toro

8 Jenny Jackson, "Beaten Gays Keep Quiet, Fearing Recriminations," *Edmonton Journal*, January 16, 1980, B2.

9 Jackson, "Beaten Gays," B2.

10 "Gay Prostitutes Warn of Bloodbath," *Edmonton Journal*, 11 August 1980, B1.

11 Graham Slaughter, "'The Canadian Stonewall': Toronto Police 'Expresses its Regret' for Gay Bathhouse Raids," CTV News, 23 June 2016, https://www.ctvnews.ca/canada/the-canadian-stonewall-toronto-police-expresses-its-regret-for-gay-bathhouse-raids-1.2956225

12 Gilbert Bouchard, "Effects of '81 Spa Raid Still Concern Local Gays," *Edmonton Journal*, 30 May 1986, G12.

13 Bouchard, "Effects of '81," G12.

14 Bouchard, "Effects of '81," G12.

15 *Edmonton Police Service LGBTQ Community Liaison Committee Newsletter*, Summer 2005.

16 Farhan Memon, "Opening Lines of Communication; Police, Gays Strike Panel to Address Concerns," *Edmonton Journal*, 27 June 1993, B3.

17 Tom Arnold, "Police, Gays Seek Better Relationship; 'Fair Treatment' the Goal," *Edmonton Journal*, 11 July 1993, B3.

18 Arnold, "Police, Gays," B3.

19 Memon, "Opening," B3.

20 Ian Hamilton, "Province Drops Park Sex Cases," *Edmonton Journal*, 27 November 1993, B1.

21 Hamilton, "Province Drops," B1.

22 Helen Plischke, "Art Raises Awareness of Gay Bashing," *Edmonton Journal*, 13 January 1996, B3.

23 Plischke, "Art Raises," B3.

24 Lisa Gregoire, "Police Use Bus Posters to Tackle Crime of Gay Bashing," *Edmonton Journal*, 10 June 1999, B3.

25 "Gregoire, "Police," B3.

26 "Edmonton Police Investigate Attacks on Gay Men," *CBC News*, 30 June 2005. https://www.cbc.ca/news/canada/edmonton-police-investigate-attacks-on-gay-men-1.540013.

27 David Howell, "Gay Stroll Eye-Opener for Recruits," *Edmonton Journal*, 2 January 2004, B7.

28 Matthew Hays, "Straight Cops, Gay 101," *The Advocate*, 24, March 16, 2004.

29 Danielle Campbell, personal communication, May 31, 2021.

30 Mike Sadava, "Gay Leader Joins Police Commission," *Edmonton Journal*, 8 January 2005, B6.

31 Scott McKeen, "Billett's Commitment Strengthened Police Commission," *Edmonton Journal*, 19 October 2009, A7.

32 Beginning in 1989, Campbell would ask each year to march in uniform in the Pride parade. The request was finally granted in 2006 under Chief

Mike Boyd. EPS participation in the Pride parade grew each year, including of the historic EPS ceremonial Pipes and Drums band.

33 Doug Johnson, "Police March with Pride: Edmonton Police Service Officers Walk and Roll Showing their Support of Pride During Parade," *Edmonton Examiner*, 11 June 2014, 59.

34 Claire Theobald, "Edmonton Police Strip off Uniforms for Pride Parade," *Toronto Star* (Online), 21 May 2018.

35 Fida Kashmala, "Edmonton Police will Not Participate in this Year's Pride Parade," *Toronto Star* (Online), 4 April 2019.

THE STRAND AND PANTAGES THEATRE

1 This article has been adapted with permission of Darrin Hagen. See Darrin Hagen, "Pantages and The Strand," *Edmonton City as Museum Project*, 15 November 2020. https://citymuseumedmonton.ca/2021/11/15/pantages-and-the-strand

2 W.R. Morrison, "The North-West Mounted Police and the Klondike Gold Rush," *Journal of Contemporary History*, vol. 9 no. 2 (1974): 93–105 (see p. 97).

3 Peter Lester, "Alexander Pantages," *The Canadian Encyclopedia*, 16 December 2013. https://www.thecanadianencyclopedia.ca/en/article/alexander-pantages

4 "Pantages x 2," *Dance Collection Danse*, https://web.archive.org/web/20200304081224/https://www.dcd.ca/exhibitions/vancouver/pantagesx2.html.

5 "The Life of Alexander Pantages," *J. Willard Marriott Library*, https://pta.lib.utah.edu/alexander-pantages/.

6 Finn J.D. John, "Vaudeville's Famous 'Klondike Kate' Became a Central Oregon Legend, *Offbeat Oregon History*, 14 August 2011. http://www.offbeatoregon.com/o1108b-vaudeville-legend-klondike-kate-bends-most-colorful-homesteader.html

7 Taso G. Lagos, "Forgotten Movie Theatre Pioneer: Alexander Pantages and Immigrant Hollywood," *The Journal of Modern Hellenism* 32 (2016): 96–114. https://journals.sfu.ca/jmh/index.php/jmh/article/view/299

8 "Pantages Theatre," Edmonton Historical Board, https://www.edmontonhistoricalboard.ca/structures/pantages-theatre/https://www.edmontonhistoricalboard.ca/structures/pantages-theatre

9 "Strand Theatre," *Cinema Treasures*, http://cinematreasures.org/theaters/14090.

10 Judy Schultz, "Spicy Tidbits of Dining," *Edmonton Journal*, 4 October 1979, 19.

11 Pantages Theatre Opened by Mayor Short in Presence of Huge Crowd," *Edmonton Journal*, 13 May 1913, 7.

12 "Pantages Theatre Sign," *City of Edmonton*, https://www.edmonton.ca/city_government/edmonton_archives/pantages-theatre-sign.aspx.

13 "Old Strand Theatre Saved from Wreckers," *Edmonton Journal*, 7 February 1976, 11.

14 "Strand Theatre," *Cinema Treasures*, http://cinematreasures.org/theaters/14090.

15 To learn more about the Edmonton Little Theatre and the history of theatre in Edmonton, see Mary Ross Glenfield, "The Growth of Theatre in Edmonton: From the Early 1920s to 1965" (Master's Thesis, University of Alberta, 2001). https://www.collectionscanada.gc.ca/obj/s4/f2/dsk3/ftp04/MQ60377.pdf

16 "Pantages Theatre Sign."

17 "Pantages Theatre Sign."

18 "Kagna Given Three Years on Indecent Assault Count," *Edmonton Journal*, 25 September 1942, 1.

19 Lyle Dick, "The 1942 Same-Sex Trials in Edmonton: On the State's Repression of Sexual Minorities, Archives, and Human Rights," *Archivaria* 68 (2009): 1–35.

20 Between 1942 and the trials in 1944, the *Edmonton Bulletin* and *Edmonton Journal* are reported to have published forty-eight news stories about the cases, including on the front page.

21 "8th Man is Held on Morals Count," *Edmonton Journal*, 27 June 1942, 13.

22 "Pair Remanded on Morals Counts," *Edmonton Journal*, 15 July 1942, 9.

23 "Kagna Is Given Three Year Term," *Edmonton Journal*, 25 September 1942, 2.

24 "Pantages Theatre Sign."

25 "A Guide for the Naive Homosexual" was a never-published but much-shared underground volume describing gay life in Canada written by early Vancouver GATE founder Roedy Green that discreetly made the rounds in the late 1960s and early 1970s.

26 Green, "Guide for the Naive Homosexual," 40.

27 "Strand Theatre."

28 Parts of the majestic Pantages Theatre live on. Upon demolition, plaster figurines were removed and moulds were taken of the inside of the theatre with the hope its former glory might one day be reconstructed as an exhibit in Fort Edmonton Park.

CENTENNIAL PLAZA

1 "Silly Six Proclaim a Gay Day Anyway," *Edmonton Journal*, 28 June 1986, B4. The previous rally was in 1981 and protested the police raid of the Pisces Health Spa.

2 Camp Harris, located just west of the city on Winterburn Road (about 2.5 miles south of Highway 16A), was originally used by the Loyal Edmonton Regiment for training exercises. By the 1980s, the camp had expanded and included a full-time live-in caretaker who managed the property and rented the facilities to various groups. It is believed that Edmonton's first Pride event took place at Camp Harris in 1980 with a picnic as the community wanted a discreet location where they could gather and celebrate. Pride events were often held at Camp Harris in the early 1980s, which included potlucks, barbeques, softball games, ecumenical worship services, and, of course, a campfire. Eventually, the majority of Pride celebrations moved to the city as people wanted to be more public and visible and didn't want to travel so far to celebrate.

3 Lois Sweet, "Comic's Humour is Radical and Outrageous," *Edmonton Journal*, 11 June 1982, A6.

4 "Gay Pride 82: Plain Old Intoxicating Fun," *The Body Politic*, September 1982, 11.

5 Ron Chalmers, "Gays and Lesbians Stage Pride Week," *Edmonton Journal*, 22 June 1983, D9.

6 Chris Zdeb, "Gay-Days Unlikely to Win City Blessing," *Edmonton Journal*, 8 June 1984, B2.

7 R.C. Jorgenson, "Do Autos Get Precedence Over People?" [Opinion], *Edmonton Journal*, 5 March 1985, A7.

8 "Coming Together," *The Body Politic*, June 1985, 5, https://archive.org/details/bodypolitic115toro.

9 "Silly Six," B4.

10 Lynda Shorten, "Gay Day Would Drive Kinisky Down Under," *Edmonton Journal*, 10 May 1989, A1.

11 Stephen Erwin, "Gays Parade with Pride; Big Turnout Pleases Organizers," *Edmonton Journal*, 28 June 1992, B1.

12 Student-led initiatives brought additional visibility with two three-day LGBTQ+ film festivals in March 1992 and March 1993 to coincide with University Pride Week celebrations. Michelle Lavoie, working through Gays and Lesbian on Campus (GALOC) and supported by the National Film Board of Canada (NFB) and Latitude 53 Gallery, curated the film festivals: *The Voice and Vision* (1992) and *Speaking in Tongues* (1993).

Both festivals found huge support, with Edmonton's LGBTQ+ community filling theatres to capacity each night. *The Voice and Vision* premiered John Greyson's controversial film about gay bashing, *The Making of Monsters*; Edmonton's premiere closely followed the films' debuts at the Berlin International Film Festival, Toronto International Film Festival, and in Vancouver's *Out on Film* and Montreal's *Image+Nation*. See Bob Remington, "Film Festival Gives Voice to Gays," *Edmonton Journal*, 10 March 1992, B6; Marc Horton, "Gay, Lesbian Film Festival Out to Educate: If People Are Open We're Here ... and Yes, Diane Mirosh is Invited," *Edmonton Journal*, 18 March 1993, D3.

13 "Mayor's Gay Day Proclamation Has Edmontonians in a Tizzy," *Edmonton Journal*, 8 June 1993, B1.

14 Marta Gold, "Reimer's Gay-Day Proclamation Criticized," *Edmonton Journal*, 27 May 1993, A1.

15 Mairi MacLean, "Mood Upbeat at Gay Pride Thanks to Ruling," *Edmonton Journal*, 16 June 2003, B1.

16 "Prairie Pride," *Perceptions Magazine*, 10 June 1998.

17 "Gay Pride Marches On," *Edmonton Journal*, 12 June 1999.

18 Andy Ogle, "City Pride Parade Marks Gains by Gays and Lesbians," *Edmonton Journal*, 17 June 2001, B1.

19 Angelique Rodrigues, "Redford to Take Part in Edmonton Gay Pride Fest," *Edmonton Sun*, 2 June 2012. https://edmontonsun.com/2012/06/02/redford-to-take-part-in-edmonton-gay-pride-fest

20 Patricia Kozicka, "City of Edmonton, Alberta Legislature Raise Pride Flags for Duration of Sochi Olympics," *Global News*, 7 February 2014. https://globalnews.ca/news/1135739/city-of-edmonton-raises-rainbow-flag-for-duration-of-sochi-olympics

21 "Premier Notley, Justin Trudeau at Edmonton Pride Parade," *CBC News* 6 June 2015. https://www.cbc.ca/news/canada/edmonton/premier-rachel-notley-justin-trudeau-at-edmonton-pride-parade-1.3103411

22 John MacKinnon, "Socially Aware Captain Andrew Ference Becomes First Oiler to March in Edmonton Pride Parade," *Edmonton Journal*, 3 June 2014. https://edmontonjournal.com/sports/socially-aware-captain-andrew-ference-becomes-first-oiler-to-march-in-edmonton-pride-parade

23 Caley Ramsay, "LGBTQ Community to Mark 35 Years of Edmonton Pride with History Project," *Global News* 11 January 2015, https://globalnews.ca/news/1767700/lgbtq-community-to-mark-35-years-of-edmonton-pride-with-history-project. The origins of Edmonton's Pride festival are hotly debated, with some suggesting it started with a small gathering at Camp Harris in 1980 and others claiming it started years earlier.

24 "Pride," *Fringe Theatre* 15 June 2017, https://www.fringetheatre.ca/blog/pride/

25 "A first for pride week," *Edmonton Examiner*, 3 June 2015.

26 Julia Parish, "A Canadian First, CFB Edmonton the First to Fly Gay Pride Flag," *CTV News* 7 June 2013. https://edmonton.ctvnews.ca/a-canadian-first-cfb-edmonton-the-first-to-fly-gay-pride-flag-1.1316592

27 Phil Heidenreich, "2019 Edmonton Pride Festival Cancelled," *Global News*, 10 April 2019. https://globalnews.ca/news/5154261/2019-edmonton-pride-festival-cancelled-email-april

28 Jasmine Graf, "Alternate Pride Events Following Cancellation of Edmonton Festival," *Global News*, 7 June 2019. https://globalnews.ca/news/5258890/pride-festival-alternate-events-edmonton-cancelled/

WOMONSPACE

1 Womonspace began in 1981 and was incorporated as a non-profit society in 1982; the first Womonspace dance was held October 23, 1982 at Hazeldean Hall and the last on October 26, 2018 at Bellevue Hall.

2 Shane, "The Originators of Womonspace," *Womonspace News*, December 1982, 2, https://archive.org/details/womonspace-1982-12. Many Womonspace members chose to remain anonymous for privacy and safety reasons. In *Womonspace News*, some contributors used only their first names, initials, or pseudonyms when contributing and when referring to other members. The need for anonymity and secrecy highlights the discrimination, the high degree of stigma, and the repercussions lesbians faced in the 1980s and 1990s in Edmonton and throughout Canada.

3 Shane, "Originators."

4 Shane, "Originators."

5 This information originates from Maureen Irwin's and Michael Phair's *Edmonton Queer History Timeline 1970–1991.*

6 In the early 1980s Womonspace met at and maintained an office and resource library for lesbians in the Oliver area, housed within another organization called Every Woman's Place (9926 112 Street). Addresses and approximate occupancy for the Womonspace offices over the years included Every Woman's Place, 9926 112 Street (1982–1985); Womyn's Building, 10055 110 Street (1986); Women's Building, 10826 124 Street (1987); Women's Building, #30, 9930 106 Street (1988–1996); and the Gay Lesbian Community Centre of Edmonton (GLCCE), #103, 10612 124 Street (1997–2000+).

7 Josephine Boxwell, "Womonspace: Creating Space for Edmonton's Lesbian Community in the 80s," *Edmonton City as Museum Project (ECAMP)*, 12 August 2020, https://citymuseumedmonton.ca/2020/08/12/womonspace-creating-space-for-edmontons-lesbian-community-in-the-1980s. Womanspace dances took place in a variety of community leagues and halls over the years, including Odd Fellows Hall, Riverdale Hall, Hazeldean Community League, Bonnie Doon Community League, Hellenic Hall, and Bellevue Community League. The Option Room (see page 258) was often the site of Womonspace pool tournaments and Womonspace's Tuesday night women-only pool and dancing drop-ins in the 1990s.

8 *Womonspace News*, October 1982. *Womonspace News*, November 1982. *Womonspace News*, December 1982.

9 *Womonspace News* was delivered to local gay bars every month. Darrin Hagen remembers reading *Womonspace News* at Flashback when he worked there; he recalls, "There was always a stack of them on the deli counter and my bar" (personal communication, 24 April 2021). Lindy Pratch, "Womonspace News," *Rise Up: A Digital Archive of Feminist Activism*, https://www.riseupfeministarchive.ca/publications/womonspace.

10 Karen, *"Confused? " Womonspace News*, December 1982, 1, https://archive.org/details/womonspace-1982-12.

11 Lindy Pratch, personal communication, 17 April 2021. Both Boots 'N Saddle and the Roost began as private men's clubs. The Roost permitted access to women a year after opening to increase income and patrons, while Boots 'N Saddle opened to women as guests in 1983.

12 Darrin Hagen recalls that Ladies' and Men's Night at the Roost and Flashback were short-lived experiments that evolved out of competition for customers; Hagen states that when one bar did one thing, the other bar responded—usually by doing the opposite (personal communication, 24 April 2021).

13 Karen, *Womonspace News*, "Flash Meets with Women," October 1983, 2–3, https://archive.org/details/womonspace-1983-10; Noelle Lucas, "Womonspace: Building a Lesbian Community in Edmonton, Alberta, 1970–1990" (Master's Thesis, University of Saskatchewan, 2002), 34.

14 Lindy Pratch, personal communication, 17 April 2021.

15 Edmonton Called Unresponsive to Lesbians," *Edmonton Journal*, 25 May 1983, C15.

16 Maureen Irwin and Michael Phair, "Edmonton Queer History Timeline: 1970–1991," 28 June 1996; Coreen Douglas and Kathy Baker, "Letter to the Editors: Open Letter to Boots N' Saddle," *Womonspace News*, July 1983, 1, https://archive.org/details/womonspace-1983-07.

17 See Lindy Pratch, "#Nightlife," produced by *Edmonton Queer History Project*, 9 June 2015, YouTube video, 5:20-6:33, https://youtu.be/3FQ_rgG7jmU.

18 Lindy Pratch interviewed in Boxwell, "Womonspace."

19 For many lesbians in Edmonton, Womonspace represented what bell hooks might have called a *beloved community*: a site for rest, refuge, and resistance; see bell hooks, *Yearning: Race Gender and Cultural Politics* (Boston: South End Press, 1990) or bell hooks, *Teaching Community: A Pedagogy of Hope* (New York and London: Routledge, 2003). See also interviews by Lindy Pratch, Agathe Gaulin, and Liz Massiah in "#Nightlife" and "#Community," produced by the Edmonton Queer History Project, https://www.youtube.com/watch?v=IuoZ5eI3pL8.

20 Nancy Fraser might call Womonspace a "subaltern counterpublic" or a public that emerged in response to exclusions within the dominant public sphere. From Fraser's perspective, *Womonspace News* can be viewed as a "parallel discursive arena where members ... [would] invent and circulate *counterdiscourses*, which in turn [would] permit them to formulate oppositional interpretations of their identities, interests, and needs" ("Rethinking the Public Sphere: A Contribution to the Critique of Actually Existing Democracy," *Social Text* 25/26 (1990): 67).

21 Jean (Bobby) Noble, "Editorial: If One is Cheated, We All Suffer!," *Womonspace News*, July 1984. 1; Carol Allen, "#Community."

22 Laura Lee, "How We Deal with Our Differences," *Womonspace News*, June 1984, 6, https://archive.org/details/womonspace-1984-06.

23 Noble, "Editorial."

24 Lucas, "Womonspace," 113.

25 Agathe Gaulin interviewed in Boxwell, "Womonspace."

26 Lucas, "Womonspace," 111.

29 Lucas, "Womonspace," 80.

28 Liz Massiah interviewed in Boxwell, "Womonspace."

29 Boxwell, "Womonspace"; Lucas, "Womonspace," 80.

WALLBRIDGE & IMRIE

1 "Women Architects Leave Friday for Tour of European Countries," *Edmonton Journal*, 26 July 1947. 13.

2 Ezra Dominey, "Les Girls," in *Edmonton: The Life of a City*, eds. Bob Hesketh and Frances Swyripa (Edmonton: NeWest Press, 1995), 226–233.

3 Dominey, "Les Girls," 230.

4 Dominey, "Les Girls," 231.

5 Dominey, "Les Girls," 232.

6 Dominey, "Les Girls," 231.

7 Dominey, "Les Girls," 233.

8 Dominey, "Les Girls," 231.

9 Dominey, "Les Girls," 232.

10 "Woman Architect Dies," *Edmonton Journal*, 5 October 1979, C4.

11 Gordon Kent, "Down-to-Earth Millionaire Loved Nature More than Money: She Left Roughly $1 Million to Preserve Alberta Wilderness," *Edmonton Journal*, 5 October 1979, B3.

12 "Claim to Fame," *Edmonton Journal*, November 2, 2003, 82.

13 Kerry Powell, "Pioneer Spirit Helped Women Build a Career," *Edmonton Journal*, 15 May 1995, B1.

14 "Jean Louise Emberly Wallbridge & Mary Louise Imrie," *Women Building Alberta*. https://womenbuildingalberta.wordpress.com/jean-louise-emberly-wallbridge-mary-louise-imrie/

15 Powell, "Pioneer Spirit."

16 "Jean Louise Emberly Wallbridge & Mary Louise Imrie," *Women Building Alberta*.

17 "Jean Louise Emberly Wallbridge & Mary Louise Imrie," *Women Building Alberta*.

COMMON WOMAN BOOKS, ORLANDO BOOKS, AND AUDREYS

1 *Common Woman Books 1983 Catalogue*, 3.

2 "Common Woman Books by Sheryl Ackerman," Edmonton Queer History Project, 29 July 2015. https://edmontonqueerhistoryproject.wordpress.com/2015/07/29/common-woman-books-by-sheryl-ackerman/comment-page-1/

3 "Common Woman Books by Sheryl Ackerman."

4 "Alternative bookstore closes its doors for good after 13 years in business," *Toronto Star*, 18 January 1992, G8.

5 "Common Woman Books by Sheryl Ackerman."

6 Jacqueline Dumas, "Orlando Books (1993–2002)," Edmonton Queer History Project, 1 January 2015. https://edmontonqueerhistoryproject.wordpress.com/2015/01/29/orlando-books-1993-2002/comment-page-1/

7 "Orlando Books," produced by Edmonton Public Library, 13 August 2020, YouTube video, 11:57. https://www.youtube.com/watch?v=fcTI29JtMhY

8 Dumas, "Orlando Books."

9 Paula Simons, "How the Vriend case established LGBTQ rights 20 years ago in Alberta—and across Canada," *Edmonton Journal*, 15 March 2008, https://edmontonjournal.com/news/insight/paula-simons-how-the-vriend-case-established-lgbtq-rights-20-years-ago-in-alberta-and-across-canada. In 1997 an Edmonton woman known as Ms. T, an exemplary foster parent for seventeen years who had opened her home to seventy-four children, was denied status as a foster parent when she left her heterosexual relationship and came out as a lesbian. Ms. T took the Alberta government to court and won a landmark legal battle in 1999, which made same-sex adoption legal in Alberta. See John Zazula Nov. 26, 1999 Decision makes adoption a reality for same-sex couples," *CBC News*, 24 November 2016, https://www.cbc.ca/news/canada/edmonton/nov-26-1999-decision-makes-adoption-a-reality-for-same-sex-couples-1.3865894.

10 "Orlando Books (1993–2002)."

11 "Orlando Books (1993–2002)."

12 The Orlando Books Collective Entrance Award is offered by the University of Alberta and was endowed by Dr. Dianne Oberg, a long-time University of Alberta education professor and one of the authors of the ATA guidebook developed by the Orlando Books Collective.

13 "Orlando Books (1993–2002)."

14 "Orlando Books (1993–2002)."

15 See this summary of Little Sisters v. Canada: https://web.archive.org/web/20031118113138/http:/www.mapleleafweb.com/scc/public3/decisions/2000_2scr_1120_02.html. See also Bruce Ryder, "The Little Sister's Case, Administrative Censorship, and Obscenity Law," *Osgoode Hall Law Journal* 39 (2001): 207–228; and Karen Busby, "The Queer Sensitive Interveners in the Little Sister's Case: A Response to Dr. Kendall," *Journal of Homosexuality*, 47, no. 3–4 (2004): 129–150.

16 "Orlando Corner Launch," *Times.10*, February 2003, 15. https://archive.org/details/times-10-2003-02

17 "Orlando Corner Launch."

KING EDWARD HOTEL

1 Valerie J. Korinek, *Prairie Fairies: A History of Queer Communities and People in Western Canada, 1930-1985* (Toronto: University of Toronto Press, 2018).

2 Korinek, *Prairie Fairies*, 222.

3   Korinek, *Prairie Fairies*, 227.

4   Korinek, *Prairie Fairies*, 225.

5   Ron Byers and Rob Browatzke, "History of Edmonton's Gay Bars, Part 1: The Beginning." Edmonton City as Museum Project, 23 September 2020. https://citymuseumedmonton.ca/2020/09/23/history-of-edmontons-gay-bars-part-1-the-beginning

6   Byers and Browatzke, "History of Edmonton's Gay Bars, Part 1."

7   Jarron Williams, "King Edward Hotel," *Lost Edmonton*. https://lostyeg.wordpress.com/2014/05/04/king-edward-hotel-10180-101-st.

8   "Experienced Italian Chef at King Edward Creates Many Appealing Dishes for Guests," *Edmonton Journal*, 24 October 1969, 83.

9   "Two men die in fire at Edmonton hotel," *The Globe and Mail*, 24 April 1978, 13.

10 "Claim to Fame," *Edmonton Journal*, 2 November 2003, 24.

11 Ric Dolphin, "Abe Cristall: Success by the Spoonful," *Edmonton Journal*, 27 June 1999, B1.

12 Dolphin, "Abe Cristall," B1.

13 "Claim to Fame."

14 Misty Harris, "Style Proves to be Genetic in Edmonton's Singer Clan," *Edmonton Journal*, 13 July 2002, A1.

15 "Corona Completes Renovations," *Edmonton Journal*, 21 June 1968, 54.

16 "Today in History," *Edmonton Journal*, 21 February 1997, F6.

17 Anne Elliott, "He Takes 'Em Off for His Bread," *Edmonton Journal*, 15 May 1975, 3.

18 Doug Swanson, "Self-Defence Is Claimed in Paquette Murder Trial," *Edmonton Journal*, 13 May 1980, B2.

19 "First 'Drive-In' Hotel Features Underground Parking for 50 Cars," *Edmonton Journal*, 5 July 1955, 7.

20 "First 'Drive-In.'"

21 Bob Harvey, "Goodbye to the Pub with No Cheer," *Edmonton Journal*, 13 September 1968, 57.

22 Byers and Browatzke, "History of Edmonton's Gay Bars, Part 1."]

CLUB '70

1   Club '70's Second Anniversary," *Club '70 News*, 2 February 1972, 2. https://archive.org/details/70newsvol3no131unse

2   Valerie J. Korinek, *Prairie Fairies: A History of Queer Communities and People in Western Canada, 1930–1985* (Toronto: University of Toronto Press, 2018), 226–30.

3   Billy Bob Bumbalo, "#Nightlife," produced by Edmonton Queer History Project, 9 June 2015, YouTube video, 8:04, https://youtu.be/3FQ_rgG7jmU. The rescue of the membership list is contested by some Club '70 members, who suggest it was never at risk.

4   Korinek, *Prairie Fairies*, 226–30.

5   *Club '70 News*, 13 September 1972, 3, https://archive.org/details/club70newsvol3no37unse

6   Korinek, *Prairie Fairies*, 227.

7   *Club '70 News*, 15 September, 1971, 1, https://archive.org/details/70newsvol2no727unse; *The Inside Track* Vol. 1, no. 12, 25 November, 1970, 2, https://archive.org/details/insidetrackvol1n112unse.

8   *The Inside Track*, vol. 1, no. 12, 4.

9   Ron Byers and Rob Browatzke, "History of Edmonton's Gay Bars, Part 1: The Beginning," Edmonton City as Museum Project, 23 September 2020, https://citymuseumedmonton.ca/2020/09/23/history-of-edmontons-gay-bars-part-1-the-beginning.

10 Barb C. Plaumann, "Viewpoint," *Carousel Capers*, August 1972, reprinted in *Club '70 News*, 13 September, 1972, 1, https://archive.org/details/club70newsvol3no37unse.

11 Korinek, *Prairie Fairies*, 226.

12 Liz Millward. "Making a Scene: Struggles over Lesbian Place-Making in Anglophone Canada,1964–1984." *Women's History Review*, 21, no.4 (2012): 563.

13 Millward, "Making a Scene," 563–4.

14 Millward, "Making a Scene," 564.

15 Kevin Allen, "Why I'm Celebrating 1969 and Calgary's Anti-Gay Rights Hero: Everett Kilppert Changed Canadian Society," The Sprawl, 26 August 2019. https://www.sprawlcalgary.com/why-im-celebrating-calgary-gay-rights-anti-hero

16 "Trudeau: 'There's No Place For the State in the Bedrooms of the Nation,'" CBC Digital Archives, https://www.cbc.ca/archives/no-place-for-the-state-in-the-bedrooms-of-the-nation-1.4681298.

17 "Roy: Guest Article," *Club '70 News*, July 1971, 2, https://archive.org/details/70newsvol2no525unse.

18 *Club '70 News*, 13 September 1972, 5, https://archive.org/details/club70newsvol3no37unse.

19 "Minutes of the Board of Directors Meeting of Club '70 Held at the Club—Edmonton," 24 January, 1977, MS-595 GALA, Series 11, Box 28, File 7, City of Edmonton Archives, Prince of Wales Armouries Heritage Centre, Edmonton, Alberta, Canada.

20 "Minutes of the Board of Directors Meeting of Club '70 Held at the Club—Edmonton," 12 December, 1977, MS-595, GALA, Series 11, Box 28, File 7, City of Edmonton Archives, Prince of Wales Armouries Heritage Centre, Edmonton, Alberta, Canada. See also: MS-GALA, Series 11, Box 28, File 8 for more information on the Club '70–GATE joint venture.

21 Korinek, *Prairie Fairies*, 233; Chris Bearchell, "Edmonton: Taking Chances, Facing Changes," *The Body Politic*, October 1984, 13.

FLASHBACK

1   Scott McConnell, "fineconversation: An interview with John Reid," *Fine Print*, June 1983, 11. https://archive.org/details/fine-print-1983-06/page/n11/

2   McConnell, "fineconversation."

3   "A Thwell Time," *Edmonton Sun*, May 23, 1982.

4   Brad Fraser, *All the Rage* (New York: Penguin Random House, 2021).

5   Darrin Hagen, "Flash Memory," *See Magazine*, 16–22 June 2005, 10–12.

6   Michael Phair, "Flashback and the Gay Drag Races," *Edmonton City as Museum Project*, 16 September 2014, https://citymuseumedmonton.ca/2014/09/16/flashback-and-the-gay-drag-races.

7   This moment may be relived by watching Fruit Loop's dramatic "drag race" recreation by Darrin Hagen, featuring Trevor Schmidt, Jake Tkaczyk, and Jason Hardwick. See "Segment 8, Flashback," *Fruit Loop: Augmented Reality Pride Tour*, https://vimeo.com/544357946/eb062fa959

8   Bob Remington, "Calling All Gays," *Edmonton Journal*, 4 March 1981, B2.

9   "Question of the Day," *Edmonton Sun*, 3 August 1982; "Johnny You're Tho Thweet," *Edmonton Sun*, 24 March 1982

10 M. Anderson. "Alberta Beef," *Fine Print*, April 1983, 2, https://archive.org/details/fine-print-1983-04/page/2/

11 McConnell, "fineconversation," 11.

12 McConnell, "fineconversation," 11.

13 Hagen, "Flash memory."

14 For more about these legal battles, see *History of Edmonton's Gay Bars Part 2: A Flashback to Flashback* | Edmonton City as Museum Project ECAMP (citymuseumedmonton.ca.

15 Hagen, "Flash memory."

16 Hagen, "Flash memory."

17 "Johnny You're Tho Thweet."

18 R. Bremner, "Awareness key to war on AIDS." *Edmonton Journal*, 2

December 1991, B2; A. Tanner, "Arts community back AIDS day with blackout." *Edmonton Journal*, 29 November 1991, B1.

19 See "Flashback Documentary" at https://www.flashbackdocumentary.ca.

THE ROOST

1 Paul Tilroe, personal communication, 18 February 2021.
2 Alice Echols, *Hot Stuff: Disco and the Remaking of American Culture* (New York: W.W. Norton, 2010), 40. As cultural studies scholar Tim Lawrence clarifies, this backlash was not necessarily experienced as homophobic by those in the gay community; see *Love Saves the Day: A History of American Dance Music Culture 1970–1979* (Durham and London: Duke University Press, 2004), 423.
3 Ron Byers and Rob Browatzke, "History of Edmonton's Gay Bars, Part 3: The Long-Running," *Edmonton City as Museum Project*, 2 October 2020. https://citymuseumedmonton.ca/2020/10/02/history-of-edmontons-gay-bars-part-3-the-long-running
4 Tilroe, personal communication.
5 Lindy Pratch, "#Nightlife," produced by *Edmonton Queer History Project*, 9 June 2015, YouTube video, 8:04, https://youtu.be/3FQ_rgG7jmU.
6 Carl Austin, personal communication, 5 April 2021.
7 Ron Byers and Rob Browatzke, "History of Edmonton's Gay Bars, Part 3: The Long-Running."
8 Austin, personal communication.
9 Shawna Mochnacz, "Interview with Dow Hicks," *Times.*10, November 2002, 30.
10 Tilroe, personal communication.
11 Austin, personal communication.
12 Stephen Erwin, "Free-Ride-for-Sex Offer Alleged in Letter: Taxi Firm Rejects Gay Men's Claims," *Edmonton Journal*, 17 September 1992, B3.
13 The Roost and Flashback played an important role in helping to support and mobilize community outreach and education during the HIV/AIDS epidemic. Both bars frequently supported community fundraisers and allowed outreach workers to share information and distribute safer-sex materials at the clubs.
14 There is a discrepancy over how many years this event ran. A 2006 *Gay-Calgary.com Magazine* article indicates it started in 1984. Other sources indicate November 11, 1985, as the first benefit. The 1985 date seems to fit better with the history of the Edmonton HIV/AIDS Network and Kairos House.
15 Jason Clevett, "23rd Annual AIDS Benefit," *GayCalgary.com Magazine*, November 2006, 30. http://gaycalgary.com/Magazine.aspx?id=37&article=140
16 Austin, personal communication.
17 "Better Service is the Key to Business," *Outlooks*, June 1997.
18 Austin, personal communication.
19 Joe Achtemichuk, personal communication, 24 February 2021.
20 Jason Clevett, "30 Years of the Roost," *GayCalgary.com Magazine*, September 2007, 42. http://gaycalgary.com/Magazine.aspx?id=47&article=50
21 Paul Detta, personal communication, 7 April 2021.
22 "The Party Is Over," *Edmonton Journal*, 29 December 2007, B5.
23 "The Party Is Over."
24 A. Harley, "Opinion," *Edmonton Journal*, 2 January 2008.
25 Detta, personal communication.

SECRETS AND PRISM

1 Noelle M. Lucas, "Womonspace: Building A Lesbian Community In Edmonton, Alberta, 1970–1990" (Master's Thesis, University of Saskatchewan, 2002), 70–76, http://hdl.handle.net/10388/etd-11042009-093447.

2   This bar appears as either Cha Cha Palace or Cha Cha Place in different sources.

3   Ron Byers and Rob Browatzke, "History of Edmonton's Gay Bars, Part 4: The Expanding Scene," Edmonton City as Museum Project (ECAMP), 7 October 2020, https://citymuseumedmonton.ca/2020/10/07/edmontons-gay-bars-part-4-the-expanding-scene.

4   Sandy Correia, "Want to Hear a Secret?" Times.10, October 1998, 25. https://archive.org/details/times-10-1998-10/.

5   Josephine Boxwell, "Womonspace: Creating Space for Edmonton's Lesbian Community in the 80s," Edmonton City as Museum Project (ECAMP), 12 August 2020, https://citymuseumedmonton.ca/2020/08/12/womonspace-creating-space-for-edmontons-lesbian-community-in-the-1980s.

6   Marilyn Moysa, "Coming Out: The Struggles to Break Through the Stereotypes," Edmonton Journal, 2 March 1993, C7.

7   Moysa, "Coming Out."

8   Sandy Correia, "Want to Hear a Secret?" Times.10, October 1998, 25. https://archive.org/details/times-10-1998-10/.

9   Times.10, July 1999, back cover. https://archive.org/details/times-10-1999-07

10 Ron Byers and Rob Browatzke, "List of Edmonton Gay Bars," Edmonton City as Museum Project, 9 October 2020. https://citymuseumedmonton.ca/2020/10/09/list-of-edmontons-gay-bars/

11 Jason Clevett, "Prism Bar and Grill: Edmonton's Lesbian Lair," Gay Calgary.com Magazine, January 2007, 35. http://gaycalgary.com/Magazine.aspx?id=39&article=231

12 Stephen Lock, "Straight to Diva 2: Straight Guys Become Radiant Divas," GayCalgary.com Magazine, March 2006, 30. http://gaycalgary.com/Magazine.aspx?id=29&article=1135

13 See Sarah Marloff, "The Rise and Fall of America's Lesbian Bars," Smithsonian Magazine, 21 January 2021. https://www.smithsonianmag.com/travel/rise-and-fall-americas-lesbian-bars-180976801.

SAX AND THE OPTION ROOM

1   "The Journal Dine Out Directory," Edmonton Journal, 29 December 1985, C12.

2   Ron Byers and Rob Browatzke, "History of Edmonton's Gay Bars, Part 4: The Expanding Scene," Edmonton City as Museum, 7 October 2020. https://citymuseumedmonton.ca/2020/10/07/edmontons-gay-bars-part-4-the-expanding-scene.

3   Kim McLeod, "Nightclub Confessions Upset Priest," Edmonton Journal, 17 June 1987, B6.

4   "ALCB Suspends Lounges' License," Edmonton Journal, 22 December 1988, B3.

5   Sherri Aikenhead, "Restaurant's boast of 'no gays' permitted by gap in Alberta law," Edmonton Journal, 10 May 1989, B1.

6   Richard Helm and Sherri Aikenhead, "Human Rights Chairman Says Nightclub is Unfair to Gays," Edmonton Journal, 12 May 1989, B1.

7   Don Retson, "Bloody Scuffle with Gays Worries Club Owner," Edmonton Journal, 11 May 1989, B1.

8   "Neighbors Diary," Edmonton Journal, 12–18 March 1989, 8.

9   See the items "$3,500 in Stolen Goods Recovered at Night Club," Edmonton Journal, 24 May 1989, F8; "Man Shot in Leg at Downtown Nightclub," Edmonton Journal, 16 August 1989, B4; and "Two Charged with Cocaine Trafficking," Edmonton Journal, 19 January 1990, B2, for example.

10 Tom Arnold, "Court Orders Triple 5 to Hand Over Premises to Gay-Oriented Club," Edmonton Journal, 8 October 1993, B3.

11 Arnold, "Court Orders."

12 The Option Room was also an early performance space for Edmonton's Village People Revue. The troupe began in 1994 as part of the build-up

to the Coronation Ball of the Imperial Sovereign Court of the Wild Rose. The revue's July debut was only the beginning; they would go on to perform in venues across Canada as part of the Imperial Sovereign Court of the Wild Rose and in support of other fundraising causes. The troupe would also perform at Edmonton's Pride festivities in 2007 and 2009 and would later partner with Womonspace for an all-lesbian version of their ensemble in 2013.

13 "Explore Edmonton," *Edmonton Journal*, Summer 1999, 20.

14 "Lap Dance for Ladies," *Fort McMurray Today*, 3 March 2011, A2.

EVOLUTION WONDERLOUNGE

1 The Pure parties were Pure: Heat (July), Pure: Desire (August), and Pure: Stephan (September).

2 Todd Babiak, "Dance Club a Place to Meet ... for Now; Successful Bar Owners Vie to Fill Gaping Hole in City's Gay and Lesbian Club Scene," *Edmonton Journal*, 15 July 2008, D1.

3 Todd Babiak, "Debut of Play Nightclub for the 'Just Queer Enough' Marks an Evolution; Lounge is Headed in Direction Downtown Should Go," *Edmonton Journal*, 18 September 2008, B1.

4 Babiak, "Debut of Play Nightclub."

5 Jason Clevett, "Play Nightclub: Edmonton's Newest Hot Spot," Gay Calgary.com Magazine, October 2008, 11. http://www.gaycalgary.com/Magazine.aspx?id=60&article=562.

6 Michelle Thompson, "Play Nightclub Vows 'Safe, Fun Time,'" *Edmonton Sun*, 20 September 2008, 4.

7 Thompson, "Play Nightclub."

8 Rob Diaz-Marino, "Up and Down Alberta," GayCalgary.com Magazine, October 2013, 5. http://www.gaycalgary.com/Magazine.aspx?id=120&article=3697

9 Diaz-Marino, "Up and Down."

10 Fish Griwkowsky, "Kicking up Their Many Heels; Burlesque Show Funny, Inspiring," *Edmonton Journal*, 20 August 2015, C3.

11 See https://community.igla.org/c/archive-championships/2016-igla-edmonton

12 Ralph Ellis et al., "Orlando Shooting: 49 Killed, Shooter Pledged ISIS Allegiance," CNN, 13 June 2016. https://www.cnn.com/2016/06/12/us/orlando-nightclub-shooting/index.html

13 Ellis, "Orlando Shooting."

14 Kevin Maimann, "After Edmonton Pride Cancelled, New Festivities Springing Up Amid 'Tension' in Edmonton's LGBTQ Community," *Toronto Star Online*, 26 May 2019. https://www.thestar.com/edmonton/2019/05/26/after-edmonton-pride-cancelled-new-festivities-springing-up-amid-tension-in-edmontons-lgbtq-community.html

15 Members of the 2SLGBTQ+ community were less likely to have savings to help manage unforeseen circumstances such as employment disruptions. See Elena Prokopenko and Christina Kevins, "Vulnerabilities Related to COVID-19 Among 2SLGBTQ+ Canadians," *StatsCan COVID-19: Data to insights for a better Canada*. https://www150.statcan.gc.ca/n1/en/pub/45-28-0001/2020001/article/00075-eng.pdf?st=e22FMkjs

THE CITADEL THEATRE

1 Joe Shoctor, Sandy Mactaggart, Ralph MacMillan, John Soprovich, and J.L. Martin bought the Salvation Army Citadel for one hundred thousand dollars to establish the Citadel Theatre in 1965. The owners retained the name Citadel, often used by the Salvation Army to refer to its buildings. See https://www.edmontonhistoricalboard.ca/structures/salvation-army-citadel and https://en.m.wikipedia.org/wiki/The_Salvation_Army.

2 Robin Phillips (1990–95), Duncan McIntosh (1995–99), and Bob Baker (1999–2016).

3 The play centres on a caustic relationship between a husband and wife that explodes into the open with the arrival of a second heterosexual couple, a professor and his wife. Although multiple theatre companies over the years sought to adapt the play to include two gay couples, Albee never allowed productions featuring same-sex couples (Victoria R. Bowles, "Theatre Cancels Homosexual Version of 'Virginia Woolf,'" UPI, 3 August 1984, https://www.upi.com/Archives/1984/08/03/Theater-cancels-homosexual-version-of-Virginia-Woolf/9659460353600).

4 Albee's public comments at the 23rd Lambda Literary Awards sparked controversy when he stated, "I am not a gay writer. I am a writer who happens to be gay" (Renee Montagne, "Author Interviews: Playwright Albee Defends 'Gay Writer' Remarks," 6 June 2011, https://www.npr.org/2011/06/06/136923478/playwright-edward-albee-defends-remarks). Colin McLean, "Playbill" for the Citadel Theatre, 2004–2005 Season, *Cat on a Hot Tin Roof*, 27.

5 "Citadel Playbill," 32. Written in 1944, this play focusses on dysfunctional family relationships without overt queer themes. Post Stonewall, Williams, who was openly gay, spoke about the autobiographical quality of his work. ("Tennessee Williams, 1911–1983," *Queer Portraits in History*, https://www.queerportraits.com/bio/williams).

6 Darrin Hagen, *The Edmonton Queen: The Final Voyage* (Victoria: Brindle and Glass Publishing, 1997), 201. *Hosanna* was produced at the Citadel Theatre for the 1975–76 and 1992–93 seasons. *Hosanna* was also produced by Workshop West and presented in the Rice Theatre.

7 The Citadel's production of *Hosanna* in 1976, starring Patrick Christopher as Hosanna and Jean-Pierre Fournier as Cuirette, was the first English-language performance of the play in Canada. Jean-Pierre Fournier remembers that censors came to opening night ready to shut the show down if it became too racy, but they were allowed to complete the run. In the second week, Fournier remembers three nuns turning up thinking the show might have a religious theme and shares a hilarious anecdote from the end of Act 1. He recalls entering the scene returning from a motorcycle ride and undressing to get in bed with Hosanna. The bed, Fournier recounts, was angled and left only a foot of space for him to pass. On that night, the nuns were sitting right in that spot. He recalls, "one nun, very relaxed and apparently caught up in and enjoying the show, was sitting with her legs stretched out touching the corner of the bed. I had to pass that corner to get in my side of the bed. So, in my bikini briefs, I approached the corner. The nun, completely absorbed in the proceedings, just watched. To get by I had to say, 'Excuse me, Sister.' She looked up at me, briefly and almost apologetically so, and tucked her feet in so that I might pass and get into the bed. We thought they would be gone for Act 2, but they were right back in their spot!" (personal communication, 29 September 2021).

8 The play has been criticized by Viviane Namaste, a trans scholar and activist, as being transphobic because Hosanna comes out as a gay man; Namaste argues that Tremblay erases trans subject positions by defaulting to gay male subject positions. See Viviane Namaste, *Invisible Lives: The Erasure of Transgendered and Transsexual People* (Chicago: University of Chicago Press, 2000).

9 Suzanne Jill Levine, *Manuel Puig and the Spider Woman: His Life and Fictions* (Madison: University of Wisconsin Press, 2001).

10 Liz Nicholls, "In Praise of Angels: Conservative Indignation Is Nothing New when Moralists Are Challenged to Think," *Edmonton Journal*, 18 September 1996, B9.

11 Charlotte Von Mahlsdorf, *I Am My Own Woman: The Outlaw Life of Charlotte Von Mahlsdorf*, Jean Hollander, trans. (San Francisco: Cleis Pres, 1995).

12 Some of these works include Raymond Storey (*South of China* 1996–97); Ronnie Burkett (*Billy Twinkle*, 2008–09; *Penny Plain*, 2011–12; *Daisy Theatre*, 2013–14 and 2014–15); Morris Panych (*The Overcoat* [with Wendy Gorling], 2006–07; *What Lies Before Us*, 2006–07); Brad Fraser (*True Love Lies*, 2010–11); Damien Atkins, with Andrew Kushnir and Paul Dunn (*The Gay Heritage Project*, 2015–2016); and Tom Wood (*A Christmas Carol*, 2000–18; *The Servant of Two Masters*, 2002–03; *Vanya*, 2004–05; *Peter Pan*, 2005–06; *Pride and Prejudice*, 2008–09; *The Three Musketeers*, 2010–11; *Make Mine Love*, 2013–14; *Sense and Sensibility*, 2016–17).

13 Mieko Ouchi, associate artistic director of the Citadel Theatre, personal communication, 21 June 2021.

14 Ouchi, personal communication.

15 For more information on the Names Project in Edmonton, see https://www.theworks.ab.ca/archive-1990.

16 "The Works and the Edmonton AIDS Network: The Names Project Quilt," The Works: Fifth Year Anniversary: 'Riveting,' June 22–July 4, 1990, https://www.theworks.ab.ca/archive-1990.

17 Edmonton's first 2SLGBTQ+ Film Festival, The Voice and the Vision, March 10, 1992, premiered *The Making of Monsters* following the film's debut at the Berlin International Film Festival, the Toronto International Film Festival (TIFF), and two other Canadian LGBT film festivals: Vancouver's Out on Film and Montreal's Image+ Nation. See https://en.m.wikipedia.org/wiki/The_Making-of_Monsters. For more see: Bob Remington "Film Festival Gives Voice to Gays," *Edmonton Journal*, 10 March 1992, B6.

18 Loud 'N Proud: A Community Celebration Launching Gay Pride Week," *Times.10*, June 1997, 21, https://archive.org/details/times-10-1997-06/

19 *In On It*, written in 2001, is a play with 2SLGBTQ+ themes that centres around several characters and intersecting storylines: a man who is dying and making final preparations, a couple working on their relationship, and two writers collaborating on a play.

GEORGIA BATHS

1 Damien Atkins, "No Heterosexual Equivalent: Why Bathhouse Has a Role," *Edmonton Journal*, 22 January 1998, A17.

2 "Georgia Baths Sign," "City of Edmonton," https://www.edmonton.ca/city_government/edmonton_archives/georgia-baths-sign.aspx.

3 David R. Johnston, "Georgia Baths: A Steamy History," Ornamentum, http://ornamentum.novakovics.com/georgia-baths-a-steamy-history.

4 "Georgia Baths: A Steamy History."

5 Gordon Kent, "There's No Place Like Georgia Baths; A Reflection of an Era Gone By, Edmonton's Last Public Bath Creaks Along," *Edmonton Journal*, 18 February 1991, B1.

6 Kent, "There's No Place."

7 Kent, "There's No Place."

8 James Adams, "The Steamy World of Public Baths," *Edmonton Journal*, 14 June 1978, B13.

9 "Steamy World."

10 "Steamy World."

11 The Pisces Bathhouse Raid | Edmonton City as Museum Project ECAMP, https://citymuseumedmonton.ca/2015/05/28/the-pisces-bathhouse-raid/.

12 "Georgia Baths Sign."

13 "Health Officer Pulls Plug on City's Oldest Public Steam Bath," *Edmonton Journal*, 9 November 2005, B4.

14 Conal Mullen, "City Will Get More Peep-Shows, 'Adult Industry' Consultant Says," *Edmonton Journal*, 1 November 1990, B3.

15 John Geiger, "Lapse Gave Live Peep Shows Edge," *Edmonton Journal*, 13 July 1994, A12.

16 "Obscenity? What's That? How Canada's High Courts Unleashed Live Peep-Shows on the West and What's Next," *Western Report*, 25 July 1994, 26–30.

17 "A New Twist in Sleaze: Lap Dancing Comes to Alberta By Dodging the Liquor Laws," *Western Report*, August 1995, 12.

18 Raquel Exner, "Neighbours Steamed About Gay Baths; Owner Says New Facility Won't Be a Problem," *Edmonton Journal*, 8 January 1998, B1.

19 Exner, "Neighbours."

20 Exner, "Neighbours."

21 Exner, "Neighbours."

THE HILL

1 Roedy Green, "A Guide for the Naive Homosexual," Eleventh Revision. (Vancouver: Author, 1971). For a digital copy of this guide, see the Edmonton Queer History Project archives on the Internet Archive, https://archive.org/details/guidefornaivehom00roed.

2 Philosopher Michel Foucault might have referred to The Hill as a heterotopia. Heterotopias are layered spaces that contradict normative understandings of space by challenging and inverting what the general public deems normal or acceptable. They are utopic, transgressive, and often exist out of necessity. The heterotopic element of The Hill inheres in the fact that cruising, public sex, and sometimes sex work occurred within its unofficial borders, especially at night. See Michel Foucault, *The Archaeology of Knowledge* (London and New York: Routledge, 1989), xvi.

3 As Tom Warner has argued, the "promiscuity of gay men, their engaging in sexual acts in places the state deems public, and their celebration of such activity have long been features of gay male culture," resulting "from the ability of men, whether heterosexual or homosexual, to move about with relative freedom even late at night, and of the historic, underground nature of gay sexuality." See *Never Going Back: A History of Queer Activism in Canada* (Toronto: University of Toronto Press, 2002), 128.

4 Warner, *Never Going Back*, 128.

5 Patrick Califia, *Speaking Sex to Power: The Politics of Queer Sex* (New York: Cleis Press, 2002), 216.

6 Valerie J. Korinek, *Prairie Fairies: A History of Queer Communities and People in Western Canada, 1930–1985* (Toronto: University of Toronto Press, 2018), 227.

7 "Gay Prostitutes Warn of Blood Bath," *Edmonton Journal*, 11 August 1980, B1.

8 Ross Henderson, "Court Told Gay Broke Date," *Edmonton Journal*, 2 May 1987, B8.

DAPPLE GREY CAFÉ

1 Jodie Sinnema, "Edmonton Leads Way Tracking Gay Bashing," *Edmonton Journal*, 14 October 2005, A6.

2 Sinnema, "Edmonton Leads."

3 Darrin Hagen, "10024-102 Street: Rony's / Dapple Gray Cafe / Appleby / Cheddars / Cafe Elite," Edmonton City as Museum, 9 July 2020. https://citymuseumedmonton.ca/2020/07/09/10024-102-street-ronys-dapple-gray-cafe-appleby-cheddars-cafe-elite.

4 Vince Coady, "Gays Reject Weapons for Self-Defence," *Edmonton Journal*, 12 August 1980, B1.

5   David Staples, "Exhibit Condemns Rage, Violence Against City Gays," *Edmonton Journal*, 7 February 1996, B1.
6   Lisa Gregoire, "Police Use Bus Posters to Tackle Crime of Gay Bashing," *Edmonton Journal*, 10 June 1999, B3.
7   Sinnema, "Edmonton Lead."
8   David Howell, "Gay Stroll Eye-Opener for Recruits," *Edmonton Journal*, 2 January 2004, B7.
9   The Canadian Press, "Hundreds rally in Edmonton to support victim of anti-gay beating," *National Post*, 3 August 2013. https://nationalpost.com/news/canada/hundreds-rally-in-edmonton-to-support-victim-of-anti-gay-beating
10 Dylan Short, "Man Arrested for Throwing Rocks in B.C. Last Week Now Charged with Edmonton Killing," *Edmonton Journal*, 27 February 2020. https://edmontonjournal.com/news/crime/man-arrested-throwing-rocks-in-b-c-last-week-now-charged-with-edmonton-killing
11 Terry Haig, "Shocking Statistics Released About Assaults Against LGBTQ People in Canada," Radio Canada, 10 September 2020. https://www.rcinet.ca/en/2020/09/10/shocking-statistics-released-about-assaults-against-lgbtq-people-in-canada

PRIDE TIMELINE

1   "Gay Pride '83," *Fineprint*, July 1983, 14. https://archive.org/details/fineprint-1983-07.
2   Ron Chalmers, "Gays and lesbians stage pride week," *Edmonton Journal*, 22 June 1983, D9.
3   Chalmers "Gays and lesbians."
4   Chris Zdeb, "Gay-Days unlikely to win city blessing," *Edmonton Journal*, 8 June 1984, B2.
5   "Loud and Proud," *Edmonton Sun*, 26 June 1984, 10.
6   Jeff Winkelaar, "A political moment," *The Body Politic*, September 1985, 23. https://archive.org/details/bodypolitic118toro
7   Maxine Ruvinsky, "Council denies request for gay awareness day," *Edmonton Journal*, 19 June 1985, B8.
8   Ruvinsky, "Council denies request."
9   "GALA '86 to promote gay and lesbian awareness," *Edmonton Journal*, 14 June 1986, C4.
10 "Neighborhood Calendar," *Edmonton Journal*, 24 June 1987, 86.
11 Conal Mullen, "Thumbs down for gay day," *Edmonton Journal*, 23 April 1989, A1; "Silly six proclaim a gay day," *Edmonton Journal*, 28 June 1989, B4.
12 Lynda Shorten, "Gay Day would drive Kinisky Down Under," *Edmonton Journal*, 10 May 1989, A1.
13 Marilyn Moysa and Florence Loyie, "Gay rights backed by McCoy," *Edmonton Journal*, 15 May 1989, A1.
14 Marta Gold, "Council approves call to recognize Gay Pride Day," *Edmonton Journal*, 24 June 1992, B3.
15 Gold, "Council approves call."
16 Stephen Erwin, "Gays parade with pride; Big turnout pleases organizers," *Edmonton Journal*, 28 June 1992, B3.
17 Rosa Jackson, "First-ever business fair targets gay consumers," *Edmonton Journal*, 21 June 1993, B1.
18 Marta Gold, "Most callers opposed Gay Pride Day proclamation, Mayor says," *Edmonton Journal*, 28 May 1993, B6.
19 Marta Gold, "Reimer's gay-day proclamation criticized," *Edmonton Journal*, 27 May 1993, A1.
20 Gold, "Proclamation criticized."
21 Gil McGowan, "Gays, lesbians march with pride," *Edmonton Journal*, 26 June 1994, B3.

22 McGowan, "Gays, lesbians march."

23 Sharon Lindores, "Counsellor, lawyer honored by Gay Pride," *Edmonton Journal*, 17 June 1995, B2.

24 Kim Ziervogel, "A parade for awareness along Whyte," *Edmonton Journal*, 25 June 1995, B3.

25 "'Awareness Day' or 'Approval Day'? Either way, Edmonton mayor Bill Smith won't bestow one on local homosexuals," *Western Report*, 1 July 1996, 14–15.

26 "Smith won't recognize gay day," *Edmonton Journal*, 21 June 1997, B3.

27 Ashley Geddes, "Mayor applauds decision but won't proclaim gay day," *Edmonton Journal*, 4 April 1998, B3

28 Allison Hanes, "Gay Pride marches on," *Edmonton Journal*, 12 June 1999, B1.

29 "Ten best suggestions for things to do this weekend," *Edmonton Journal*, 18 June 1999, E5.

30 Florence Loyie, "Mayor's praise of Gay Pride fest gets big play in local magazine," *Edmonton Journal*, 10 June 2000, B5.

31 Andy Ogle, "City pride parade marks gains by gays and lesbians," *Edmonton Journal*, 17 June 2001, B1.

32 Duncan Thorne, "Local gays look to B.C. victory," *Edmonton Journal*, 5 August 2002, B4.

33 Sarah O'Donnell, "Smith's stand on pride week draws complaint," *Edmonton Journal*, 11 June 2003, A2.

34 Paula Simons, "Gay rights: What are Klein, Smith so afraid of?" *Edmonton Journal*, 12 June 2003, B2.

35 "Petitioners oppose gay pride parades," *Edmonton Journal*, 10 June 2004, B6.

36 "Alberta backs down on same-sex marriage," CTV News, 13 July 2005.

37 Scott McKeen, "Mandel blasé about being first mayor in gay pride parade," *Edmonton Journal*, 17 June 2005, B1.

38 Marti Maclean, "Rain can't dampen gay pride parade," *Edmonton Journal*, 19 June 2005, A12.

39 Cigdem Iltan, "Big E spills over with Gay Pride," *Edmonton Journal*, 14 June 2009, A5.

40 Mariam Ibrahim, "No shortage of gay pride in eTown," *Edmonton Journal*, 13 June 2010, A7.

41 "Two decades of proud progress," *Edmonton Journal*, 14 June 2011, A12

42 Gemma Karstens Smith, "Pride gradually triumphing over prejudice, annual festival organizers say," *Edmonton Journal*, 1 June 2012, A4.

43 Gemma Karstens Smith, "'Let's just celebrate who we are'," *Edmonton Journal*, 10 June 2012, A3.

44 Kathy Mueller, "Smith Douses 'Lake of Fire'," *Edmonton Sun*, 16 April 2012.

45 Alicja Siekierska, "Mandel praised for Pride Week support," *Edmonton Journal*, 17 June 2013, A3.

46 John MacKinnon, "Ference says Pride Parade all about inclusion," *Edmonton Journal*, 14 June 2014, A1.

47 Tyler Dawson, "Province to fund LGBT youth mentorship project," *Edmonton Journal*, 11 June 2014, A7.

48 Rachel Ward, "Thousands flood Whyte Avenue as Edmonton shows its colours at Pride Parade," *Edmonton Journal*, 7 June 2015. https://edmonton journal.com/local-news/thousands-flood-whyte-avenue-as-edmonton-shows-its-colours-at-pride-parade

49 Caley Ramsay, "LGBTQ Community to Mark 35 Years of Edmonton Pride with History Project," *Global News*, 11 January 2015. https://globalnews.ca/news/1767700/lgbtq-community-to-mark-35-years-of-edmonton-pride-with-history-project/

50 Elise Stolte, "'Lost space' revitalized to honour ex-councillor," *Edmonton Journal*, 27 May 2016, A12.

51 Jonny Wakefield, "Two-spirit community serves for first time as parade grand marshals," *Edmonton Journal*, 12 June 2017, A5.

52 Rob Csernyik, "Pride volunteers offer themselves as open books for human library," *Edmonton Journal*, 10 June 2017, A11.

53 "Pride And Prejudice [editorial]," *Edmonton Journal*, 13 June 2017, A8.

54 Clare Clancy, "UCP denied chance to march in Edmonton Pride Parade," *Edmonton Journal*, 3 May 2018. https://edmontonjournal.com/news/politics/pride-festival-recommends-ucp-be-denied-the-chance-to-march-in-june-parade

55 Emma Graney and Clare Clancy, "UCP to host its own Pride event Saturday," *Edmonton Journal*, 6 June 2018, A4.

56 Kyle Muzyka, "Mid-parade protest was necessary to be heard, Pride demonstrator says," *CBC News*, 11 June 2018. https://www.cbc.ca/news/canada/edmonton/edmonton-pride-2018-shay-lewis-1.4701693

57 Dylan Short, "Organizers cancel Pride festival; Board unable to meet demands of LGBTQ groups, sources say," *Edmonton Journal*, 11 April 2019, A1.

58 Moira Wyton, "'Vibrant and vital': Pride in Edmonton persists beyond the parade," *Edmonton Journal*, 31 May 2019. https://edmontonjournal.com/news/local-news/vibrant-and-vital-pride-in-edmonton-persists-beyond-the-parade

59 Andrew Jeffrey, "Edmonton LGBTQ non-profit takes Pride event online this weekend," *CBC News*, 9 June 2020. https://www.cbc.ca/news/canada/edmonton/edmonton-online-pride-event-1.5604143

60 Ciara Yaschuk, "Augmented reality Pride tour celebrates Edmonton's LGBTQ history, showcases performances," *Global News*, 7 July 2021. https://globalnews.ca/news/7960231/augmented-reality-pride-tour-edmonton-2021/

61 "Pride Month Kick-Off" *Edmonton Downtown Business Association*, https://www.edmontondowntown.com/events/pride-month-kick-off/

62 "Pride Month in Edmonton," *Pride Edmonton*, 1 June 2023, https://prideedmonton.ca/event/pride-month-in-edmonton/.

ABOUT THE EQHP

The Edmonton Queer History Project (EQHP) first began in 2015 as a way to help commemorate and celebrate the thirty-fifth anniversary of Edmonton's Pride festival. We started by hosting a free public exhibition at the Art Gallery of Alberta and have evolved into a grassroots community initiative that has been supported by many partners and friends. Our original team members included Dr. Kristopher Wells, Michael Phair, Dr. Alvin Schrader, Dr. Michelle Lavoie, Michael Janz, and Julia Grouch. More recently, we have expanded our work with new project members including Darrin Hagen, Remi Baker, Rob Browatzke, Morgan Evans, Paige Simpson, Elizabeth Cytko, Toryn Sudaby, Kyler Chittick, Japkaran Saroya, Sarah Dumais, Blaze Bennett, and Samantha Hegelson, among many other volunteers and contributors. Our work is truly a passionate and collective effort focussed on helping to preserve, share, and celebrate our city's rich and diverse queer and trans history and to share this history with the widest possible audience.

Our collective work has been made possible thanks to funding and generous support from the MacEwan Centre for Sexual and Gender Diversity, Canada Research Chairs program, City of Edmonton, Edmonton Heritage Council, Edmonton Downtown Business Association, Edmonton Community Foundation, and the Stollery Charitable Foundation. We are also thankful for guidance and support we have received from the City of Edmonton Archives, Provincial Archives of Alberta, University of Alberta Archives, Edmonton Public Schools Archives and Museum, MacEwan University Libraries, University of Alberta Libraries, Institute for Sexual Minority Studies and Services, Neil Richards Collection of Sexual and Gender Diversity at the University of Saskatchewan, Old Strathcona Business Association, Fruit Loop, Rainbow Story Hub, and Fort Edmonton Park.

We would also like to thank and acknowledge the many community groups and individuals who have become dedi-

cated historians, Knowledge Keepers, and archivists that have
helped to preserve our community's history in their basements,
closets, garages, and homes. Local community historians and
custodians like Maureen Irwin, Elizabeth Massiah, Michael
Phair, Darrin Hagen, Ron Byers, Rob Browatzke, Dr. Michelle
Lavoie, Kristy Harcourt, Lindy Pratch, and so many others
have helped to keep our history alive through their dedicated
work to document, preserve, and tell our stories. Whether it be
through oral history, books, plays, slide shows, exhibits, films,
walking tours, websites, podcasts, blogs, social media, or other
creative or artistic means, these efforts have all contributed to
celebrating the incredible richness, complexity, and diversity
of our 2SLGBTQ+ communities.

Yet we still need to do more to uplift and celebrate Two
Spirit, lesbian, trans, bisexual, and racialized voices. How and
why we tell our stories matters. We invite you to add to this
important history by connecting with us or by sharing your
own stories and experiences by visiting our digital stories map
(www.eqhpstories.com).

In this book, we have attempted to carefully source, cite,
and credit all the various materials we have drawn from to
help document and share Edmonton's queer and trans history.
We recognize that histories are messy and complex and have
many gaps, absences, silences, and multiple interpretations.
We welcome any corrections and suggestions for improvement
as history is a work in progress, necessarily partial, and always
somewhat incomplete.

You can learn more about our project by visiting our multimedia website (www.EdmontonQueerHistoryProject.ca),
which features our downtown queer history map, walking
tours, podcast, digital archives, stories map, *Pride vs. Prejudice*
documentary film, and so much more! Stay connected and
keep updated about project news and events by following us
on social media by searching for the Edmonton Queer History
Project on Instagram, Facebook, Twitter/X, and TikTok.

Thank you for joining us on this journey into our community's past. The future will continue to be bright and queer if we
continue to fight and advocate for it.

Portions of this text have appeared in slightly different form on the Edmonton Queer History Project website; see www.edmontonqueerhistoryproject.ca.

NeWest Press acknowledges that the land on which we operate is Treaty 6 territory and Métis Nation of Alberta Region 4, a traditional meeting ground and home for many Indigenous Peoples, including Cree, Saulteaux, Niitsitapi (Blackfoot), Métis, Dene, and Nakota Sioux, since time immemorial.

NeWest Press prohibits the use of *Cruising the Downtown* in connection with the development of any software program, including, without limitation, training a machine learning or generative artificial intelligence (AI) system.

Library and Archives Canada Cataloguing in Publication
Title: Cruising the downtown : celebrating Edmonton's queer history / edited by Kristopher Wells.
Names: Wells, Kristopher, 1971– editor
Identifiers: Canadiana (print) 20240508181 | Canadiana (ebook) 20240516141 | ISBN 9781774391181 (softcover) | ISBN 9781774391198 (epub)
Subjects: LCSH: Sexual minorities—Alberta—Edmonton—History.
LCSH: Sexual minorities—Alberta—Edmonton—Social conditions.
LCSH: Sexual minority community—Alberta—Edmonton—History.
LCSH: LGBT activism—Alberta—Edmonton—History.
LCSH: Gay business enterprises—Alberta—Edmonton—History.
Classification: LCC HQ73.3.C32 E36 2025 | DDC 306.76097123/34—DC23

Editor for the Press: Leslie Vermeer
Cover and interior design: Natalie Olsen, Kisscut Design
Cover photo © This Old Postcard/ Alamy.com
All interior images courtesy of the Edmonton Queer History Project.

NeWest Press acknowledges the support of the Canada Council for the Arts, the Government of Alberta through the Ministry of Arts, Culture and Status of Women, and the Edmonton Arts Council for support of our publishing program. We acknowledge the financial support of the Government of Canada through the Canada Book Fund for our publishing activities. The Edmonton Queer History Project acknowledges funding support received from the Edmonton Community Foundation, Edmonton Heritage Council, Stollery Charitable Foundation, and Canada Research Chairs program.

NeWest Press
#201, 10131 97 Street Edmonton, Alberta T5J 0L2 www.newestpress.com

No bison were harmed in the making of this book.
Printed and bound in Canada. 1 2 3 4 28 27 26 25